A CONCISE GUIDE TO READING THE NEW TESTAMENT

A Canonical Introduction

David R. Nienhuis

Baker Academic
a division of Baker Publishing Group
Grand Rapids, Michigan

Published by Baker Academic
a division of Baker Publishing Group
P.O. Box 6287, Grand Rapids, MI 49516-6287
www.bakeracademic.com

Printed in the United States of America

Library of Congress Cataloging-in-Publication Data
Names: Nienhuis, David R., 1968– author.
Title: A concise guide to reading the New Testament : a canonical introduction / David R. Nienhuis.
Description: Grand Rapids : Baker Academic, 2018. | Includes index.
Identifiers: LCCN 2017022592 | ISBN 9780801097638 (pbk. : alk. paper)
Subjects: LCSH: Bible. New Testament—Canon. | Bible. New Testament—Criticism, interpretation, etc.
Classification: LCC BS2320 .N54 2018 | DDC 225.6/1—dc23
LC record available at https://lccn.loc.gov/2017022592

18   19   20   21   22   23   24   7   6   5   4   3   2   1

In keeping with biblical principles of creation stewardship, Baker Publishing Group advocates the responsible use of our natural resources. As a member of the Green Press Initiative, our company uses recycled paper when possible. The text paper of this book is composed in part of post-consumer waste.

This book is dedicated to the many faithful
witnesses who have helped
to lead me along the way of the Word,
including especially

Lanny and Diane, Cathy, Arvin and Barb,
Ross, Dean, Rob, Frank, Gene,
Teresa, Richard, Francis, and Brenda

Contents

Acknowledgments   vii

1. Introduction: The Form and Function of the
   New Testament Canon   1
   Following the Way of the Word

2. The Gospel according to Matthew: The Call to
   Discipleship   17
   "Take my yoke upon you, and learn from me."

3. The Gospel according to Mark: The Cost of
   Discipleship   33
   "Take up your cross and follow me."

4. The Gospel according to Luke: The Scope of
   Discipleship   51
   "The kingdom of God is among you."

5. The Gospel according to John: The Center of
   Discipleship   67
   *"I, when I am lifted up from the earth, will draw
   all people to myself."*

6. The Acts of the Apostles: The Community
   of Discipleship   87
   *"In the last days it will be . . . that I will pour out my
   Spirit upon all flesh."*

7. The Letters of Paul: The Pattern of Discipleship   109
   *"I have been crucified with Christ; and it is no longer I
   who live, but it is Christ who lives in me."*

8. The Catholic Epistles: The Tradition of
   Discipleship   133
   *"Whoever says 'I abide in him' ought to walk just as he
   walked."*

9. The Revelation to John: The Conquering
   Disciple   153
   "These follow the Lamb wherever he goes."

Glossary   173
Suggestions for Further Reading   184
Scripture Index   187
Subject Index   194

Acknowledgments

Teaching others is part of the life of **discipleship** (Matt. 28:19–20). As such, it is a practice involving equal parts imitation, adaptation, innovation, and, of course, **inspiration**. I do not know whether this book qualifies as innovative, though I've certainly tried to create something unique that would fill what I perceive to be a gap in the already saturated market of introductory texts. And I will of course leave it to others to determine what, if any of it, might be considered inspired (though it was certainly an inspiring experience to write it). What I can say without any reservation is that much of what you are about to read amounts to my own distinctive adaptation of what I have learned from those who have taught me how to read Scripture over the course of my life. This book is lovingly dedicated to all of them.

I am especially grateful for my many teachers. Like preaching, the instructive task of introducing complex material to the uninitiated is a distinctive ability that is learned, at least in part, by observing masters of the craft who ply their trade with grace and skill. Thus I owe a huge debt to the many teachers and scholars who have left their mark on me and my work.

Because this is an introductory, nonscholarly text, I have kept footnotes to a minimum. Nevertheless, readers should know that hardly a page goes by that isn't influenced in one way or another by studies produced over the last thirty years by those working at the forefront of the contemporary movement in biblical studies commonly known as "the theological interpretation of Scripture." I am in their debt. This is perhaps most especially the case with Rob Wall, my friend, colleague, and collaborator at Seattle Pacific University. Many of the ideas I've put into play in this introductory book—especially those having to do with the interpretive significance of the actual sequence of biblical texts—were sharpened as a result of the rich body of scholarly work he has produced over the years.

On those occasions where I've been directly dependent on one of my teacher-colleague's works, I've given credit in a footnote; otherwise I've let my words flow from the computer keys the way I would speak as a teacher in the classroom, communicating as openly as I could in the full knowledge that some variation of my words undoubtedly came first out of the mouths of one of my teachers. I suppose it is like this for every professor, but I'm grateful nonetheless. Of course, any half-truths, poorly conceived ideas, or outright falsehoods are my responsibility alone.

I'm also exceedingly thankful to my colleagues in the School of Theology at Seattle Pacific University and Seminary, especially the members of the Bible department with whom I work so closely: Rob Wall, Gene Lemcio, Frank Spina, Sara Koenig, Bo Lim, Laura Holmes, J. J. Leese, and Jamie Coles. It is truly an honor to work alongside such lovely and talented people. Thanks also go to Dr. Brenda Salter-McNeil, my teaching companion in SPU's Introduction to Christian Reconciliation course; our collaboration continues to teach me anew how the Word of God we proclaim meets ground, for good or for ill, in particular bodies that walk a distinctive way in the world.

I remain so very grateful for my students. These chapters have been tested out on a number of classes over the last year and a half (especially the 2014–15 sections of the Four Gospels, One Jesus course), and the feedback I've received from them has made this a far better book than it would otherwise have been. Among my students, particular thanks go to the members of my weekly small group: Adrienne Elliott, Maddie Haugen, Caitlin Heinly, Macie Mooney, Caitlin Tallungen, and especially Kierstin Brown and Jessie Comfort, who reviewed chapters and helped me think through relevant discussion questions. These amazing women have invited me into their personal lives and afforded me countless hours of rich reflection on how the Word might be made flesh in our world today. Similar editorial thanks go to David Meade, Elaine Nguyen, and my wife, Teresa Osborn, all of whom have helped revise drafts, suggest discussion questions, and identify useful terms for the glossary (these terms are in **boldface font**).

I am also appreciative of my friend James Ernest, former executive editor at Baker Academic, who suggested that I write this book and guided me through the initial stages of its development. His duty was handed off to Bryan Dyer and Eric Salo, both of whom worked very hard to make this a better book than it would have been without their help. I'm deeply thankful to all of them and to everyone else at Baker Academic for the parts they have played in bringing this work to light.

Last, though by far not least, is a word of gratitude to God. I am sometimes embarrassed by the privileged life I lead as a teacher and scholar of the Bible. The fact is, I make a modest yet very comfortable living teaching others about a Lord who gave up everything for my sake. I spend my days reading Christian Scripture in community with faithful others, sharpening and being sharpened. I get to walk alongside an apparently never-ending throng of bright and earnest emerging adults whose many questions about life keep my head busy and my heart tender. I often fear that I am getting more than I am giving. So I submit this book as an offering in humble gratitude to God for a good life I did little to earn. I do so in the hope that it would play some small part in God's far grander call for everyone to come and walk the way of the Word, that the peace of God might be spread far and wide across this troubled earth.

Soli Deo gloria.

David R. Nienhuis
Seattle Pacific University
Autumn 2016

1

Introduction

The Form and Function of the New Testament Canon

Following the Way of the Word

Each passing year sees the publication of more and more texts that aim to introduce students and laypeople to the **Bible** (see Glossary for terms in boldface). What could possibly justify the production of yet another book? Aren't there enough choices available already?

Those of us who teach the Bible to undergraduates and seminarians know that the answer is no, actually. Certainly there is a wide range of excellent and reputable texts to choose from. But teachers who work in contexts that are both academically serious and confessionally Christian face unique problems. On the one hand, we want our students to spend the bulk of their study time reading the Bible. On the other, there are so many introductory matters to cover in order to help students understand what they are reading that there often isn't enough time in a standard class period *both* to cover introductory concepts *and* to work through the text with students. Hence appears the need for an appropriate textbook to inform their homework experience.

But here is where a new and different set of problems arises. Most introductory textbooks seek to be as exhaustive as possible, addressing as many historical and literary elements of analysis as they are able. The result, obviously, is a large text with thick, substantive chapters. What professor wouldn't be happy with that? I was, for many years, until I discovered some things that concerned me. First, when given an assignment to read the introductory text along with sections from **Scripture**, I discovered too many students were reading the textbook and skimming (or skipping) the assigned Bible reading. Because students have limited time, they often default to what is perceived to be the shortest possible route to the goal. And because their educational experience has trained them to be assessment oriented, they perceive the goal to be a grade that is determined by homework and exams; so they rush to "the expert" to help them get "the important parts" instead of reading the Scripture on their own. This results in too many students spending their time reading *about* the Bible instead of actually learning to read the Bible themselves.

Second, most introductory textbooks present students with a Bible that differs rather sharply from the one received by the **church**. For centuries now, biblical scholarship has privileged the reconstruction of an "original context" for the biblical texts, using historical criteria as a means to regulate contemporary interpretive possibilities. One of the results of this project has been a dismantling of the Bible's final form. When it comes to the New Testament (NT), students learn that they should actually read Mark first, not Matthew, since the former is the earlier text. They learn that Luke and Acts should be rearranged to be read alongside each other as two parts of an authorial whole; that John's **Gospel** should be read alongside the Letters of John; that Paul's Letters should be rearranged to begin with 1 Thessalonians; and that there are indeed a number of letters attributed to Paul that are not actually written by him at all.

The inevitable result is the suspicion that there is something wrong with the Bible as we have received it. Whoever put it together must have arranged it incorrectly! Worse, they left out all the important historical information we need in order to make any sense of it. How could we ever understand the intention of the original authors without first being introduced to the social, cultural, religious, and political realities that shaped the composition of their text and informed its reception by the original hearers? And who can provide us with this information but the academically trained expert in biblical studies?

Once students start thinking this way, a final realization creeps in. They discover that the quest to read the Bible "correctly" requires them to take it out of the hands of Christians, and out of the context of the church (which is, of course, the community that introduced most of them to the Bible in the first place) and place it instead into the hands of the scholarly expert, to be studied in the context of the university classroom.[1] Thus, the hope of most Christian institutions of higher education risks being thwarted: we require courses in the Bible in order to help our students become better Scripture readers and, hopefully, better Christians; but by replacing the Christian Scripture with the scholars' Bible, we inadvertently create an existential chasm between students' intellectual formation and spiritual formation. Confusion is the inevitable result when *what* they hear in class and read in their textbook is out of step with *how* they read in church and what they hear from the pulpit.

Of course, the actual use of the Bible in many churches presents a different set of problems. Some of my students attend popular non-denominational churches led by entrepreneurial leaders who claim to be "Bible believing" and strive to offer sermons that are "relevant" for successful Christian living. Unfortunately, in too many cases this formula results in a preacher appealing to a short text of Scripture, out of context, in order to support a predetermined set of "biblical principles" to guide the congregants' daily lives. The only Bible these students encounter, sadly, is the version that is carefully distilled according to the **theological** and ideological concerns that have shaped the spiritual formation of the lead pastor.

On the other side of the continuum are more "traditional" churches, which use the readings from a **lectionary** in worship. Students who attend these churches—especially Episcopalian, **Roman Catholic**, and **Eastern Orthodox** students—typically encounter a huge amount of

1. The story of how the church's Scripture was transformed into the scholars' Bible is powerfully narrated by Michael C. Legaspi, *The Death of Scripture and the Rise of Biblical Studies* (Oxford: Oxford University Press, 2011).

Scripture each Sunday, including an **Old Testament** (OT) reading, a **psalm,** a reading from the NT, and a passage from one of the four Gospels. These four readings are usually arranged **typologically,** with the first three chosen for their thematic correspondence with the assigned Gospel text. While students in these churches typically hear a lot of Scripture read over their lifetime, they often lack a detailed narrative framework for understanding how all these various texts fit together. They may be able to recognize Scripture when they hear it read, but they are usually unable to place the story they heard within the larger story of God narrated in the Bible.

A wide range of **Protestant** churches exists between these two poles, and many of their leaders labor to communicate the important role Scripture plays in the life of a Jesus follower. Students memorize the names of the biblical books in order. They learn the basic plotline of the larger biblical story. They are encouraged to set aside time each day for devotions. They memorize a variety of Bible verses. By the standards of most contemporary Christians, these students know their Bible well.

And yet these same students typically struggle in my classes as much as the others, if not more so. This is the case because most of them have been trained to be Bible *quoters,* not Bible *readers.* They have the capacity to recall a relevant biblical text in support of a particular doctrinal point, or in opposition to a hot spot in the cultural wars, or in hope of emotional support when times get tough. They approach the Bible as a sort of reference book, a collection of useful God-quotes that can be looked up as one would locate a word in a dictionary or an entry in an encyclopedia. What they are not trained to do is read a biblical book from beginning to end, to trace its narrative arc, to discern its main themes, and to wonder about how it shapes our faith lives today. Indeed, oftentimes these students find themselves dismayed when they read a beloved Bible quote in its actual literary context and discover that it does not seem to bear the meaning they thought it did when they quoted the verse in isolation.

To summarize, the problem as I see it is this: the university frequently introduces students to a Bible they don't recognize, and the church often teaches students to be devoted to a Bible they don't know how to read.

In my years of teaching I have found that what is most helpful is a kind of concise reading guide, one capable of providing a relatively straightforward bird's-eye view of the text to orient readers so they can get down to the business of building a life habit of reading the Bible carefully for themselves. This is precisely why Rob Wall and I partnered with our Scripture department colleagues at Seattle Pacific University to produce *The Compact Guide to the Whole Bible: Learning to Read Scripture's Story* (Grand Rapids: Baker Academic, 2013), and why I have gone on to compose this reading guide focused specifically on the NT.

The chapters of this book are held together by a thematic refrain that echoes throughout. I consistently refer to the form of the New Testament itself, as well as the contents of the story it tells, as *the way of the Word*. The logic behind that refrain can be stated simply:

> The Bible, which has been provided for us to be the written Word of God, is intentionally designed to guide readers through a process of learning the way of Jesus, who is the embodied Word of God.

This conception of the Bible's intended purpose is grounded in the Bible's own articulation of Scripture's function: "All scripture is **inspired** by God and is useful for teaching, for reproof, for correction, and for training in **righteousness**, so that everyone who belongs to God may be proficient, equipped for every good work" (2 Tim. 3:16–17). These verses have far less to say about the *original authorship* of Scripture than about its *contemporary function*: Scripture's primary target is the **revelation** of God for the formation of faith.

The subtitle describes this book as *A Canonical Introduction*. What makes a NT introduction **canonical**? Four orienting convictions drive the reading articulated here: a canonical introduction will read the Bible as *Scripture*; it will approach the Bible as an authoritative *collection*; it will privilege the interpretive significance of the Bible's *final form*; and it will focus on the Bible's function as a *faith-forming narrative*. Each of these convictions requires further elaboration before we can start our journey on the way of the Word.

Reading the Bible as Scripture

Christians turn to the Bible for a number of different reasons. Some do so to gather biblical support for doctrinal positions. Others search it for propositional truth claims that can be used in arguing political or ethical matters. Still others seek inspirational quotations or stories in search of emotional support. All of these readers undoubtedly conceive of the Bible as an authoritative text, but they are not necessarily approaching the Bible as Scripture.

Reading the Bible as Scripture requires a recognition of the Bible's orienting identity. The Bible is the **canon** of Christian Scripture, a collection of **holy** writings set apart by God's people in recognition of their Spirit-empowered capacity to mediate the transforming presence of God to the community of faith. Those who approach the Bible as Scripture, then, do so in company with faithful others in order to be transformed by God. They will be less interested in having their own questions answered than in opening themselves up to the questions God has in store for them. They will not think of the Bible as a tool to be used like an inert object, but as a divinely appointed setting for encountering a living Subject (i.e., God). In short, reading the Bible as Scripture involves approaching it as an act of worship.

This means, then, that the church is the appropriate setting for reading the Bible. In using the word "church," I do not merely refer to the buildings we gather in on Sunday mornings, but to the transhistoric community of God's people who received this text long ago and have been gathering to attend to its message ever since. Yet I do not mean to say that the classroom, the living room, or the bus is somehow the *wrong* location for reading. No, reading the Bible with the church means reading the Bible knowing that we are always reading in company with a very particular community. It means reading as members of a body, knowing that interpretive meaning is discovered in conversation, not in isolation. It requires an awareness of the contemporary diversity of that body, knowing that we will never be transformed if we read only with those who already support our biases and presuppositions. It means keeping the church's ancient **theological** agreements (often called the **rule of faith**) in mind as we read, knowing that the powerful variety of Scripture's witnesses may lead us apart from one another if we do not read with the hope of fulfilling **Christ**'s prayer that his followers "may all be one" (John 17:21).

Chief among these theological agreements is a proper understanding of the God who brought Scripture into being and speaks through it today: this is the Creator of all things, the faithful **covenant** partner to Israel who became flesh in Jesus and comes to us today by means of the Holy Spirit, who takes away our bent toward sinning and sets our hearts at liberty for service to God.

Thus, this book will not include extensive historical analyses of the factors that brought individual NT texts into being. We do not presume that a singular "real meaning" is hidden away in a past "original context" that must be unearthed by a professional historian. In place of reconstructed portraits of ancient authors and original audiences to whom we no longer have direct access, the reader will find a close analysis of the text that stands before us, with one reader's careful reflection on what the Word has to teach us about the way of Christ and how the Holy Spirit might help us walk in that way today.

Approaching the Bible as a Collection

The previous section identified the Bible as the canon of Christian Scripture. The word "canon" comes from a Greek word used initially to describe a "rule" (as in a ruler with which one measures things). Over time it came to refer to an official, approved "list" or "collection" of authorities by which truth might be measured. To approach the Bible as a canon, then, is to read it in the recognition that the Bible is actually an authoritative book full of books, a collection of writings edited together into a unified whole.

The Bible's "collectedness" bears a number of important implications for our reading. Just as approaching the Bible as Scripture disallows interpretation in isolation from other Christians, so also approaching the Bible as a canon disallows the reading of one biblical text in isolation from another. Though each book of the Bible had its own discrete origin in a particular place and time, they were each ultimately received as parts of a canonical whole in the expectation that they would continue to be read as such. Thus, reading Matthew in canonical context leads us to spend less time considering its point of historic composition and more time on the logic of its placement in the canon: How does Matthew help us transition out of the Old Testament and into the New? How does Matthew prepare the way for Mark? What is Matthew's distinctive contribution to the fourfold Gospel collection?

These sorts of questions presume that the placement of the NT books is the result of intentional choices on the part of the ancient collectors. There is, in fact, plenty of evidence in support of such a claim. But first, to whom are we referring when we speak of "the ancient collectors"? Much could be said here, but for our purposes a brief explanation will have to do.[2] Though it was common in the past to search for this or that figure or crisis that instigated the formation of the NT canon, it is now widely recognized to have been a far more multifaceted and organic process. In the decades following their initial composition, the texts that would eventually form the NT were copied and disseminated to churches across the Mediterranean world. In this context illiteracy was the norm, and reading and writing was a professional skill. Since the copying of texts was extremely costly, only the most highly valued documents could be reproduced. While it is clear that a wide variety of ancient Christian texts were deemed valuable at one time or another in this or that corner of early Christendom, the ones that survived long enough to be deemed "canonical" were those that (1) emerged from the earliest generation of **apostles**, (2) gained the widest recognition of scriptural authority, and (3) combined well together with others to communicate the whole apostolic story of God's salvation in Christ and through the Spirit.

This "decision," if it can be called that, came about as the result of a collective and gradual process guided by the Holy Spirit. Indeed, when thinking of how the process played out, "discernment" ends

2. Anyone interested in the history of NT canonization should start with what has become the classic text on the subject, Bruce Metzger's *The Canon of the New Testament: Its Origin, Development, and Significance* (Oxford: Clarendon Press, repr. 1997). For a more detailed and updated account of the formation of the whole Christian Scripture, see Lee Martin McDonald, *The Biblical Canon: Its Origin, Transmission, and Authority* (Grand Rapids: Baker Academic, 2006).

up providing a better conception than "decision." As far as we can tell from the written testimony of early **church fathers**, the indirect witness of the **scribes** who published the texts, and the evidence of intentional design in the NT we have received, we gather that apostolic writings initially circulated among the churches in smaller collections of varying size and shape. These were subjected to a long process of arrangement and rearrangement: individual texts entered the emerging canon by means of subcollections that were tested over generations of use in the worshiping communities until a final contents and sequence gained purchase across the majority of churches. By the time powerful church leaders stepped up in the later 300s to bring the canonization process to a close, the decisions were mostly already made for them: the "canon lists" of the mid- to late-fourth century show widespread acceptance of a collection very closely resembling the very same NT canon we have today.[3]

The final form of the NT, then, is neither accidental nor incidental. Indeed, the Word as it has come down to us appears to have a way to it, a reading logic designed to form readers into the sort of **disciples** capable of hearing the Spirit as the Spirit leads them along the way of Jesus.

The Interpretive Significance of the Bible's Final Form

The NT abounds with evidence pointing to the intentionality of its design. Two types of evidence, historical and artistic, can be offered to convince us of the meaningfulness of the canon's final shape.

The historical evidence can be categorized into internal and external types. Internal evidence (that is, evidence discerned from the form and contents of the NT itself) shows that the NT texts were carefully arranged according to a narrative structure that was imposed by the

---

3. The primary differences, where they existed, had mostly to do with (a) whether or not to include Revelation; (b) whether to include all seven Catholic Epistles (CE) or only James, 1 Peter, and 1 John; and (c) whether to place the Pauline Letters immediately after Acts, as was the habit in the West, or after the CE, as was the habit in the East. Most of these issues will be addressed in one way or another in the chapters that follow. Suffice it to say at this point that the *contents* at least of the NT canon were widely agreed upon by the fifth century.

editors: the canon begins with the story of God's work in Jesus (the four Gospels), follows with the Holy Spirit's empowerment of the church subsequent to Jesus's **ascension** (the Acts of the Apostles), continues with the story of the first churches as communicated through twenty-one apostolic letters, and concludes with a vision of God's **consummation** of all things in the Revelation to John. This structure does not correspond at all with the historical emergence of these individual texts: if it did, most of the letters would come *before* the Gospels. As it stands, the individual texts have been artistically arranged into larger subcollections designed to communicate the story of the Creator God's work in Christ and the Holy Spirit to bring about the restoration of all creation.

Though the external historical evidence is admittedly sparse, what we do have also provides us with insight into the meaningfulness of the final form. Indeed, throughout this book we will consider the words of the church fathers from the early centuries who bear witness to the development of our canon. We will learn, for instance, that John, which is so very different than the other three Gospels (which are typically called the **Synoptic Gospels**[4]), comes at the end of the Gospel collection to function as a closing "spiritual" reflection on the story of Jesus. We learn that Acts was separated from Luke in order to function as an introduction to the NT letter collection. We will learn one leader's view that the **Catholic Epistles** (CE) collection was added because a "perplexing problem in the writings of the Apostle Paul"[5] was leading some readers to believe that one could have faith without also being obedient. Complete historical clarity is lacking, of course, but by paying attention to the reflections of those who lived in the days of the canon's formation, we gain insight into its nature and function.

There is also clear artistic evidence of design within the subcollections. For example, consider the fourfold Gospel collection. As we will see, though Matthew's Gospel does not appear to have been the first Gospel written, it comes first in the canon because it is the one most

---

4. Since the nineteenth century, Matthew, Mark, and Luke have been called Synoptic Gospels because they share a common view of Jesus's words and deeds.

5. Augustine, *Faith and Works*, in *Saint Augustine: Treatises on Marriage and Other Subjects*, trans. Marie Ligouri, ed. R. J. Deferrari, Fathers of the Church 27 (Washington, DC: Catholic University of America Press, 1955), 213–82.

capable of transitioning readers out of the OT and into the New. It also sets the stage well by offering readers the clearest portrayal of the call to discipleship. This relatively straightforward Gospel is followed by Mark, which sounds a cautionary note to emphasize the dark side of discipleship: ours is a Lord who came to die on a cross and calls us to do the same. Luke then follows to expand the scope of God's salvation, showing that this Lord is not simply the **Messiah** of Israel, but also the Savior of the whole world. John then concludes the Gospel collection with an extended meditation on Jesus's identity as the Word of God, the one who is the way, the truth, and the life, the one means of access to God. We can see, then, that the four Gospels combine to tell us the whole story of Jesus, the Messiah of Israel (Matthew) who came to give his life as a ransom for many (Mark) so that everyone in the whole world (Luke) would find salvation in him (John).

There is also the simple fact that there are *four* Gospels. Though modern readers tend to think of number symbolism as insignificant, ancient readers believed numbers corresponded to spiritual realities. Ancient Jews noted with fascination how God provided detailed instructions for the building of things like Noah's ark (Gen. 6), the temple and its accessories (Exod. 25–27), and even the new Jerusalem (Rev. 21). After all, if God is the Creator of all things, it must mean that we can learn about God by studying the actual form of things that God makes. The number four, it turns out, was understood to be the number symbol for created things. So just as there are four points on the compass, four physical elements (earth, water, wind, and fire), four rivers in the paradise of creation (Gen. 2:10–14), four points on the cross, and four creatures attending God in the visions of Ezekiel and John (Ezek. 1; Rev. 4), it makes perfect sense that there should be four *created* Gospels to articulate the one gospel of Jesus Christ.

After the Gospels comes the Acts of the Apostles. This book tells the story of the earliest church as it grew and spread abroad by the power of the Holy Spirit working in its midst. In particular, it tells the story of the earliest Jewish Christian mission to Jews in and around Jerusalem (chaps. 1–8), its scattering abroad because of persecution (chap. 8 and following), its expansion among **gentiles** (chaps. 10–14), and the eventual development of a full-blown mission to the gentile world (chaps. 15–28). This sets the stage for the letters that follow:

the latter half of Acts is almost entirely about the apostle Paul in order to prepare us to read his letters. After the Pauline collection we return to where Acts started by reading letters from the leaders of that first Jewish mission (the letters of James, Peter, John, and Jude). The canon then concludes with the Revelation to John, which tells the story of God's victorious conclusion of salvation.

Once again, number symbolism matters. The church fathers often noticed that Paul's thirteen letters address *seven* churches—Rome, Corinth, Galatia, Ephesus, Philippi, Colossae, and Thessalonica. The Catholic Epistles, which follow Paul, offer up *seven* letters of their own. Finally, as if to crown the sequence, the Revelation to John begins with the risen Lord Jesus addressing seven letters to seven churches. Since seven is the biblical number for completion and perfection, the numerical form of the apostolic letters is reflective of a complete and perfect communication of apostolic teaching.

Then also, the number three is the number of divinity, reflecting the three persons of God. There are twenty-one letters in the NT (three sets of seven), and the pattern of seven repeats three times (Paul to seven churches, seven Catholic Epistles, seven letters to seven churches in Revelation). On top of all that, the number seven is the product of four plus three, as if to suggest that the God who is one in *three* has inspired the *four*fold Gospel to produce all these perfect apostolic *sevens*.

In sum, the sequence of NT books is meaningful, and reading the books in sequence communicates a message that is greater than the sum of its constituent parts. Each chapter that follows, then, will open with a "canonical transition" section that highlights the meaningfulness of the transition from one book or collection to the next. As we will see, these texts can be seen to hang together like links on a chain, or better, like way markers on a trail leading the reader further along the path of discipleship.

The Bible's Function as a Faith-Forming Narrative

The books of the NT are not disinterested, journalistic stories reporting ancient events from an unbiased point of view. All of them are driven by a single agenda: the formation of faith in the lives of those who read. At every point the NT texts call out to the reader to make decisions, to rethink positions, to increase faith, and ultimately to follow the call of God in Christ and the Holy Spirit. Near the conclusion of the fourfold Gospel, the author says,

> Now Jesus did many other signs in the presence of his disciples, which are not written in this book. But these are written so that you may come to believe that Jesus is the Messiah, the Son of God, and that through believing you may have life in his name. (John 20:30–31)

So also Acts opens with Jesus telling his disciples, "You will be my witnesses" (Acts 1:8), and Paul, in his turn, opens his collection of letters with the claim that he has been charged "to bring about the obedience of faith among all the Gentiles for the sake of his name" (Rom. 1:5). Everywhere we turn in the NT, we are reminded that Scripture's function is the equipping of God's people so that everyone will be ready to perform the good works God has called us to do. We might even go so far as to say that Scripture was formed in order to be performed by those who read it. As it turns out, narrative is the perfect mode of discourse for achieving this end.

Modern biblical scholarship's myopic focus on historical reconstruction had the effect of obscuring the now widely recognized fact that the Bible is, at its base, a story. Even the nonnarrative elements of the text (like legal code, proverbs, or letters) are only meaningful to us because they have the larger biblical story as their backdrop. Our older, more rationalistic orientation toward the Bible led us to seek deeper, propositional truths buried beneath the surface of the biblical narrative. What we have learned, of course, is that no moral or summary of a story can take the place of the story itself. Stories, it turns out, are "irreducible": they cannot be distilled down into a purer, simpler, "truer" form. We can try to explain them, summarize them, or turn them into timeless "principles," but doing so will always be an attempt to turn the story into something other than what it is in itself.

The irreducibility of narrative makes it one of the most powerful forms of discourse that humans possess. Stories do not provide us with simplistic answers to life. Instead, they spark the imagination and evoke our capacity to wonder; in doing so, they ignite a personal meaning-making process in the reader. There are many reasons for this, but one of the more important is the fact that stories provide us with a vicarious experience of life. The word "vicarious" comes from the Latin word for "substitute"; stories allow us to experience the feelings or actions of another person in the realm of the imagination. Whether the story is about something real or imaginary, good stories temporarily provide us with a substitute existence: they present us with realistic characters in situations we can relate to; we come to love them or hate them, worry about them or wonder what they're going to do; we experience pleasure when they surprise us, anger when they are abused, disgust when they abuse others, and shock when they do something unexpected. And as we observe this substitute life, we cannot help but reflect on the story of our own lives. We learn from their choices, and if they are good characters, we are inspired by their virtue. Stories immerse us temporarily in a world other than our own, and in doing so, they provide us with a deeper understanding of our own identities, values, choices, and purpose.

The gospel is a particularly potent story. In it Jesus is presented as the Word of God who "became flesh and lived among us" (John 1:14), the Creator taking the form of a creature like us, one who lived a life like our own as an example, so that we "should follow in his steps" (1 Pet. 2:21). As we read his story, we are inspired by the truth of his message and his life, and thus he becomes our hero, our model, our Lord. We also read about others as they follow his way. Some are able to do so, others fail miserably, most stumble along as best they can—and through it all our conception of what it might be like for *us* to follow is clarified. The story of earliest Christianity provided in the NT offers us models for how Christianity is embodied and practiced in the real world. And as we immerse ourselves in this life-shaping story, as we return to it again and again, reading in order to let it spur our imagination and generate our meaning-making, we are slowly transformed: a story about a God who became flesh for our sake ends up being made flesh in our daily lives.

Calling Christianity a story-shaped performance might lead us to suppose that the imitation of Christ is a simple matter of repeating his words and replicating his deeds. But real life doesn't work that way, not least because our world is so considerably different from the one into which Jesus was born. It is not enough to quote Jesus (or one of his apostles) in response to a particular situation; the story calls us to *embody* Jesus, participate in his life, and take up his character as our own. This is undoubtedly what Paul means when he says, "I have been crucified with Christ; and it is no longer I who live, but it is Christ who lives in me. And the life I now live in the flesh I live by faith in the Son of God, who loved me and gave himself for me" (Gal. 2:19–20). Paul does not mean he has literally been crucified as Jesus was; he means he is living his life according to the pattern of the one who loved us so much that he gave his life away to save others.

No, the Christian life is not to take the form of a wooden impersonation of Jesus (as if we could do that anyway!). The faith-forming narrative of Scripture provides us with a plotline within which we may orient our own lives today. We are disciples, no less so than Peter or John or Thomas. We are the church, no less so than the people of Philippi or Rome or Corinth. We are the **saints** yearning together with the **martyrs** of Revelation that Jesus will come again to destroy death once and for all. We read these stories as our own; the characters we encounter hold up a mirror before us. We learn from their mistakes, internalize their virtues, and take their hope as our own, so that we might assume our rightful place as characters playing our part in the unfolding drama of God's **reconciliation** of all things.

The book you are reading approaches the NT as a holy book that was intentionally formed by a particular community to function as a faith-forming narrative. The NT is a word with a distinctive way to it, a literary path designed to lead readers along the living way of the Word, who is Christ Jesus our Lord. The goal is neither to unearth a history of "what really happened" way back when, nor to memorize powerful verses and distill timeless principles for life, but to hear the call to take up the way of the Word for ourselves, to let it sink in until we are able to embody his character in our lives, in the hope that we might participate in the **redemption** that God is bringing into being.

What all this means is that it isn't enough for Christians to emphasize the authoritative character of the Bible. We must also attend very carefully to the character of those who read it. If the Bible is indeed *Scripture*, a holy text set apart by God, then we must approach it with the humility of those who are seeking to have their lives and their world changed. We must speak the truth to one another, being quick to confess our shortcomings and even quicker to overlook those of others, knowing that "love covers a multitude of sins" (James 5:19–20; 1 Pet. 4:8). If the Bible is indeed the *church's* Scripture, we must develop the sort of character traits that will enable us to approach the task with honest relational openness, knowing that God is addressing all of us, not just me and my self-selected tribe of those who already agree with me. This is precisely why the Lord placed the **Communion** table at the center of our worship: it is absolutely imperative that Christians be the sort of people who are capable of sitting together with those with whom we disagree. If the Bible is indeed a *collection of different texts intentionally formed together* to communicate a whole truth about God, it means we must develop the patience to linger long before the mirror of the Word—to struggle through its varieties, its puzzles, and its challenges—and to stay put until we are transformed from mere hearers into "doers of the word," whose creed actually matches our deeds (James 1:22–25).

In short, if the Bible is indeed a faith-forming narrative, as this introduction assumes it is, we must approach it with open ears and open hearts, ready to be transformed. No other posture will do if we are to take up the way of the Word as our way of life.

Questions for Discussion

1. Having read this introduction, what questions do you have? What do you want to know more about? Make a list to share with your class or reading group.

2. How does this approach to the Bible differ from the approach(es) you've learned? What is to be gained by following this approach? What sort of assumptions might need to be given up?

2

The Gospel according to Matthew

The Call to Discipleship

**"Take my yoke upon you,
and learn from me."**

(MATTHEW 11:29)

The way of the Word begins with the Gospel according to Matthew. Since the premise of this introduction is that the sequence of the NT books is intentionally designed to shape interpretation, we should begin by asking why it is that Matthew is placed first among the Gospels.

The tradition of the ancient **church** was that Matthew was first in line because it was the earliest of the four written Gospels. In fact, they believed it was addressed to Jews, originally written in Aramaic, and only later translated into Greek. Careful analysis of the Gospels, however, has convinced modern scholars that the Matthew we possess was *not* translated from an Aramaic original and also was not the first of the four to be composed. Most would now say that Matthew's *literary* priority among the four was established very early on, and the story of its *historical* priority was created to support what had become the customary scribal practice.

So what might account for the early, widespread tendency to publish the fourfold Gospel with Matthew as its lead text? The later fourth-century sermons of **John Chrysostom** may provide us with a clue. He begins his first sermon on Matthew by complaining about what he takes to be the complexity and immorality of the Greek philosophical tradition. But turning from them to Matthew, he contends,

> Our lessons are not such; rather **Christ** hath taught us what is just, and what is seemly, and what is expedient, and all virtue in general, comprising it in few and plain words: at one time saying that, on two commandments hang the **Law** and the **Prophets** (Matt. 22:40), that is to say, on the love of God and on the love of our neighbor: at another time, Whatsoever ye would that men should do to you, do ye also to them; for this is the Law and the Prophets (Matt. 7:12).

In contrast to the esoteric philosophy of the day, John Chrysostom insists that the Gospel of Matthew presents Christian teaching in a clear and straightforward manner for the benefit of everyone.

> And these things even to a laborer, and to a servant, and to a widow woman, and to a very child, and to him that appears to be exceedingly slow of understanding, are all plain to comprehend and easy to learn. For the lessons of the truth are like this; and the actual result bears witness thereto. All at least have learned what things they are to do.[1]

Matthew's Gospel is first among the four because it offers the most straightforward introduction to the way of the Word. As we will see, the other Gospels will fill out the complexity and scope of the mission, but not before Matthew provides readers with a clear understanding of the call to **discipleship**.

Canonical Transition: From the Old Testament to Matthew

I begin with a basic claim: among the four **canonical** Gospels, none is better suited than Matthew to help readers transition out of the Old

---

1. John Chrysostom, *Homilies on Matthew* 1.12, in *A Select Library of Nicene and Post-Nicene Fathers of the Christian Church*, 1st series, trans. George Prevost, ed. Philip Schaff, 14 vols. (1886–1889; repr., Peabody, MA: Hendrickson, 1994), 10:5.

Testament (OT) and into the New Testament (NT). It is sometimes referred to as a transition or "bridge" text, or even the "hinge" on which the two Testaments pivot and swing.

Matthew has this reputation because of the way his Gospel connects God's work in and through the people of Israel to what God has accomplished in Christ and the church. On the one hand, numerous elements in Matthew's Gospel provide the reader with a powerful sense of continuity with what has come before in Israel's history: God's work in Jesus is not to be received as a novel thing; Jesus has *not* come because Israel failed, and the church is not inaugurated to *replace* Israel. In Matthew's Gospel, Jesus becomes the *embodiment* of faithful Israel, and the church is to be understood as Israel being *restored* by its powerful **Messiah**.

On the other hand, there are persistent *discontinuities* with what has come before in order to make it plain that God's work in the way of the Word is something distinctive and exclusively new. Jesus is not just one more reforming Israelite in a long line of forebears; the church is not a restored Israel waiting to falter and be restored again later. No, Jesus is God's unique representative, the Son of Man, the Lord of the Sabbath, God with us. The church, by extension, is the one solid rock on which faithfulness to God is established and secured.

It is this continuity-discontinuity pattern that creates the hinge effect in this Gospel, and it is apparent throughout. In what follows I provide a few examples to demonstrate the function of Matthew's canonical transition, which clearly roots Christianity in historic Israel while simultaneously proclaiming that God's work in Christ Jesus is the fulfillment of a history that will transition God's people into a new situation.

Let's begin with a close look at the opening **genealogy** (Matt. 1:1–17). Readers of the OT are familiar with genealogies, those long lists of father-son pairings included to demonstrate lineage and make a case for the origins of certain people groups.[2] Most Bible readers skim

---

2. Notice, for example, the genealogy in Gen. 10, which includes names like Tarshish, Egypt, Canaan, and Cush. Are these historic individuals or simply ways of accounting for the rise of cities and nations?

these or skip them altogether, but doing so is a big mistake: the material in these long lists communicates crucial **theological** information.

Matthew's Gospel begins with an "account of the genealogy [*geneseōs*, "genesis"] of Jesus the Messiah, son of David, son of Abraham" (1:1). Matthew is going to tell us of the genesis, the "beginning" or "birth" of Jesus. Our minds are drawn back to the first book of the Bible and its many genealogies; in this way Bible readers find themselves oriented on familiar ground. But then again, this opening narration of "the beginning of Jesus" is also the introduction to a story proclaiming "the new beginning" Jesus is about to inaugurate. Matthew's Gospel narrates both the beginning of Jesus (continuity) and the new beginning Jesus brings (discontinuity).

Turning to the genealogy itself, we find that it too is continuous with what Bible readers come to expect, yet also strikingly discontinuous. On the one hand, this genealogy is clearly a who's who of Israel's history, designed to state without ambiguity that Jesus is a true Jew of royal lineage. His line is continuous both with Abraham, the one to whom God said, "In you all the families of the earth shall be blessed" (Gen. 12:3), and also with David, the one of whom God said, "I will establish the throne of his **kingdom** forever. I will be a father to him, and he shall be a son to me" (2 Sam. 7:13–14). The figure of David appears to be a key for understanding why the genealogy is structured according to three sets of fourteen. Ancient Jews learned from others the art of **gematria**, where letters of the alphabet are assigned numerical values. A word then can have a number, which can be related mystically to other words with the same value, or to the occurrence of the same number in nature or history. The numerical value of the three consonants in the Hebrew for "David" is fourteen; David is the fourteenth person listed in the genealogy; and David's name precedes (1:1) and concludes the list (1:17). The gematria thereby intensifies the claim that God has sent Jesus to be the son of David, Israel's king.

But there is more to this pattern of fourteens than meets the eye. What is the significance of *three* sets of fourteen? Has Matthew included a deeper riddle within the gematria? We might observe that three sets of fourteen generations are the same as six sets of seven generations, which means Jesus marks the seventh of seven generations, the "perfection," we might say, of the generations of Israel. As Paul puts it, "When the fullness of time had come, God sent his Son, born of a woman, born under the law, in order to **redeem** those who were under the law, so that we might receive adoption as children" (Gal. 4:4–5). Jesus is the long-expected new David (continuity), but he's not just another David or Davidic figure. He is the culmination and completion of the Davidic line (discontinuity), the King of kings.

Even if one doesn't catch the genealogical number riddle, one cannot help but notice the presence of four women in this list—something highly unusual in genealogies of the day, which typically include men only. The four women all have two things in common. First, they are of **gentile** origin. Tamar and Rahab were Canaanites, Ruth was a Moabite, and Bathsheba ("the wife of Uriah") was married to a Hittite. Matthew wants us to remember that within the continuity of Israel's history there has always been the (apparently discontinuous) presence of gentiles. Abraham himself, the very progenitor of Israel, both *was* and *was not* a Jew, for he was called out from the Chaldeans to become the father of Israel. We should not be surprised, therefore, when the first people to recognize the birth of the "king of the Jews" end up being gentile astrologers (Matt. 2:1–12). Indeed, gentiles are some of the greatest exemplars of faithfulness in this Gospel (e.g., 8:5–13).

Further, all four of these women had some sexual irregularity about them. Tamar seduced her father-in-law, Judah, in order to continue the lineage of God's people; Rahab was a prostitute; Ruth was a widow who could be viewed as having secured her marriage to Boaz through seduction (see Ruth 3:1–18); and David begat Solomon through Bathsheba, but only after David committed adultery with her and then arranged to have her husband be killed. By the time we read of Mary's predicament, the continuity-discontinuity pattern is established: in *continuity* with Israel's history, Mary's case is not the first time God has made use of a serious sexual irregularity to further God's plans for God's people. In discontinuity with that history, however, is Mary's purity: her pregnancy is not the result of a human act but because she is with "child . . . from the Holy Spirit" (1:20). Something very new is going on in the person of Jesus.

The hinge effect continues as we move on from the genealogy. The narrator of Matthew's Gospel exhibits a repeated concern to identify particular events in Jesus's life as the direct fulfillments of specific Jewish Scriptures.[3] On multiple occasions either Matthew himself or someone in the Gospel narrative pauses to point out that ancient scriptural prophecies are being fulfilled in Jesus.[4] All told, Matthew quotes the OT over sixty times and alludes to it beyond our capacity to count; he does this far more often than the other Gospel writers do. It is obvious that Matthew wants to present the OT as the firm foundation upon which the way of the Word is walked. The constant emphasis on fulfillment provides the sense that the world is governed by God's design, that everything that occurs represents the continuous timely unfolding of an ancient plan revealed long ago to God's people Israel.

By the time we arrive at Jesus's inaugural sermon and hear him insist, "Do not think I have come to abolish the law or the prophets; I have come not to abolish but to fulfill" (Matt. 5:17), we are not surprised. God is doing something very new in Jesus, but on Matthew's terms, this new work cannot be understood apart from the work God had been doing all along in and through the people of Israel. Only Matthew's Gospel is capable of making this strong transitional assertion. To begin the NT canon with Matthew is to begin a *New Testament* that can be understood only as the fulfillment of what has come before.

The Shape of Matthew's Gospel

There are yet other reasons why Matthew's Gospel comes first among the canonical four. In fact, it is immediately recognizable as an ex-

3. Earliest Christianity used a Greek translation of the Jewish Scriptures known as the **Septuagint**, a name derived from a tradition about the "seventy" translators who produced it (hence it is also typically abbreviated by using the Roman numeral for seventy, **LXX**). This translation was produced as a result of the widespread **hellenization** of the ancient world in the centuries before the birth of Christ. Once Greek became the common tongue of the Mediterranean world, Jews required a Greek translation of their Scriptures. When NT authors quote the OT, they are almost always quoting the LXX. Since modern English versions of the Bible translate the OT from the Hebrew, usually the NT quotation does not line up exactly with the text as it is found in the English OT.

4. See reference to fulfillment in Matt. 1:22–23; 2:5–6, 15, 17–18, 23; 3:3–4; 4:14–16; 8:17; 11:10; 12:17–21; 13:14–15, 35; 15:7–9; 21:4–5; 26:54–56; 27:9–10.

tremely *well-ordered* Gospel. Though Matthew follows Mark's narrative structure very closely,[5] he rearranges stories and incorporates a good many others into a narrative structure designed to communicate Gospel events and teachings in a helpful, straightforward manner.

Though numerous literary structures have been discerned in Matthew, the simplest recognizes the way in which Matthew integrates narrative and teaching discourse in an alternating structure.

The five sermons (possibly an allusion to the five books of Moses) are each designed to address a particular aspect of Christian discipleship. The fact that Mark and Luke include much of this material in different locations in their Gospels makes it rather clear that these sermons are the result of Matthew's creative editorial activity. He wants to present readers with a clear, well-ordered articulation of Jesus's teaching. Nothing could be more appropriate for the first Gospel in the collection.

As it turns out, Matthew's ordering strategy reflects a deep interest in number patterns, a feature typical of ancient **rabbinic literature**. There are nine (3 × 3) miracle stories gathered neatly together in chapters 8–9, and seven **parables** in chapter 13. We find twelve fulfillment citations of OT **Scripture** and seven denunciations of the **Pharisees** in chapter 23. The nine Beatitudes in chapter 5 are gathered into three groups: two groups of four, plus one culminating beatitude. The two groups of four each contain precisely 36 words in Greek (3 × 12, the number 12 being for God's people). These few number patterns I've mentioned are just the tip of the iceberg, for this Gospel is populated with triads and patterns of sevens and twelves. The number arrangements do more than point to an obsessive author; they also convey a sense of order and predictability. Like the recurring references to the fulfillment of OT Scripture, the number patterns provide the sense that God is in control and all things are working out in an orderly fashion and completely according to plan.

5. Around 90 percent of Mark's Gospel is replicated in Matthew, who only omits seven passages from Mark's narration: Mark 1:23–28, the encounter with the demon in the **synagogue**; 1:35–39, Jesus's departure from Capernaum; 4:26–29, the **parable** of the seed growing secretly; 7:32–37, the healing of the deaf man; 8:22–26, the two-stage healing of a blind man at Bethsaida; 9:38–40, the disciples forbidding an "outsider" exorcist; and 12:41–44, the widow's mite.

The Structure of Matthew

A Basic Outline
Introduction (1:1–2:23)
Ministry in Galilee (4:1–18:35)
Ministry in Judea (19:1–20:33)
Confrontation in Jerusalem (21:1–27:66)
Resurrection (28:1–20)

Alternating Structure of Narrative and Sermon		
1:1–4:25	NARRATIVE	introducing Jesus
5:1–7:29	SERMON	on the character of Christian discipleship
8:1–9:38	NARRATIVE	collection of nine miracle stories
10:1–42	SERMON	on the mission of Christian disciples
11:1–12:50	NARRATIVE	on Jesus's actions and people's responses
13:1–53	SERMON	of parables, exploring why people reject discipleship
13:54–17:27	NARRATIVE	on the formation of the Christian community
18:1–35	SERMON	on Christian community as discipleship
19:1–23:39	NARRATIVE	confrontation with the religious authorities
24:1–25:46	SERMON	on living in light of the end
26:1–28:20	NARRATIVE	of betrayal, arrest, suffering, death, resurrection, and commission

What Does Matthew Teach Us about God's Work in Christ Jesus?

Jesus is many things in Matthew's Gospel—healer, master, and most certainly a teacher—but he is, first and foremost, the Son of God. By Jesus's day, calling someone "the Son of God" was basically equivalent to calling him "the King of Israel."[6] We've already observed that the very first verse of Matthew's Gospel proclaims Jesus to be "the Son of

6. See Matt. 27:42; Pss. 2:6–7; 89:26–27; 2 Sam. 7:13–14; Isa. 9:6. The terms "Messiah" (from Hebrew) and "Christ" (from Greek) both mean "anointed," which by Jesus's day had come to refer to the one anointed to lead Israel, meaning the new king.

David" (1:1). The title "Son of David" occurs ten times in Matthew, but seven of those occurrences involve characters in the story calling Jesus by this title.[7] Likewise Jesus is called "Son of God" seven times.[8] Of further significance is the fact that in comparison to Mark, Matthew adds ten additional references to Jesus as "the Son" and forty additional references to God as "Father." As if to underscore the fact, in the familiar **Synoptic** confession of Peter, "You are the Messiah [Christ]" (Mark 8:29; Luke 9:20), Matthew has, "You are the Messiah [Christ], *the Son of the living God*" (16:16, emphasis added).

But Matthew means more than "King of Israel" when he uses the title "Son of God." One of its earliest occurrences comes in a quotation of Jewish Scripture: when Jesus's family finds refuge in Egypt and later returns to Palestine, Matthew declares that the movement fulfills the prophecy of Hosea 11:1, "When Israel was a child, I loved him, and out of Egypt I called my son." Matthew's reference to the exodus story also brings to mind the scene in that book in which God tells the Pharaoh, "Israel is my firstborn son" (Exod. 4:22). This echo inaugurates a series of parallels between Jesus and ancient Israel: both come up out of Egypt; both pass through water (Red Sea for Israel, **baptism** in the Jordan for Jesus) and enter a wilderness of temptation (40 years for Israel, 40 days for Jesus) as preparation before inaugurating their mission (entry into Canaan for Israel, beginning of ministry for Jesus).

In this way we come to see that Jesus is more than just another Israelite in a succession of Israelites. He becomes the actual embodiment of Israel, the fullness of God's will for God's people concentrated into a single human being. He is the Word of God presented to us as a way of being. Because of this, although Israel fell when tempted in the wilderness, Jesus remains faithful to God's "word" in "the wilderness" (4:1–11). To culminate a history that included many duplicitous kings, Jesus will be the one to lead God's people faithfully and to teach them the way of **righteousness**. Jesus is a human who is so completely aligned with God's will and power that he can

7. In Matt. 9:27; 12:23; 15:22; 20:30, 31; 21:9, 15.
8. In Matt. 4:3; 4:6; 8:29; 14:33; 16:16; 26:63; 27:40.

truly say of himself, "No one knows the Father except the Son and anyone to whom the Son chooses to reveal him" (11:27).

Accordingly, this is not a distant, absentee king, a ruler who hides in the comfort of his palace while his people struggle through life. No, this King is "Emmanuel," which we are told means "God is *with us*" (1:23). Jesus comes not to rule *over* people from afar, but to walk the way of the Word with them, teaching them the ways of faithful covenant relationship with God. Indeed, the theme of God's presence in Jesus, and Jesus's presence with us, dominates Matthew's Gospel from beginning to end. The opening claim that Jesus is God with us (1:23) forms a striking bookend with the very last words of this Gospel, where Jesus says, "I am with you always, to the end of the age" (28:20). Jesus's ascension to heaven is not recorded in this Gospel; on Matthew's terms, Jesus continues to be God with us, present to us for all time. Notice that Matthew alone preserves Jesus's words to the church that "where two or three are gathered in my name, I am there among them" (18:20). Likewise, this Gospel alone includes the description of the final judgment of the nations, where the Son of Man separates people into groups of those who have cared for the needy and those who did not, saying, "Just as you did it [or failed to do it] to one of the least of these who are members of my family, you did it to me" (25:31–46). Elsewhere in Matthew we are told that welcoming an impoverished disciple (10:40) or a small child (18:5) is the same as welcoming Jesus. The message seems to be that Jesus became God with us so that those who follow him might be enabled to perform the work of God's people with Jesus present as both model and guide.

What Does Matthew Teach Us about the Spiritual Formation of Christian Disciples?

What we claim about Jesus will determine our understanding of what it is to follow him. Matthew's Christology emphasizes Jesus's model and presence because Matthew's portrait of Christian spiritual formation centers on discipleship. All four Gospels recount Jesus calling disciples to follow him, but Matthew's Gospel makes this theme its central focus.

First, both Jesus and his disciples are portrayed as teachers who teach others the way of the Word. Matthew structures his Gospel into five sermons on various aspects of Christian discipleship, as if to create an authoritative compendium of teaching on the subject. The first and longest of these sermons, traditionally titled the Sermon on the Mount (chaps. 5–7), provides a portrait of the character and habits of the Christian disciple. Here we catch a sense of how serious the call is in the plan of God: though Jesus will call himself "the light of the world" in John's Gospel (John 8:12), here in Matthew the *disciples* are identified as "the light of the world" (5:14–16). The disciples are the ones whose task it is to model Jesus's way of righteousness for subsequent generations.

Jesus places this role on his disciples with the highest degree of seriousness:

> Whoever breaks one of the least of these commandments, and teaches others to do the same, will be called least in the **kingdom of heaven**; but whoever does them and teaches them will be called great in the kingdom of heaven. For I tell you, unless your righteousness exceeds that of the scribes and Pharisees, you will never enter the kingdom of heaven. (5:19–20)

"Whoever *does them* and *teaches them*." Disciples are described here less like students in a classroom and more like a community of practitioners honing a skill under a coach or a craft under a master. In fact, Matthew's Gospel plainly seeks to establish the notion that Jesus came not only to teach, heal, die, and rise again, but also to establish a messianically reformed Israel, a community called "church" that would continue to practice and proclaim his teaching after his resurrection. It is a conspicuous thing that this term "church," which is used so frequently in the rest of the NT, occurs among the canonical Gospels only in Matthew. The first of the four Gospels thus ensures readers of the NT that the church was established by Jesus himself and not as an afterthought by a later movement of Christians.

Matthew's portrait of Jesus's teaching makes it plain that this community called church must be characterized by two primary features: it must insist on careful obedience to the way of the Word, and it must do so in a way that makes evident the radical mercy of God. Many throughout history have stumbled over the strident demands of the inaugural sermon on discipleship (chaps. 5–7), even wondering if its high call to perfection in service and self-giving (5:43–48) stands in contradiction to the gospel of grace. Rather than resolve the issue easily for us in this Gospel, Jesus simply increases the pressure: "Not everyone who says to me, 'Lord, Lord,' will enter the kingdom of heaven, but only the one who does the will of my Father in heaven" (7:21). The sermon ends with a sharp contrast between those who hear Jesus's words *and act on them* and those who do not: "The rain fell, and the floods came, and the winds blew and beat against that house, and it fell—and great was its fall!" (7:27). Apparently only those who *obey* Jesus will be able to stand amid the storms of life.

Thirteen of the seventeen occurrences of the word "hypocrite" in the NT occur in Matthew. The word literally means "actor" in Greek, making it quite appropriate for a Gospel focused on obedience. The scribes and Pharisees are the primary target of this charge, "for they do not practice what they teach" (23:3). One of the best illustrations of the contrast between faithfulness and hypocrisy, however, comes in the form of one of Jesus's parables:

> What do you think? A man had two sons; he went to the first and said, "Son, go and work in the vineyard today." He answered, "I will not"; but later he changed his mind and went. The father went to the second and said the same; and he answered, "I go, sir"; but he did not go. Which of the two did the will of his father? (21:28–31)

If obedience is the bottom line, neither right association nor right confession will do. Going to church doesn't make one faithful before God. Neither does believing the right things. The only way to do the will of the Father, it turns out, is to actually do it! The church is to be a community of careful obedience to Jesus's way of life. How else can it rightly fulfill its function as the light of the world? Hence the Gospel of Matthew ends with a Great Commission, charging the church with the task of making disciples of all nations, "teaching them to obey everything that I have commanded you" (28:20).

And yet, in the face of this strident call to a demanding obedience, Jesus can say, "Take my yoke upon you, and learn from me; for I am gentle and humble in heart, and you will find rest for your souls. For my yoke is easy, and my burden is light" (Matt. 11:29–30). This is the case because Jesus is God with us, the one sent into the world out of the abundance of God's mercy, not only to show us the way of righteousness, but also to empower us to actually walk in the way of righteousness.

The "mercy" theme in Matthew emerges before Jesus even arrives on the narrative stage. Before Joseph finds out that Mary is pregnant by the power of the Holy Spirit, he does not fulfill the letter of **Torah** in regard to Mary (death by stoning, Deut. 22:13–30), but "being a righteous man and unwilling to expose her to public disgrace, planned to dismiss her quietly" (1:19). Apparently righteousness has less to do with rigid outward compliance with the law and more to do with being merciful.

Jesus himself will underscore this theme at key points in the Gospel. His Beatitudes include the line, "Blessed are the merciful, for they will receive mercy" (5:7). Later, when Jesus is criticized for eating with unworthy tax collectors and sinners, Matthew alone of the Gospel writers has Jesus respond by quoting Hosea 6:6, "Go and learn what this means, 'I desire mercy, not sacrifice'" (9:13). Later, when the disciples are criticized for plucking grain on the Sabbath, Matthew alone has Jesus again quoting Hosea 6:6: "If you had known what this means, 'I desire mercy, not sacrifice,' you would not have condemned the guiltless" (12:7). In all these instances, mercy triumphs over judgment. Put sharply, in Matthew's Gospel mercy is revealed to be the basis on which God's law rests, and thus mercy takes priority over strict obedience. Indeed, the primary act of obedience *is* being merciful. The emphasis is made quite clear in Jesus's long denunciation of the scribes and Pharisees (chap. 23), where at one point Jesus says,

Woe to you, scribes and Pharisees, hypocrites! For you tithe mint, dill, and cumin, and have neglected the weightier matters of the law: justice and mercy and faith. It is these you ought to have practiced without neglecting the others. You blind guides! You strain out a gnat but swallow a camel! (23:23–24)

Apparently some commands of Scripture are weightier than others, and in the scale of determination are things like justice, mercy, and faith. If a choice is to be made between performing an act of religious piety and showing mercy on another human being, the faithful witness to God's rule will show mercy. "In everything," Jesus says, "do to others as you would have them do to you; for this is the law and the prophets" (7:12).

At this point readers may wonder how the church is supposed to balance this call to careful obedience with the habit of radical mercy. The balance has proved difficult for most congregations; we tend to either insist on strict obedience to the point of being exclusionary, or emphasize mercy in the name of inclusion with the result that Christian distinctiveness is threatened. The Gospel of Matthew offers us no easy resolution apart from the promise of Jesus: "Where two or three are gathered in my name, I am there among them" (18:20). Only the church that is carefully focused on mediating the presence of the living Lord will be able to lead Christians in the way of merciful obedience.

We'll end this chapter with a powerful passage that illustrates the "presence" theme in action: the well-known scene of Jesus walking on the water.[9] The story is quite similar in the three Gospels that include it: the disciples are in a boat in a storm, Jesus walks to them on the water, they are afraid, and Jesus says, "It is I [*egō eimi*]; do not be afraid" (14:27). *Egō eimi*, "I am," is the OT name for God; not just any human is performing this superhuman task: it is the Lord of sea and sky, the Creator of the universe somehow fully present with humanity in the person of Jesus. Matthew's Gospel alone, however, has Peter respond, "Lord, if it is you [*ei sy ei*, literally, "if you are"], command me to come to you on the water" (14:28). "If you are truly God with us," Peter seems to say, "your empowering presence can enable me to do what you do, to speak with your words and walk in your steps. If you are with me, I will be empowered to walk the way of the Word." And Peter *does* walk on water: he *is* enabled to imitate this godlike act—until he takes his eyes off Jesus's presence, remembers the storm, and sinks like a stone.

9. See Matt. 14:22–33; Mark 6:45–52; John 6:15–21.

Jesus is God present with us. When Christians are gathered in Jesus's name, Jesus is there in their midst, and he brings with him the power of God. The church mediates Jesus's powerful presence as it performs the work that God has given it to do with merciful gladness and humble obedience.

—————————— Questions for Discussion ——————————

1. Now that you've read this chapter on Matthew, what questions do you have? What do you want to know more about? Make a list to share with your class or reading group.

2. What does it mean for the Gospel of Matthew to serve as a hinge between the Testaments? In what important ways is Matthew both continuous and discontinuous with the OT?

3. What is new or significant to you about the Son of God title in Matthew as portrayed in this chapter? Does it change your conception of Jesus in any way? If yes, how?

4. How does the story of Jesus walking on the water, as presented in Matthew, exemplify this Gospel's depiction of the call to discipleship?

5. This Gospel launches the NT with the emphatic claim that Jesus started a *church*. What is your understanding of the role of the church in the Christian life? How has this Gospel affirmed, challenged, or reshaped your view?

6. If Matthew's Gospel had been left out of the NT, what would be missing?

7. Where does this book locate you on the way of the Word? How has it helped you along? Where has it warned you to slow down? What in your discipleship requires acceleration? Has the route to your destination been at all clarified?

3

The Gospel according to Mark

The Cost of Discipleship

"Take up your cross and follow me."

(MARK 8:34)

In his *Harmony of the Gospels*, **Augustine of Hippo** records his understanding of the relationship between the Gospels of Matthew and Mark:

> Matthew is understood to have taken it in hand to construct the record of the incarnation of the Lord according to the royal lineage, and to give an account of most part of His deeds and words as they stood in relation to this present life of men. Mark follows him closely, and looks like his attendant and epitomizer. . . . By himself separately, he has little to record; in conjunction with Luke, as distinguished from the rest, he has still less; but in concord with Matthew, he has a very large number of passages. Much, too, he narrates in words almost numerically and identically the same as those used by Matthew, where the agreement is either with that **evangelist** alone, or with him in connection with the rest.[1]

---

1. Augustine, *Harmony of the Gospels* 1.2.4, in *A Select Library of Nicene and Post-Nicene Fathers of the Christian Church*, 1st series, trans. S. D. F. Salmond, ed. Philip Schaff, 14 vols. (1886–1889; repr., Peabody, MA: Hendrickson, 1994), 6:78.

According to this ancient understanding, Matthew wrote first, and Mark was an "attendant and epitomizer" who provided the **church** with little more than an abbreviated version of Matthew. This view held sway for most of church history and accounts for the scarcity of commentaries on Mark's Gospel before the modern period.

Upon closer examination, scholars have determined that Augustine's assumption was incorrect: it was not Mark who abbreviated Matthew, but Matthew who expanded upon Mark. This recovery of Mark's historical priority had the effect of pulling Mark out of the shadows, which led, in turn, to a rediscovery of the immense power and distinctiveness of Mark's Gospel. Far from being Matthew's epitomizer, Mark offers us a unique and challenging portrait of Jesus—and by extension, a stunning portrayal of the cost involved for those who follow the way of the Word.

Canonical Transition: From Matthew to Mark

As the last chapter made plain, Matthew's Gospel launches the NT with a clear, well-ordered Gospel focused on calling people to follow Jesus. It was a challenging call, no doubt, but it was a call to which people were able to faithfully respond. **Disciples** may be people of "little faith" (Matthew's favorite designation for disciples: 6:30; 8:26; 14:31; 16:8; 17:20), but apparently even a very little faith is enough to move mountains (21:21–22). In Matthew's Gospel, disciples can follow Jesus and do what he can do—even walk on water (14:28–33). In Matthew's Gospel, disciples make mistakes, but they understand who Jesus is (14:33) and receive his teaching "with joy" (13:20, 51–52). By the time we come to the end of Matthew and receive the call "Go therefore and make disciples of all nations" (28:19), readers feel equipped for the task and ready to begin the mission.

Then we turn the page and find ourselves reading another Gospel. But where Matthew's Gospel was clear and orderly, this is a stripped-down and fast-paced Gospel. Instead of a patient articulation of Jesus's lineage and origin, we find ourselves in the middle of the action right at the very beginning: After a one-line introduction (Mark 1:1), we read a quick version of John's work (1:2–8) before Jesus appears rather suddenly (1:9); he is quickly **baptized** and "thrown" (literal translation of Greek *ekballō*, not gently "led" as in the other Gospels) into the wilderness by the Spirit to face temptation (1:12; cf. Matt. 4:1); he immediately begins his ministry (1:14–15), calls a few disciples (1:16–20), and heads into a **synagogue** to pick a fight with a demon who is suddenly revealed to have been residing there right alongside the religious folks (1:21–28). All this storyline, which requires four chapters to convey in Matthew, takes place in the first twenty-eight verses of Mark. At this point, readers of Matthew may find themselves joining in the chorus of amazed witnesses in the synagogue who "kept on asking one another, 'What is this? A new teaching—with authority!'" (1:27). Yes, Mark follows Matthew to provide readers with a new Gospel teaching, and in **canonical** sequence it reads as a cautionary note following on the optimism of Matthew. As we will see, where Matthew's Gospel presented us with the *call* to discipleship, Mark presents us with a stark portrayal of discipleship's *cost*.

Numerous points of contrast illustrate the difference between the two Gospels. We ended the last chapter with a look at the walking-on-water scene, where Peter quite literally steps out in faith at Jesus's command (Matt. 14:28–33). In Mark's Gospel the scene plays out exactly as in Matthew: the disciples are caught in a boat in a storm, Jesus walks out to them on the water, they are afraid, and as before Jesus responds, "It is I; do not be afraid"—but here there is no faithful disciple joining Jesus on the water. Instead, "he got into the boat with them and the wind ceased. And they were utterly astounded, for they did not understand, . . . but their hearts were hardened" (Mark 6:51–52). Where the scene in Matthew's Gospel ended in worship (Matt. 14:33), Mark ends with the disciples lost in confusion and fear. Throughout the whole of Mark's Gospel, the disciples do not understand who Jesus is or comprehend what he is doing. In Matthew, disciples are the light of the world, but in Mark's Gospel the disciples find themselves stumbling along in a world of darkness where illumination is hard to come by.

It would be incorrect, however, for us to characterize Matthew as an optimistic Gospel and Mark as a pessimistic one. Mark does not insist that humans are incapable of understanding who Jesus is: Mark insists that humans are *prevented* from doing so by God. Notice the following contrasts:

> Nothing is covered up that will not be uncovered, and nothing secret that will not become known. (Matt. 10:26)

> For there is nothing hidden, except [*in order*] to be disclosed; nor is anything secret, except to come to light.[2] (Mark 4:22)

Where Matthew's Jesus reveals that which is hidden, Mark has Jesus concealing things *as a means of* **revelation**. Consider these parallel statements on the reason Jesus speaks in **parables**:

> The reason I speak to them in parables is *that* "seeing they do not perceive, and hearing they do not listen, nor do they understand." (Matt. 13:13, emphasis added)

> Everything comes in parables, *in order that* they may indeed look, but not perceive, and may indeed listen, but not understand; so that they may not turn again and be forgiven. (Mark 4:11–12, emphasis added)

In Matthew, Jesus justifies teaching in parables because those who are not listening carefully aren't going to understand anyway. In Mark, Jesus tells parables *in order that* people won't understand and change their ways. The sharp contrast between the two is evident when the parallel scenes are set side by side: when Jesus finishes telling his parables in Matthew's Gospel, he asks his disciples, "'Have you understood all this?' They answered, 'Yes'" (Matt. 13:51). When Jesus finishes his parable in the same scene in Mark's Gospel, he berates the disciples for their lack of understanding: "Do you not understand this parable? Then how will you understand all the parables?" (Mark 4:13).

The **church fathers** had a set of terms for describing the difference we encounter here: **kataphasis** and **apophasis**. Kataphasis combines

---

2. By including *hina*, "in order to," which is not translated in the NRSV here, my rendition, as well as this reading of Mark 4 in general, follows Richard B. Hays, *Reading Backwards: Figural Christology and the Fourfold Gospel Witness* (Waco: Baylor University Press, 2014), 28–33.

the Greek prefix *kata-* (an intensifier in this instance) with the verb *phanai*, meaning "to speak"; kataphatic **theology** underscores what can be known of God. It involves making *affirmations* about God, describing who God is. God *is* love. God *is* merciful. God *is* present with us. Apophasis, by contrast, combines the Greek prefix *apo-* (meaning "off" or "away from") with *phanai*; it underscores the *unknowability* of God and describes God according to what God is not. God *is not* like us. God *is not* reducible to our preferred ways of thinking. God works in mysterious ways that sometimes leave us befuddled and scared. Kataphasis describes God as knowable. Apophasis reminds us that true knowledge of God forces us to acknowledge that there is so much we do not and cannot know about God.

Taken together, Matthew and Mark seem to represent these two sides of God's revelation in **Christ**. With Matthew's Gospel alone, disciples may fall into the trap of thinking they fully understand God and God's call on their lives. Mark's Gospel follows Matthew as a kind of canonical speed bump, requiring us to slow down to reconsider what we've read from another perspective. Mark reminds disciples that the yoke of discipleship is not always easy, and the burden of following not always light. Matthew teaches us how to swim, but Mark leads us out into deep, dark waters. Matthew informs us of what to expect of God's *presence* in our lives. Mark insists that we should not be at all surprised when God seems *absent*—and that when God does act, we should expect the unexpected.

The Shape of Mark's Gospel

One need not read much of Mark to notice the difference between it and Matthew. Matthew presents us with a well-lit path through a Gospel that is plainly structured and well-ordered in its presentation of Jesus's words and deeds. Mark, by contrast, is a shadowy Gospel where the reader often feels lost and disoriented. There are many reasons for this. Mark's Gospel rushes along at breakneck pace, with almost no transitional scenes to introduce the stories. There are too few references to the passing of time, leaving the reader unable to place the stories in a meaningful chronological frame. And with the absence of extensive teaching material, Jesus often inhabits an obscure and ambiguous persona.

As we've already noticed, Matthew and Mark share the same basic narrative plotline.

Matthew	Mark
Introduction (1:1–3:17)	Introduction (1:1–15)
Ministry in Galilee (4:1–18:35)	Ministry in Galilee (1:16–10:52)
Ministry in Judea (19:1–20:33)	Ministry in Judea (11:1–13:37)
Confrontation in Jerusalem (21:1–27:66)	Confrontation in Jerusalem (14:1–15:47)
Resurrection (28:1–20)	Resurrection (16:1–20)

What Mark doesn't include are Jesus's five teaching sermons recorded in Matthew. With Mark, the focus is almost always on the *deeds* of Jesus. Many of Jesus's famous *words* are missing here, but Mark's versions of the major **Synoptic** miracle stories are typically longer and are often told in greater detail.

A particularly telling feature of Mark's miracle stories is their placement in the plotline of the Gospel as a whole. The majority of Mark's miracles—seventeen of the total nineteen—take place in the first eight chapters. Indeed, the miracles come along so frequently in the first half of Mark that the reader is left with the sense that Jesus has come primarily to be a worker of wonders who casts out demons, stills storms, heals paralytics, and feeds multitudes. And yet, after Jesus has performed one miracle after another, no one seems to understand who he is. He casts out demons, and the religious authorities think he's demon possessed (Mark 3:22). He walks on water, and his disciples think he's a ghost (6:49). Just after multiplying a few loaves and fishes to feed thousands, the **Pharisees** have the nerve to come to Jesus and demand that he provide a sign from heaven! Flabbergasted, Jesus "sighed deeply in his spirit and said, 'Why does this generation ask for a sign? Truly I tell you, no sign will be given to this generation'" (8:12). Right after that, when the disciples reveal that they don't understand what is happening either, Jesus launches into an angry rebuke: "Do you still not perceive or understand? Are your hearts hardened? Do you have eyes, and fail to see? Do you have ears, and fail to hear?" (8:17–18).

This plot point marks the beginning of a major shift in Jesus's perceived attitude toward the performance of miracles. He heals one more person at the end of chapter 8, another in chapter 9 (where he responds to the healing request with a grumpy, "You faithless generation, how much longer must I be among you?" [Mark 9:19]), and then one final healing in chapter 10—but by that time, Jesus's role has clearly shifted from being a public wonder-worker: Jesus is moving about in secret, teaching his disciples in private.

Certain structural features help us make further sense of this significant transition in Mark's Gospel. The seventeenth miracle occurs immediately after Jesus rebukes his disciples for their lack of understanding (8:22–26), and it is a strange one: it is the first healing of a blind man, who regains his sight only after Jesus makes *two* attempts to heal him. The first attempt leaves him seeing only partially, with blurry vision. The second heals him completely, such that "he saw everything clearly" (8:25). This stumbled, two-stage healing is found nowhere in the other Gospels; why would Jesus require *two* attempts to enable someone to see?

Right after this, as Jesus and his disciples make their way through Caesarea Philippi, Jesus asks a *perception* question: "Who do people say that I am?" (Mark 8:27). While the majority of people *see* Jesus as a **prophet**, Peter confesses that he *sees* Jesus as the **Messiah** (8:29). At that moment Jesus reveals, for the very first time, that he must go to Jerusalem to confront the religious authorities, be executed at their behest, and "after three days rise again" (8:31). Mark notes that "he said all this quite openly," quite *clearly*, without any hiddenness. But this new revelation of Jesus's plan is not at all clear to Peter, who immediately begins to rebuke Jesus for suggesting such a thing. Apparently Peter *sees* that Jesus is the Messiah, but he does not see clearly; his vision is blurred by his own hopes for Jesus's kingship, a vision where Messiahs conquer their enemies and do not allow themselves to be conquered. Could it be that the double healing of the blind man mirrors the partial healing of

Peter, who has only a partial, hazy vision of Jesus's identity and mission?

This interpretive hunch is confirmed over the next couple chapters as another pattern emerges. On three separate occasions Jesus will announce his intention to die and rise again (Mark 8:31; 9:30–32; 10:32–34). On each occasion the disciples will immediately reveal their misunderstanding of Jesus's intention (8:32; 9:33–34; 10:35–41), and Jesus will follow each with a corrective teaching designed to heal them of their distorted vision of his mission (8:33–9:1; 9:35–37; 10:42–45). Amazingly, this process ends with the second healing of a blind person in Mark (10:46–52), the last miracle performed by Jesus in the Gospel. In contrast with the first, this man is healed "immediately . . . and followed [Jesus] on the way" (10:52).

So here we find a pattern of Jesus teaching his disciples about the way of the cross, framed on either side by two stories of people regaining their sight. The first sees only partially, until a second healing makes him well; Jesus teaches about the cross; a final healing of a blind man enables him to see everything such that he can follow the way of the Word without stumbling.

After so many miracles, what does this structural pattern suggest? It seems that those who come to Jesus to see signs and wonders will only understand him partially. They may receive *some* healing, but their understanding will be limited, and they'll have a hard time following because of their blurred vision. Only those who receive Jesus's difficult teaching about the cross will be able to "see" him clearly and follow him faithfully on his way.

Let's consider how this pattern fits within the Gospel of Mark as a whole. If we take Jesus's frustration over miracles and the two-stage healing as a midpoint (8:11–26), we discover something else. Immediately after these scenes Jesus asks his disciples, "Who do people say that I am?" (8:27). This is not the first time the question of Jesus's identity has come up. In fact, up to this point many people have been wondering who Jesus is (1:7, 27; 2:7; 3:22; 4:41; 6:2–3, 49–50). The only ones who know Jesus's identity are the readers, who are told in the very first verse (1:1); God, who announces it aloud twice (1:11; 9:7); and, amazingly, the demons whom Jesus encounters (1:24, 34; 3:11; 5:7). For his part, Jesus has spent most of his time trying to *keep* people from knowing who he is! He silences the demons who announce his identity (1:23–25, 34; 3:11–12), speaks in parables so that his hearers won't understand (4:10–12), and demands that those he heals say nothing to anyone about what happened to them (1:40–44; 5:43; 7:36; 8:26).

We see, then, that this is a Gospel focused quite intensely on the question of Jesus's identity. Prior to chapter 8, every human in the story is wondering who Jesus is. After the frustration over miracles, Jesus announces his identity plainly to the disciples (Mark 8:32) and spends the next few chapters teaching them privately what following him involves (see, e.g., 9:30–31). Through all this we may discern that Mark is a two-part Gospel: in the first part, Jesus is a public wonder-worker, but he is ironically focused on *concealing* who he is, so everyone is left confused; in the second part, Jesus devotes his time to private instruction about the way of the cross, *revealing clearly* who he is, but this leaves the disciples more confused than ever.

The Structure of Mark

Part One—1:1–8:26—miracles in public, identity concealed	
1:1	Readers are informed of Jesus's identity.
1:11	God identifies Jesus at his baptism.
1:21–28	Demon says, "I know who you are!," and onlookers ask, "Who is this?"
1:21–8:21	Sixteen miracles proclaim Jesus's identity as the embodiment of God's power.
8:22–26	Seventeenth miracle is the healing of someone blind who sees, but only partially at first.
Part Two—8:27–16:20—teaching in private, identity revealed	
8:27	Jesus asks, "Who do people say that I am?" and Peter proclaims his identity.
9:7	God identifies Jesus at the transfiguration.
8:31–10:45	Pattern: Jesus describes the way of the cross, disciples see partially, Jesus corrects.
10:46–52	Final miracle: blind man regains his sight and is able to follow Jesus.
11:1–16:20	Jesus enters Jerusalem and completes his journey to the cross.

Despite the differences between Mark's Gospel and Matthew's, one of the key emphases has remained the same: those who claim to be Christian must correctly understand Jesus's identity if they are to follow the way of the Word.

What Does Mark Teach Us about God's Work in Christ Jesus?

Thus far we have seen that Mark's Jesus is enigmatic and hard to understand. But why? What would God's purpose be in sending a Messiah no one would be able to receive or understand? Why would Jesus speak in parables "in order that they may indeed look, but not perceive, and may indeed listen, but not understand; so that they may not turn again and be forgiven" (4:11–12)? Why would Jesus silence those who recognize him and insist that those he heals say nothing to anyone about what has happened to them?

Let's look again at Mark's version of Jesus walking on water (6:47–52). The scene is strikingly similar in the other two Gospels that include the story (cf. Matt. 14:22–33; John 6:15–21), but in contrast to Matthew's memorable inclusion of Peter joining Jesus on the water, Mark includes one minute detail that is easily overlooked: as Jesus is walking on the water within sight of his disciples, the narrator says that Jesus "intended to pass them by" (6:48). Jesus did not aim to join the disciples in the boat; he wanted to pass by in front of them, to let them witness his display of the Creator's power, but *not* to invite them to participate in that power as he does in Matthew's version of the story. Why would he do that?

Those who are familiar with the **Scriptures** of Israel will pick up on the resonance these words create with OT scenes where God is revealed in an indirect fashion. In the book of Exodus, just after the Lord proclaims his commitment to Moses (33:17), Moses asks God, "Show me your glory" (33:18). God responds,

"I will make all my goodness *pass before you*, and will proclaim before you the name, 'The LORD'. . . . But," he said, "you cannot see my face; for no one shall see me and live." And the LORD continued, "See, there is a place by me where you shall stand on the rock; and while my glory *passes by* I will put you in a cleft of the rock, and I will cover you with my hand until I have *passed by*; then I will take away

my hand, and you shall see my back; but my face shall not be seen."
(Exod. 33:19–23, emphasis added)

Moses gets to catch a glimpse of God, but not directly; God can be seen from behind, passing by: but to look directly at God, to see God's glory in its fullness, is beyond human capacity.

Later in Israel's history, the prophet Elijah will find himself suffering persecution under a corrupt king. He retreats into the wilderness, travels to Mount Horeb (the same place Moses encountered God), and hides in a cave. God meets him there and says,

> "Go out and stand on the mountain before the LORD, for *the LORD is about to pass by*." Now there was a great wind, so strong that it was splitting mountains and breaking rocks in pieces before the LORD, but the LORD was not in the wind; and after the wind an earthquake, but the LORD was not in the earthquake; and after the earthquake a fire, but the LORD was not in the fire; and after the fire a sound of sheer silence. When Elijah heard it, he wrapped his face in his mantle and went out and stood at the entrance of the cave. (1 Kings 19:11–13, emphasis added)

This is a striking moment in the history of God's revelation. Israel was used to encountering the presence and power of "the LORD" through cataclysms in creation, through fire,[3] earthquakes,[4] and wind.[5] This was particularly the case in the central salvation story of Israel, the exodus from Egypt, where God demonstrated who alone had the right to be known as King of kings and the Ruler of all creation. Nevertheless, in this scene with Elijah, God is not revealed according to Israel's expectation; instead, God is made known in "a sound of sheer silence." This Hebrew phrase—which brings together the words for *voice*, *silent* or *still*, and *thin*—is notoriously difficult to translate into English: it has been rendered "a still small voice" (KJV/RSV), "a sound of a gentle blowing" (NASB), "the sound of a low whisper" (ESV), or simply "a gentle whisper" (NIV). Whatever it is, it

---

3. Fire, as in Gen. 19:24; Exod. 3:2; 9:13–23; 13:21–22; 19:18; Lev. 10:2; Num. 16:35; 1 Kings 18:23–40; Ps. 18:8.

4. Earthquakes, as in Exod. 19:18; Pss. 18:7; 68:8; 2 Sam. 22:8.

5. Wind, as in Gen. 8:1; Exod. 13:21–22; 15:10; Ps. 78:26.

is an experience that exceeds normal human expression; it is a *sound* that is *silent*, a *void* that is *palpable*, a *something* that is knowable but cannot be grasped.

This destabilizing experience of God is expressed most powerfully in the story of Job, who knows that God is present and able to save, but cannot understand what God is up to when God *doesn't* save him from pain and loss. In the midst of his confusion, Job complains,

> If one wished to contend with him, one could not answer him once in a thousand. He is wise in heart, and mighty in strength—who has resisted him, and succeeded?—he who removes mountains, and they do not know it, when he overturns them in his anger; who shakes the earth out of its place, and its pillars tremble; who commands the sun, and it does not rise; who seals up the stars; who alone stretched out the heavens and *trampled the waves of the Sea*; who made the Bear and Orion, the Pleiades and the chambers of the south; who does great things beyond understanding, and marvelous things without number. Look, *he passes by me*, and I do not see him; he moves on, but I do not perceive him. He snatches away; who can stop him? Who will say to him, "What are you doing?" (Job 9:3–12, emphasis added)

"He tramples the waves of the sea. . . . He passes by me, and I do not see him; he moves on, but I do not perceive him." In a clear echo of this very scene, Mark's portrayal of Jesus appears to underscore a crucial truth about God, one that God's people must understand if their faith is to withstand the storms of life: God may be "with us" in Jesus, as Matthew proclaims, but that presence is often experienced indirectly and ambiguously. Indeed, sometimes it is known only as a sound of sheer silence, an experience of absence and alienation where the only thing that feels truly real is the hole torn in our hearts when God cannot be seen or heard.

Disciples trained to know Jesus through the Gospel of Mark will come to expect this experience in their lives. They will know that God's ways are not our ways, nor are God's thoughts our thoughts (Isa. 55:8–9). They will know that God's power is expressed in self-giving service, and God's victory takes the form of self-denial and loss. Indeed, disciples shaped by Mark will be ready to be astonished by God. The women who come to Jesus's tomb at the end of Mark's

Gospel do not expect to encounter anything other than a dead body, but instead are surprised by an angel telling them, "You are looking for Jesus of Nazareth, who was crucified. He has been raised; *he is not here*" (16:6, emphasis added). This is an unexpected, shocking experience of Jesus's absence, but it comes with a promise: "*He is going ahead of you* to Galilee; *there you will see him*, just as he told you" (16:7, emphasis added).

Jesus is not here, but we are not abandoned; Jesus may be experienced as absent, but that does not mean we are forsaken. As **Dietrich Bonhoeffer** knew so well, "Those who have found God in the cross of Jesus Christ know how wonderfully God hides himself in this world and how he is closest precisely when we believe him to be most distant."[6] The call to walk the way of the Word involves walking "by faith, not by sight" (2 Cor. 5:7), knowing that one day when we least expect it, Jesus will pass us by in a rich demonstration of divine power—provided we have eyes that are trained to see his deeds and ears that are skilled at hearing his word. But what habits and practices will prepare us to be available to this elusive God?

What Does Mark Teach Us about the Spiritual Formation of Christian Disciples?

If there is one thing we learn about discipleship from Mark's Gospel, it is this: followers of Jesus should not expect to fully understand God's will and God's ways. Consider how often those around Jesus are confused by what they hear or see:

> "Do you not understand this parable? Then how will you understand all the parables?" (4:13)

> For they did not understand about the loaves, but their hearts were hardened. (6:52)

> "Then do you also fail to understand?" (7:18)

6. Dietrich Bonhoeffer, *God Is on the Cross: Reflections on Lent and Easter* (Louisville: Westminster John Knox, 2012), 62.

"Why are you talking about having no bread? Do you still not perceive or understand?" (8:17)

But they did not understand what he was saying and were afraid to ask him. (9:32)

The preeminent sin of God's people throughout Scripture is idolatry, the human tendency to put something created in the position of authority that belongs to the Creator alone. Among the various false gods we worship in our lives, none is more deadly than the pocket-sized, preferred versions of God that we carry around with us. We are fearful and uncertain, so we give preference to kataphatic notions of God's identity, with the result that God is reduced into categories that fit our expectations and serve our ends. We fail to remember that God is also known apophatically and that a true encounter with God should take us to a new and perhaps even unsettling place. As Augustine once said, "Why wonder that you do not understand? For if you understand, it is not God."[7] Or more positively, in the words of **Gregory of Nyssa**: "This is truly the vision of God: never to be satisfied in the desire to see him."[8]

Mark's Gospel reminds us that God is at work even when we don't see or understand God's work. But it also reminds us that our vision is vastly improved when we attend to the pattern of God's mysterious character and behavior as it is witnessed throughout the Scriptures of Israel and as we watch the disciples struggle in Mark. When the storms of life assail us, those who know their Scripture will not scream at the sky, "Do you not care that we are perishing?" (Mark 4:38); and when the storm subsides and the seas are stilled, those who know their Scripture will not wonder, "Who then is this, that even the wind and the sea obey him?" (4:41). They will calm their fear with the knowledge that the Lord of sea and sky is there with them in the storm and is more than able to calm anything that threatens

7. Augustine, *Sermon* 117.5, quoted in John Paul II, *Augustinum Hipponsensem*, apostolic letter, August 28, 1986, http://w2.vatican.va/content/john-paul-ii/en/apost_letters/1986/documents/hf_jp-ii_apl_26081986_augustinum-hipponensem.html.

8. Gregory of Nyssa, *The Life of Moses* 2.239, in *Gregory of Nyssa: The Life of Moses*, trans. Abraham J. Malherbe and Everett Ferguson, Classics of Western Spirituality (Mahwah, NJ: Paulist Press, 1978), 116.

to overtake us (cf. Pss. 65:5–7; 89:9; 104:7; 107:23–29). When we are wandering in the wilderness and lacking sustenance, those who know their Scripture will recall the provisions of the past (Mark 6:30–44; cf. Exod. 16:13–35; 2 Kings 4:42–44; Ps. 23) and will not be like the disciples who ask "How can one feed these people with bread here in the desert?" (Mark 8:4). And when we feel abandoned by God, we will remember the bare honesty of the psalmist who was not afraid to say, "My God, my God, why have you forsaken me?" (Ps. 22:1; Mark 15:34), recalling as Jesus did what happened with the ancestors who trusted in God: "They trusted, and you delivered them. To you they cried, and were saved; in you they trusted, and were not put to shame" (Ps. 22:4–5).

Even when we know our Scripture, we will still get it wrong sometimes. Mark's Gospel reminds us, contrary to the contemporary slogan "Failure is not an option," that failure *is* in fact an option—and indeed it has to be, "so that the cross of Christ might not be emptied of its power" (1 Cor. 1:17–18). Matthew's Gospel may portray Peter striding godlike on the waves of the sea, but we will be in serious trouble if we ever forget how quickly Peter sank once he took his eyes off Jesus (Matt. 14:28–31). Mark's Gospel portrays a Jesus who passes us by "to give his life as a ransom for many" (Mark 10:45), one who walks along a way where only the Word can lead. When Jesus feels absent, Mark asks us to remember the promise of the angel: he is not here but has gone on before us and promises to meet us at the end if we will follow where he leads. As Gregory reminds us,

> To follow God wherever he might lead *is* to behold God. His passing by signifies his guiding the one who follows, for someone who does not know the way cannot complete his journey safely in any other way than by following behind his guide. He who leads, then, by his guidance shows the way to the one following. He who follows will not turn aside from the right way if he always keeps the back of his leader in view. For he who moves to one side or brings himself to face his guide assumes another direction for himself than the one his guide shows him.[9]

9. Gregory of Nyssa, *Life of Moses* 2.252–53, in *Gregory of Nyssa: The Life of Moses*, trans. Malherbe and Ferguson, 119 (emphasis original).

Epilogue

One final point about Mark must be made before we conclude. Scholars have argued for some time now that Mark's Gospel originally ended at 16:8, "So [the women] went out and fled from the tomb, for terror and amazement had seized them; and they said nothing to anyone, for they were afraid." This ambiguous, unsettling ending comports well with Mark's own themes throughout the Gospel, where disciples do not understand, show no faith (4:40; 9:19), and fail to follow through on what is commanded of them. Some **scribes** apparently found this ending too abrupt, so other verses were added on to certain **manuscripts** of the Gospel.[10]

The ending the church eventually canonized includes another twelve verses that were clearly designed to bring Mark to what was deemed a more fitting conclusion. But if Mark's original ending was found to be too jarring, this longer ending introduces a series of other problems. For one thing, 16:1 tells us that two other women accompanied Mary Magdalene that morning, but 16:9 insists that Jesus appeared first to Mary Magdalene alone. That verse also informs us that Mary was the one from whom Jesus "cast out seven demons," as if the reader would recognize her by this particular feature, but neither Matthew nor Mark have said any such thing. This ending twice calls Jesus "Lord" (vv. 19–20), against Mark's preference throughout the Gospel for referring to Jesus by his name alone. This paragraph also includes around eighteen words not found elsewhere in Mark's Gospel, and it emphasizes "signs" (vv. 17–18) despite the fact that Mark's Gospel repeatedly downplays the efficacy of such things.

Rather than see this longer ending as a fitting part of Mark's Gospel, it makes more sense to read it as a "canonical" ending—not simply because it was the one eventually canonized, but also because it quite clearly points *away* from the distinctiveness of Mark's Gospel by incorporating materials found in the other three Gospels and Acts.

10. Our oldest manuscripts along with a number of other early witnesses to Mark show no evidence of 16:9–20.

A Truly Canonical Ending—Mark 16:9–20

v. 9	He appeared first to Mary Magdalene.	John 20:14
v. 9	. . . from whom he had cast out seven demons.	Luke 8:2
v. 10	She went out and told those who had been with him, while they were mourning and weeping.	John 20:18
v. 11	But when they heard that he was alive and had been seen by her, they would not believe it.	Luke 24:11
v. 12	After this he appeared in another form to two of them, as they were walking into the country.	Luke 24:13–35
v. 14	Later he appeared to the eleven themselves.	Matthew 28:16
vv. 15–16	And he said to them, "Go into all the world and proclaim the good news to the whole creation. The one who believes and is baptized will be saved."	Matthew 28:19
v. 17	"And these signs will accompany those who believe."	Acts 2:43; 5:12
v. 17	"By using my name they will cast out demons."	Acts 5:16; 8:7
v. 17	"They will speak in new tongues."	Acts 2:4
v. 18	"They will pick up snakes in their hands."	Acts 28:3–6
v. 18	"They will lay their hands on the sick, and they will recover."	Acts 9:12, 17
v. 19	So then the Lord Jesus, after he had spoken to them, was taken up into heaven.	Luke 24:51
v. 19	. . . and sat down at the right hand of God.	Acts 2:33; 5:31; 7:55–56
v. 20	And they went out and proclaimed the good news everywhere.	Acts 1:8

The longer ending of Mark does less to complete Mark's Gospel than to remind readers that there is more to read, that there are other stories, other voices to hear, other encounters with Jesus to experience. Mark's ending breaks open the apparent finality of the disciples' failure in order to prepare us for other perspectives.

Indeed, despite the claim in verse 8 that the women "said nothing to anyone," the next Gospel will begin by introducing us to an individual who had in fact received instruction in the way of Jesus and is ready for more information (Luke 1:3–4). Disciples may have "little faith" (Matt. 6:30; 8:26; 16:8) or even "no faith" at all (Mark 4:40), but that will not keep the good news from being spread abroad to reach the ends of the earth.

——————————————— Questions for Discussion ———————————————

1. Now that you've read Mark, what questions do you have? What do you want to know more about? Make a list to share with your class or reading group.

2. If so much of Mark is already found in Matthew, what is the canonical value of Mark's Gospel? Restate this Gospel's function in your own words.

3. In what ways does the interplay of *revelation* and *concealment* shape Mark's Gospel? Why is it important that the knowable God maintain some sense of unknowability?

4. How does Mark's story of Jesus's walking on water compare with Matthew's? How does this reflect Mark's contribution to the biblical canon?

5. Mark wants readers to know that we will not be able to follow Jesus faithfully if we do not follow him to the cross. How has this challenged your own discipleship or your conception of Christian discipleship?

6. If Mark's Gospel had been left out of the NT, what would be missing?

7. Where does this book locate you on the way of the Word? How has it helped you along? Where has it warned you to slow down? What in your discipleship requires acceleration? Has the route to your destination been at all clarified?

4

The Gospel according to Luke

The Scope of Discipleship

"The kingdom of God is among you."

(LUKE 17:21)

Luke's opening is strikingly different from those of the other **Gospels** we've read thus far. Where Matthew and Mark both begin with a strong christological claim—This is the gospel of Jesus Christ, the Son of God, the son of David and son of Abraham—Luke's Gospel begins with one long, carefully composed sentence that is notable *not* for its **theological** claims but for its undeniable *secularity*. Scholars have long observed that Luke has deliberately constructed this opening in imitation of the **Hellenistic** historians and biographers of his age: from the acknowledgment of other available Gospels, to the listing of his credentials as a historian and the dedication to his patron "Theophilus," this piece of Holy **Scripture** begins much the same as any worldly history would have in the first-century Greco-Roman world. The lofty language resembles an ornate marble entrance welcoming the reader to a building erected prominently in the middle of the public square. This is not a Gospel written for one subgroup of Christians or another. This is a Gospel for the public, and everyone is invited to enter in.

But who is this "Theophilus" fellow? The reference to him at the beginning of the work suggests that he is the author's patron, the person who supported the writing and publication of the Gospel. Yet the name itself means "Friend of God." It was a common enough name in Luke's day, but some have wondered if perhaps the dedication is simply a literary device to describe all Christian readers. So **Origen of Alexandria**, in his *Homilies on the Gospel of Luke*, writes, "Someone might think that Luke addressed the Gospel to a specific man named Theophilus. But, if you are the sort of people God can love, then all of you who hear us speaking are Theophiluses, and the Gospel is addressed to you."[1]

All of you are Theophiluses. As we will see, this Gospel is addressed to everyone—"Jew or Greek, . . . slave or free, . . . male and female" (Gal. 3:28)—to the widest possible scope of readers, so that all might come to know the truth about Jesus and follow him as he leads us along the way of the Word.

Canonical Transition: From Mark to Luke

As we observed at the end of the previous chapter, Mark's endings indicate a desire on the part of the scribal community to make sure readers understood that the gospel did indeed spread abroad, despite the claim that the first witnesses "fled from the tomb" and "said nothing to anyone, for they were afraid" (Mark 16:8). Luke's Gospel opens by affirming that fact and more: as it turns out, "many" have undertaken the task of setting down versions of the gospel story, and Luke intends to write one that is more carefully written and "orderly" in its presentation (1:3).

From a rhetorical perspective, Luke's long opening sentence lands hard on the final phrase. If we reconstruct the English according to Greek word order, it would be translated to read, "so that you may

---

1. Origen, *Homilies on the Gospel of Luke* 1.6, in *Origen: Homilies on Luke; Fragments on Luke*, trans. Joseph T. Lienhard, SJ, Fathers of the Church 94 (Washington, DC: Catholic University of America Press, 1996), 9.

know, concerning the things about which you have been instructed, *the truth*" (1:4). This is a fascinating line: though Theophilus has apparently already received some catechesis in the Christian faith, this instruction alone has not provided him with the particular experience of truth that Luke has in mind. The term "experience" is used intentionally here because the Greek word translated "truth" is not the most common word for "truth" in the NT. That word, *alētheia*, is typically used in relation to more conceptual truth. The word Luke uses here, however, is *asphaleia*, from which we get our English word "asphalt." *Asphaleia* is linked etymologically with the verb *sphallō*, "to make someone stumble or trip," but the "a" prefix turns the word into its opposite. To possess *asphaleia* is to possess stability or steadiness, a kind of trusting assurance that one will not fall despite the spinning unevenness of the ground.

After being challenged by Matthew only to be dizzied by Mark, most NT readers could probably use a dose of stability! Luke wants his "Theophilus" friends of God to know that his version of the gospel will provide them with the kind of stable assurance that basic, preliminary faith instruction alone cannot provide. Luke's is a *faith-strengthening* narrative, a version of the gospel designed to set Christians to work in the world with confidence. Readers have more to learn about God's work in Jesus, and Luke intends to offer further instruction.

The Shape of Luke's Gospel

Luke's Gospel maps out the full impact of God's salvation as it makes contact in creation. It accomplishes this by greatly expanding the impact of the gospel vision already set forth in the Gospels of Matthew and Mark. We can observe how he has sought to express this expansion spatially (both geographically and historically) as well as anthropologically.

Geographically speaking, the Gospel of Luke is focused intensely on the city of Jerusalem. The city is named thirty-three times in Luke (more than the other three Gospels combined), an additional sixty times in Luke's second work, the Acts of the Apostles, and

The Structure of Luke

1:1–4:13	Introduction
4:14–9:50	Ministry in Galilee
9:51–19:28	Travel Narrative
19:29–23:56	Confrontation in Jerusalem
24:1–53	Conclusion

only fourteen times elsewhere in the NT. Luke alone among the Gospels tells the story of twelve-year-old Jesus visiting Jerusalem with his parents and then sneaking back to discuss theology with the teachers in the temple, telling his parents, "Did you not know that I must be in my Father's house?" (2:41–52). Luke narrates very much the same temptation story as Matthew but changes the order of the devil's temptations to have the climax take place in Jerusalem (4:1–13). The transfiguration of Jesus is narrated in all three **Synoptic Gospels,** but only Luke relays the content of Jesus's conversation with Moses and Elijah: they "were speaking of his departure [*exodos,* "exodus"], which he was about to accomplish at Jerusalem" (9:31).

While Matthew and Mark portray Jesus ministering around Galilee and eventually ending up in Jerusalem, Luke announces Jesus's intention to head there with a somber declaration: "When the days drew near for him to be taken up, he set his face to go to Jerusalem" (9:51). This inaugurates a distinctive section in Luke often referred to as "the Travel Narrative" (9:51–19:28), where Luke does some of his most creative work; nearly 50 percent of the material in this section is found only in this Gospel. As the stories and teachings progress, we're repeatedly told that Jesus is heading "to/toward Jerusalem" or that he is "on his way," building an intensifying motif focused on the climax that will occur in that holy city.[2] Finally, at the end of the story, Luke alone among the four Gospels has Jesus ascend to the Father, but not before telling his **disciples** to "stay here in the city until you have been clothed with power from on high" (24:49).

Clearly, Luke wants us to understand the importance of Jerusalem in the drama of God's salvation. The Acts of the Apostles, in turn,

2. Luke 9:51, 52, 53, 56, 57; 10:3, 38; 13:22, 33; 17:11, 19; 18:31; 19:4, 28.

takes this theme up in reverse by carefully describing how the Gospel emerged out of Jerusalem and extended outward into the world. Jesus's pronouncement in Acts 1:8 functions as a sort of table of contents for the book as a whole: "But you will receive power when the Holy Spirit has come upon you [narrated in Acts 2:1–4]; and you will be my witnesses in Jerusalem [2:5–8:1], in all Judea and Samaria [8:1 and following], and to the ends of the earth [chaps. 13–28, narrating Paul's missionary journeys and eventual arrival in Rome]." With this framework in view, we see that Luke is interested in establishing a geographical portrait of salvation in order to score an important theological point: his Gospel focuses on the exodus of Jesus accomplished in the Holy City of Israel, and Acts focuses on taking the good news of that event outward, everywhere, to the ends of the earth. Thus Luke communicates that God's salvation emerges out of Israel and extends outward to embrace the entire creation.

Luke also wants to stabilize the gospel story within world history. He alone among the Gospel writers works to frame the events of Jesus's life in relation to the ruling powers of the day:

In the days of Herod, king of Judea . . . (1:5)

In those days a decree went out from Emperor Augustus that all the world should be registered. This was the first registration, when Quirinius was governor of Syria. (2:1–2)

In the fifteenth year of the reign of Emperor Tiberius, when Pontius Pilate was governor of Judea, and Herod was tetrarch of Galilee, and his brother Philip ruler of the region of Ituraea and Trachonitis, and Lysanias tetrarch of Abilene, in the high priesthood of Annas and Caiaphas . . . (3:1–2)

Luke is not interested in history for history's sake, however. He wants to capture for his readers the awareness that God has broken into world history, that the time is fulfilled and the day has come for God's greatest saving act to take place.

We may recall how Matthew was interested in describing the events of Jesus's life as fulfillment of *prophecy* to Israel. Luke, by contrast, is interested in celebrating the fulfillment of God's *promises* to Israel. This is most notable in the early chapters of Luke's Gospel, where with joy the characters and narrator alike proclaim that God is acting to complete the work of **redemption** begun in and through the people of Israel.

> LUKE: Many have undertaken to set down an orderly account of the events that have been fulfilled among us. (1:1)

> THE ANGEL GABRIEL: He will be great, and will be called the Son of the Most High, and the Lord God will give to him the throne of his ancestor David. He will reign over the house of Jacob forever, and of his **kingdom** there will be no end. (1:32–33)

> ELIZABETH: Blessed is she who believed that there would be a fulfillment of what was spoken to her by the Lord. (1:45)

> THE SONG OF MARY: He has helped his servant Israel, in remembrance of his mercy, according to the promise he made to our ancestors, to Abraham and to his descendants forever. (1:54–55)

> THE SONG OF ZECHARIAH: Blessed be the Lord God of Israel, for he has looked favorably on his people and redeemed them. He has raised up a mighty savior for us in the house of his servant David, as he spoke through the mouth of his holy **prophets** from of old, that we would be saved from our enemies and from the hand of all who hate us. Thus he has shown the mercy promised to our ancestors, and has remembered his holy **covenant**, the oath that he swore to our ancestor Abraham, to grant us that we, being rescued from the hands of our enemies, might serve him without fear, in **holiness** and **righteousness** before him all our days. (1:68–75)

> THE SONG OF SIMEON: Master, now you are dismissing your servant in peace, according to your word; for my eyes have seen your salvation, which you have prepared in the presence of all peoples, a light for **revelation** to the **Gentiles** and for glory to your people Israel. (2:29–32).

As if to underscore the point, Luke uses a range of "fill" words fourteen times in the first two chapters alone: when God acts at the *fullness* of time, God *fills* people with the Holy Spirit; and when the Holy Spirit is at work, hearts are *full* of joy, wombs are *filled* with new life, and hungry bodies are *filled* with food.[3] In fulfillment of past promises, God is at work in history to fill people with power to live in the world with confidence as children of God.

What Does Luke Teach Us about God's Work in Christ Jesus?

This work of God in history directs us to our third and final example of Luke's Gospel expansion. Matthew's Gospel presents Jesus as the **Messiah** of God's people, sent to the lost sheep of the house of Israel. Mark presents Jesus as an enigmatic figure who confronted the spiritual and religious powers of his day in a manner that left his followers confused and disoriented as they stumbled along the way of the Word. Luke, by contrast, is determined to take a wide-angle view on the gospel story to describe the impact of the gospel on all of humanity. Luke wants to describe what the **kingdom of God** looks like when it is made real among us (17:20–21). For example, where Matthew's **genealogy** traces the lineage *from* Abraham *to* Jesus "the Son of God" (cf. 4:3, 6) to secure Jesus's identity as an Israelite in the line of David, Luke tracks Jesus's identity in the opposite direction, moving from Jesus back through history all the way to the first human, "Adam, son of God" (3:23–38). Matthew's Jesus is the Messiah of Israel, but Luke widens the scope to insist that Israel's Messiah is in fact the Redeemer of all humanity.

The same point is scored when Luke expands the quote from Isaiah 40 as it pours from the lips of John the Baptist. Both Matthew and Mark have John identify himself as the speaker of Isaiah 40:3, as a "voice of one crying out in the wilderness, 'Prepare the way of the Lord, make his paths straight'" (Matt. 3:3; Mark 1:3). Luke, however, expands the quote through Isaiah 40:5: "Every valley shall be filled, and every mountain and hill shall be made low, and the

3. Luke 1:1, 15, 20, 23, 41, 45, 53, 57, 67; 2:6, 21, 22, 39, 40.

crooked shall be made straight, and the rough ways made smooth; and all flesh shall see the salvation of God" (3:5–6). As we read on, we may notice how Luke offers detailed descriptions of what happens when the gospel touches ground in various contexts, especially when it comes to those who fall outside the reach of Israel's dominant vision of salvation. Where Matthew's Jesus says "enter no town of the **Samaritans**" (Matt. 10:5), Luke's Jesus holds Samaritans up as models of faith (10:30–37; 17:11–19). Luke also brings in additional stories of faithful tax collectors (15:1; 18:9–14; 19:1–10) and intensifies focus on the gentiles as the ultimate focus of God's salvation (2:32; 3:23–38; 4:24–27; 7:1–10; 24:47). Hence, in Luke alone Jesus explains his actions by asserting, "The Son of Man came to seek out and to save the lost" (19:10).

Especially notable is Jesus's expressed concern for the vulnerable members of society. Widows play a prominent role in Luke,[4] along with those who are at risk of losing their "only" child (7:12; 8:42; 9:38), leaving them poor and destitute in their old age. Likewise women in general, who had very little societal or domestic power in Jesus's day, are presented as whole characters, with hopes and fears and wills of their own: women like Mary and Elizabeth, who make free choices and sing revolutionary songs of praise to God (1:26–56); Anna, who prophesies in the temple (2:36–38); and Mary and Martha, who must make difficult choices between fulfilling their prescribed gender roles or stepping forth to follow Jesus in discipleship (10:38–42). A particularly striking feature in this regard is Luke's tendency to add female examples to balance out the males. So after listing Jesus's male followers (6:12–16), Luke is careful to add a list of female followers (8:1–3); the healing of the centurion's servant (7:1–10) is followed immediately by the healing of a widow's only son (7:11–17); the **parable** of a man who loses a sheep (15:4–7) is paired with a parable of a woman who loses a coin

4. Matthew only refers to widows once, and it comes on the lips of a **Sadducee** testing Jesus (22:23–28). Mark repeats that story (12:18–23) and extends the teaching by highlighting Jesus's concern for such people (12:38–44). Though John never once refers to widows, Luke raises them to our attention on seven different occasions (2:37; 4:25–26; 7:12; 18:3–5; 20:28, 47; 21:2–3), four of which include actual widows as characters in the story.

(15:8–10). With these careful acts of literary symmetry, Luke reminds us that the humanity created and saved by God is both male *and* female.

That humanity is also often poor. Luke's Gospel begins by reminding us of God's intention to fill "the hungry with good things" (1:53) but then amazes us by presenting a Jesus who is born into a family that is actually poor.[5] Where Matthew's Gospel has *religious* outsiders receiving God's sign in the heavens inviting them to witness Jesus's birth (the Magi, Matt. 2:1–12), Luke has *economic* outsiders, poor shepherds, receiving a vision of angels proclaiming Jesus's birth as "good news of great joy for *all* the people" (2:10, emphasis added). This good news is confirmed when Jesus begins his ministry by insisting, "The Lord . . . has anointed me to bring good news to the poor" (4:18), and then proclaiming in the Beatitudes, "Blessed are *you who are poor*, for yours is the kingdom of God" (6:20, emphasis added; cf. Matt. 5:3).

In all this we see that Jesus is more than Israel's Messiah (as in Matthew), and more than a mysterious wonder-worker and teacher who has come "to give his life a ransom for many" (as in Mark 10:45). In Luke, Jesus is a deliverer for humanity, a "Savior"; in fact, all but two of the nineteen occurrences of the words "Savior," "saved," and "salvation" in the Gospels and Acts occur in Luke's writings.[6] As Zechariah sings in the Gospel's beginning, Luke's Jesus is a "mighty savior" sent "that we would be saved from our enemies" to "serve him without fear, in holiness and righteousness before him all our days" (1:69–71, 74–75). Jesus's own self-identification at the beginning of his ministry focuses on his role as a Spirit-anointed deliverer: "The Spirit of the Lord is upon me, because he has anointed me to bring good news to the poor. He has sent me to proclaim release to the captives and recovery of sight to the blind, to let the oppressed go free, to proclaim the year of the Lord's favor" (4:18–19).

---

5. Mary and Joseph's economic status is revealed when they present Jesus in the temple and offer the sacrifice designated for those who are poor (Lev. 12:8).

6. Luke repeats this title twice in the opening chapters (1:47; 2:11) and then repeats the words for "salvation" thirteen times between the Gospel and Acts (Luke 1:69, 71, 77; 2:30; 3:6; 19:9; Acts 4:12; 7:25; 13:26, 47; 16:17; 27:34; 28:28).

What Does Luke Teach Us about the Spiritual Formation of Christian Disciples?

When they are read side by side, the first two Gospels leave us with a bit of a conundrum when it comes to our understanding of the human capacity to respond faithfully to God's saving work. In Matthew, disciples are admittedly people of "little faith"[7]—but apparently a little faith is all that is needed (Matt. 17:20), for that Gospel promises that Jesus who is "God with us" will be a present partner "to the end of the age" to empower our faithfulness. In sharp contrast to this is Mark's Gospel, which presents disciples who have "no faith" (4:40) even though Jesus is present with them, disciples who do not understand his words and deeds,[8] who have eyes that fail to see and ears that fail to hear (8:18), who run from the cross, flee the empty tomb in terror, and say nothing to anyone because they are afraid. Luke, in turn, opens his Gospel from the confident perspective of one who knows that the events fulfilled in Christ Jesus are being proclaimed abroad by servants of the Word and compiled in written form by **evangelist** writers like himself. Clearly God is working in and through faulty human disciples, despite Mark's portrayal. But how?

We're afforded a clue in Luke's opening chapter. When the angel Gabriel appears to Mary, he affirms the presence of God's power just as Matthew's Gospel did, announcing, "The Lord is with you" (Luke 1:28; cf. Matt. 1:23). When Mary is informed of what God wants to do through her, however, she responds from the limits of her human perspective much like a disciple in Mark: "How can this be, since I am a virgin?" (Luke 1:34). Gabriel's response points to the resolution Luke will offer readers of the fourfold Gospel: "The Holy Spirit will come upon you, and the power of the Most High will overshadow you" (1:35). Thereafter the Spirit comes upon Elizabeth, enabling her to recognize what God has done in Mary (1:41), and again upon Zechariah (1:67) and Simeon (2:25–27) as they respond with joy to what God is doing. Soon thereafter the Spirit comes down upon Jesus at his **baptism** (3:22), enabling him to perform his ministry (4:18)—a

7. Matt. 6:30; 8:26; 14:31; 16:8; 17:20.
8. Mark 4:13; 6:52; 7:18; 8:17, 21; 9:32; 14:68.

scenario which is then echoed early in the Acts of the Apostles, when the disciples, having isolated themselves in an upper room in Jerusalem, are depicted as being unable to fulfill their divine commission until the Holy Spirit comes upon them to empower them for God's service (Acts 2).

The Holy Spirit, it turns out, is Luke's clarification for how God invests believers with active power for faithful service.[9] Much can be said about the role of the Holy Spirit in Luke (and indeed, Luke himself will have a lot more to teach us about the Holy Spirit in the Acts of the Apostles), but for our purposes it is enough to focus on three particular aspects of Luke's portrayal as they compare to the other Gospels we've surveyed thus far: in Luke, the *experience* of the Holy Spirit produces joy, the *practices* of the Holy Spirit are prayer and worship, and the *effect* of the Holy Spirit is social transformation.

First, the *experience* of the Holy Spirit. It is a striking fact that the word "joy" only shows up one time in Mark's Gospel, when Jesus is describing what happens when the gospel "seed" falls on rocky ground: "When they hear the word, they immediately receive it with joy. But they have no root, and endure only for a while; then, when trouble or persecution arises on account of the word, immediately they fall away" (Mark 4:16–17). As we have seen, Mark's Gospel is focused on the human inability to comprehend God's ways, so it makes sense for it to portray human joy as shallow and short-lived. Luke's Gospel, by contrast, insists that the Holy Spirit is the means by which God enables our right response—so it makes sense that authentic, sustained joy would be a mark of the Holy Spirit's activity in human lives.

Luke's Gospel begins and ends with scenes of joy. Every major character in the opening chapters experiences joy at God's activity: Zechariah (Luke 1:14), Elizabeth (1:44) and her neighbors and relatives (1:58), Mary (1:47), and even the shepherds (2:10). At the end of the Gospel, the disciples experience joy when Jesus enters Jerusalem (19:37) and when he appears to them after his crucifixion (24:41);

9. Matthew refers to the Spirit 13 times, 5 of which speak specifically of the "Holy Spirit"; Mark has 8 references, 4 of which are "Holy Spirit." Luke, by contrast, refers to the Spirit 22 times, 13 of which are specific references to the "Holy Spirit"; in fact, Luke speaks of the Spirit's work 14 times before Jesus even begins his ministry, which can only occur because the Spirit of the Lord is upon him (4:18).

after he ascends to heaven, the last sentence of the Gospel reports, "They returned to Jerusalem with great joy" (24:52). In between, Luke is careful to add several references to joy, such as when the seventy disciples sent on mission "returned with joy, saying, 'Lord, in your name even the demons submit to us!'" (10:17), an event that leads Jesus to rejoice in response (10:21). Though Matthew also tells the parable of the lost sheep, only in Luke does the shepherd rejoice and invite people to celebrate with him (15:4–7), a scene that is echoed soon thereafter when the woman who lost her coin rejoices (15:9) and the father of the prodigal son throws a party to "celebrate and rejoice" at the return of his long-lost son (15:32). Amazingly, these scenes are often occasions for joy in heaven as well (2:13; 15:7, 10), suggesting that the spiritual experience of joy is a foretaste of the celebration encountered eternally in the presence of God.

The experience of the Holy Spirit is necessarily related to the *practices* that cultivate that experience. In Luke, those key practices are prayer and worship. The joyful opening chapters of Luke are punctuated by scenes of worship (Mary, 1:46–55; Zechariah, 1:64–79; angels, 2:13–14; shepherds, 2:20; Simeon, 2:29–32; Anna, 2:37–38), as are its final scenes (24:50–53). Praise is a common response to healing in Luke (13:13; 17:15; 18:43). Even the centurion at the cross praises God when he witnesses Jesus's death (23:47)! But what is perhaps most arresting is Luke's portrayal of Jesus as a person who himself worships God in prayer. In fact, nearly half of all the Gospels' references to prayer are found in Luke's Gospel. Here Jesus is seen praying before almost every major event in his life: at his baptism (3:21), before choosing his disciples (6:12), at his transfiguration (9:28–29), and before his arrest (22:41–45). He is also often seen praying in his day-to-day life (5:16; 9:18; 11:1), a witness that prompts his disciples to ask him to teach them to pray as well (11:1–13). If we return for a moment to Mark's one depiction of short-lived joy, we might infer from Luke that the joy of the gospel is only sustained by a life of prayer and worship.

Finally, given Luke's interest in expanding Israel's understanding of the scope of God's salvation to include those marginalized by religious practices of the day, we shouldn't be surprised that the *effect* of the Holy Spirit's presence is social transformation. We may recall that Matthew's Gospel launched the NT by placing the establishment of

God's restored community at center stage. That community, called **church**, was recognized by the crucial characteristics of obedience and mercy. Luke extends that depiction by making it plain that where the Spirit is at work, social relationships are rearranged to reflect the values of God's **kingdom**.

The strategic site of social transformation in Luke's Gospel is the dinner table.[10] Jesus is involved in nineteen different meals in Luke, thirteen of which are found only in this Gospel. Through it all, the table is revealed to be an essential metaphor for communal life in the kingdom of God. Eating has always been an important activity for humans; despite the casualness of our fast-food culture, formal meals are still special occasions for us. We decorate our tables, use our best tableware, and prepare unique dishes. When we invite others to such meals, we're making a space for them in our lives and welcoming them into a deeper level of relationship.

Meals were even more significant occasions in Jesus's day insofar as they served as an important means of social organization: formal meals were opportunities to reinforce communal hierarchies (invitations and seating arrangements were carefully orchestrated to reflect or deny the honor due someone) and establish contexts for reciprocity (insofar as extended hospitality was a means of placing someone in a position of social debt). Thus, when we see Jesus's opponents inviting him for dinner (Luke 7:36–50; 11:37–54; 14:1–6), it isn't simply that they're trying to be nice to him; they are in fact engaging in a culturally accepted means of asserting their sense of Jesus's proper place in their midst.

For his part, Luke's Jesus changes the table practices of his day in different ways in order to transform our understanding of human relationships in God's world. In particular, Jesus uses the dinner table as a place to perform a more godly understanding of holiness. The biblical word "holy" means "separate," and the perennial temptation of religious people is to express this separation socially, thinking that holiness has to do with avoiding people deemed "ungodly," as though their sin were something contagious for "holy" people. The

10. For a closer look at Jesus's use of the table as a tool for social transformation, see Robert J. Karris, *Eating Your Way through Luke's Gospel* (Collegeville, MN: Liturgical Press, 2006).

biblical portrait, however, makes it plain that holiness has less to do with being secluded in a holy club and more to do with being *set apart* for God's service. A case to illustrate this difference is found in the well-known story of Jesus attending a banquet at the tax collector Levi's house. This was a scandalous act, for in doing so Jesus expressed his embrace of those considered to be notorious sinners.

The **Pharisees'** more conventional understanding of holiness leaves them shocked at this. Jesus's response to their outrage is instructive: "Those who are well have no need of a physician, but those who are sick; I have come to call not the righteous but sinners to repentance" (Luke 5:31–32; cf. 15:1–2). Since the word for "call" can also be translated "invite," we would be right to understand that Jesus accepted *their invitation* to dine because it provided him with an opportunity to *invite them* into discipleship. Rather than using meals to secure himself socially, then, Jesus uses meals to secure *others* socially, putting himself at great social risk in doing so.

This scenario is witnessed again and again in Luke's Gospel. When a "sinner" woman rushes in to anoint Jesus's feet during a meal, the Pharisee host is scandalized, but Jesus welcomes her act and uses it as an occasion to teach about hospitality and forgiveness (7:36–50). When Martha wants Mary to conform to socially accepted gender roles in preparing a meal, Jesus calms Martha and praises Mary's nonconformity (10:38–42). At another meal hosted by a leader of the Pharisees (14:1–24), Jesus upends the rules of hierarchy and reciprocity, criticizing those who seek seats of honor over others, and telling the host,

> When you give a luncheon or a dinner, do not invite your friends or your brothers or your relatives or rich neighbors, in case they may invite you in return, and you would be repaid. But when you give a banquet, invite the poor, the crippled, the lame, and the blind. And you will be blessed, because they cannot repay you, for you will be repaid at the resurrection of the righteous. (14:12–14)

Where the kingdom of God is made manifest, and God's rule is in effect, people receive what they *need*, not what others think they deserve. Indeed, one of Jesus's final acts before entering Jerusalem is to invite himself over for a meal at the hated tax collector Zacchaeus's house. On hearing Jesus address him, Zacchaeus responds by pledging a life dedicated to the practice of radical generosity (Luke 19:1–10). When Jesus reacts by declaring, "Today salvation has come to this house," we learn a good deal about the scope of God's saving agenda: God is interested in far more than saving disembodied souls; God's salvation seeks to transform the human social order.

On closer examination we see that Jesus's use of meals points to an even deeper truth. All of these table stories in Luke come to a climax in the final chapter of the Gospel, when two distraught disciples meet the risen Lord on the road to Emmaus (24:13–35). Though they do not recognize who is in their midst as they make their sad journey together, when they sit down at the table to eat, Jesus is suddenly "made known to them in the breaking of the bread" (24:35). Immediately our minds are drawn back to the Last Supper, when Jesus held up bread and said, "This is my body, which is given for you" (22:19). And if we go all the way back to the beginning of the Gospel to recall that the infant Jesus's first bed was a food trough for animals (2:7, 12, 16), we realize what Luke has been trying to tell us all along: in the work of Christ and the Spirit, God is providing healing nourishment for all of creation. The church is to be God's table, the place where God is at work in order to feed the world. Where God is working, hungry bellies are filled with food and hungry souls are sustained by merciful love. Where God is at work, hearts are full of joy and mouths are filled with praise. Where God is at work, dark valleys of injustice are filled with light and arrogant high walls of protected privilege are brought down so that "all flesh shall see the salvation of God" (3:6). Where God is at work, the church is filled with people from all backgrounds, ethnicities, classes, and abilities, so that the church might witness to the world the full scope of God's salvation.

Questions for Discussion

1. Now that you've read this chapter on Luke, what questions do you have? What do you want to know more about? Make a list to share with your class or reading group.

2. As we've seen, God's people, in the way they worshiped God in Jesus's day, suffered from far too narrow a view of God's saving activity. Jesus's words and deeds emphasized a *widening* of God's mercy, oftentimes going far beyond what conventional religious practice of the time allowed. What habits and expectations of Christian life and practice today have the same narrowing effect?

3. In what ways do you feel challenged by Luke's message of inclusion? What is the effect on the church if Jesus is indeed the Redeemer of *all* humanity and not simply those who participate in my church community?

4. Who is at the table in the meal stories in Luke's Gospel? What kinds of people does Jesus include at the table?

5. What is the significance of the motif of "fullness" in the shape of Luke's Gospel? How does this theme relate to history?

6. "In Luke, the *experience* of the Holy Spirit produces joy, the *practices* of the Holy Spirit are prayer and worship, and the *effect* of the Holy Spirit is social transformation." Relate these to your own life. Which of these three are true in your experience? Are any missing in your life?

7. How does this chapter challenge common notions of *holiness*? In light of this, what ought to be considered some of the key attributes of a holy life?

8. If Luke's Gospel had been left out of the NT, what would be missing?

9. Where does this book locate you on the way of the Word? How has it helped you along? Where has it warned you to slow down? What in your discipleship requires acceleration? Has the route to your destination been at all clarified?

5

The Gospel according to John

The Center of Discipleship

"I, when I am lifted up from the earth, will draw all people to myself."

(JOHN 12:32)

Luke's Gospel is part 1 of a two-part narrative that continues with the Acts of the Apostles. Luke ends with Jesus telling the **disciples** to "stay here in the city until you are clothed with power from on high" (24:49), and Acts begins with another familiar-sounding introductory prologue, again addressed to Theophilus, which picks up the action precisely where Luke left us—with Jesus's **ascension** leaving the disciples waiting in Jerusalem for God to act. When placed side by side, Luke and Acts form a smooth narrative transition from part 1 to part 2.

Nevertheless, the **canonical** sequence does not lead as expected from part 1 (Luke) into part 2 (Acts). Instead, we turn to the Gospel according to John, a version of Jesus's story that is strikingly different from the three others we've read. This transition has jarred readers from ancient times on through to the present. Indeed, these days the majority of NT scholars deny any meaningful relationship between Luke and John, choosing instead to read Luke alongside Acts, and John alongside the Johannine Letters.

What could account for this unexpected interruption of the canonical narrative flow? What is it about John's Gospel that justifies the disruption of Luke's continuous account? The great church historian **Eusebius of Caesarea** passed down **Clement of Alexandria's** account for John's distinctiveness: "John, perceiving that the external facts had been made plain in the Gospel, being urged by his friends, and **inspired** by the Spirit, composed a spiritual Gospel."[1] A generation after him, **Origen of Alexandria**, appealing to the OT image of offering up the firstfruits (i.e., the very best) at the end of the harvest as an offering to God, claimed that while all of the **Jewish Scripture** points to the gospel of Jesus, the written Gospels themselves are the "firstfruits" of all Scripture—and among them, he insisted, John's Gospel takes pride of place as the first of the firstfruits, the highest and most perfect offering to God.[2]

What did these **church fathers** mean by these statements? Did they believe that John's Gospel was *superior* to the others? Or perhaps written to *interpret* the others? What *is* plain is this: readers moving from the **Synoptics** to John *before* moving to Acts require some kind of interpretive approach that will account for the presence of this very different Gospel in the larger canonical matrix.

Canonical Transition: From the Synoptics to John

So just how different is John's Gospel? Imagine for a moment that John was our only Gospel. We would know far less of Jesus's biography, for John's Gospel includes no story of his birth and no mention that his mother's name was Mary. We'd have no account of his **baptism** in the Jordan River or his temptation in the Judean wilderness. No

---

1. Eusebius, *Ecclesiastical History* 6.14.5–7, in *A Select Library of Nicene and Post-Nicene Fathers of the Christian Church*, 2nd series, trans. Arthur Cushman McGiffert, ed. Philip Schaff and Henry Wace, 14 vols. (1890–1900; repr., Peabody, MA: Hendrickson, 1994), 1:261.

2. Origen, *Commentary on John* 1.1–6.

scene of glorious transfiguration before Peter, James, and John. Jesus never eats with tax collectors and sinners in John, and not a single exorcism is described. Jesus clearly has twelve disciples, but they are never enumerated or listed by name. As for Jesus's final hours, there *is* a last meal with the disciples in John, but the Last Supper words that institute the new **covenant** are entirely absent. Jesus goes to a garden (not named Gethsemane) but displays no agonizing distress as he awaits his arrest. Indeed, rather than pray that the "cup" of his suffering be taken away (as he does in the Synoptics), Jesus responds incredulously to those who would defend him, saying, "Am I not to drink the cup the Father has given me?" (John 18:11). In like manner Jesus never falters while carrying his cross, so no one is forced to help him; does not appear to suffer on the cross; and does not cry out, "My God, my God, why have you forsaken me?" Taken as a whole, it seems plain that John's Gospel is *not* in the canon primarily to provide us with additional biographical details of Jesus's life.

What is missing from Jesus's biography pales in comparison to what is missing from John's account of Jesus's *teaching*. Jesus never proclaims the arriving **kingdom of God** in John, and he never tells a single **parable**. He is frequently *called* "Teacher," but he really isn't portrayed as such: Jesus never calls anyone to repent, deny themselves, or renounce possessions; he never exhorts anyone to take up their cross and follow him, offers no sermon on discipleship, says nothing about loving one's neighbor (much less one's enemy!), and teaches nothing about prayer (which means, of course, no model Lord's Prayer for us to imitate). John's Gospel is not in the canon simply to provide us with additional details of Jesus's teaching on discipleship.

But emphasizing John's omissions is not to suggest that John's Gospel is thin when compared with the Synoptics, for in fact the Gospel is rich with distinctive material. John's Jesus performs a number of miracles, typically called "signs," that are not found in the other Gospels: he changes water into wine at a wedding feast (chap. 2), heals a paralytic at the pool in Bethsaida (chap. 5), gives sight to a man who was born blind (chap. 9), and brings Lazarus back to life after he is dead for three days (chap. 11). Instead of the institution of the **Lord's Supper**, we find the memorable story of Jesus washing the disciples' feet (chap. 13). Instead of detailed calls to discipleship, we find a single "beloved disciple," who provides the reader with a portrait of a model follower of Jesus.

While there are fewer narrative scenes overall in John, those that exist are often more detailed and drawn out than the Synoptic narratives; frequently they involve a direct interchange with a single memorable character. Here we meet the **Pharisee** Nicodemus (chap. 3), who early in the Gospel comes by night, in secret, to chat with Jesus, but by the end is boldly going before Pilate for permission to care for Jesus's body. We meet a **Samaritan** woman at a well (chap. 4), who begins as an outcast in her village but eventually takes up the mantle of the first **apostle** by leading many in her village to **Christ**. Though we know Mary and Martha from a short story in Luke 10, John provides us with an extended, intimate portrait of two sisters overwhelmed by grief (chap. 11), each of them struggling to reconcile their devotion to their Lord with the fact of their beloved brother's death. In John we also get to know the disciple Thomas, whose inability to see the risen Lord limits his capacity to believe in him (chap. 20). John's Gospel ends with a final scene of Jesus reinstating the apostle Peter (chap. 21), whose shocking betrayal of Jesus remained glaringly unaddressed at the end of each of the Synoptics. Given the central role Peter plays in Acts, it's a good thing we have John's witness to this final scene!

In all this we see that John's Gospel focuses rather intensely on what happens when people encounter Jesus. This detail appears to serve a deeper, more pervasive feature of John's Gospel: it provides readers with a rich and resonant meditation on the mystery of Jesus's identity. In John alone, Jesus is identified as the Word of God through whom "all things" were made (1:3) and as the "Lamb of God who takes away the sin of the world!" (1:29). In this Gospel, Jesus provides people with "eternal life," and this not simply as a heavenly eternal inheritance, but also as a present, experienced reality (e.g., 3:15–16; 5:24; 6:54). Jesus doesn't simply predict the coming of the Holy Spirit, as in Luke: he actually *dispenses* the Holy Spirit on the disciples, personally, by breathing on them (20:22–23).

The most arresting feature of John's identity portrait may be Jesus's repeated "I am" statements. This allusion to the personal name of God in the OT is closely related to the Hebrew verb "I am," rendered in the Greek translation as *egō eimi*. Jesus says of himself "I am" five times in Matthew and four times each in Mark and Luke, but in John, Jesus says of himself "I am" on at least twenty-four occasions. Some of these are absolute and emphatic, such as John 8:58, "Before Abraham was, I am"; but many function as a predicate for seven elaborated identity metaphors: Jesus is "the bread of life" (6:35–51); "the light of the world" (8:12; 9:5); "the gate for the sheep" (10:7, 9); "the good shepherd" (10:11, 14); "the resurrection and the life" (11:25); "the way, and the truth, and the life" (14:6); and "the vine" of God "the vinegrower" (15:1, 5).

How ought we to make sense of these extensive Johannine differences? What is John's canonical function? It has often been said that while the Synoptics portray Jesus revealing the truth about the *kingdom* of God, John seeks to depict a Jesus whose primary job is to reveal that he is the one true *Revealer* of God.[3] Put another way, the Synoptic Gospels direct our attention toward what it means to call God "Father." Hence the focus is on the emerging kingdom of God and the personal, social, and political transformation that Jesus's disciples must undergo if they are to become citizens of that kingdom. John's Gospel, by contrast, rounds out the fourfold Gospel by requiring us to meditate on what it means to call Jesus God's "Son."[4] In doing so, the Gospel collection concludes with an intense focus on Jesus as the center of God's work, the embodiment of God's mission and will, the one and only Revealer of God. "No one comes to the Father," John insists, "except through" Jesus (14:6), the Son who is "lifted up" in order "to draw all people to" himself (12:32).

The Shape of John's Gospel

It has long been observed that John's Gospel appears to be a composite built out of what once may have been two or more separate books.

3. "Jesus as the revealer of God reveals nothing but that he is the Revealer." Rudolf Bultmann, *Theology of the New Testament*, trans. Kendrick Grobel (New York: Scribner, 1955), 2:66.
4. For more on the differences in christological outlook between the Synoptics and John, see Eugene Lemcio, "Father and Son in the Synoptics and John: A Canonical Reading," in *The New Testament as Canon: A Reader in Canonical Criticism*, ed. Robert W. Wall and Eugene E. Lemcio, Journal for the Study of the New Testament Supplement 76 (Sheffield: JSOT Press, 1992), 78–108.

After a vibrantly **theological** prologue (1:1–18), a section commences that is often labeled "The Book of Signs" (1:19–12:50). It has this name because of the miracles and actions found in these chapters, often called "signs," which seem designed to tell us specific things about Jesus's identity. Of course, the vast majority of those who witness these signs do not end up believing in Jesus (12:37), and the public ministry ends in failure. The word "sign" occurs sixteen times in this part of the Gospel, but then it doesn't appear again until the end of chapter 20 in a closing statement (20:30) that some believe was originally found at the end of chapter 12. When we turn to the first verse of chapter 13, we discover that we are at the end of Jesus's life, just before the celebration of the Jewish **Passover** wherein Jesus is to be crucified. This inaugurates the second section of John's Gospel (13:1–20:31), typically called "The Book of Glory" due to Jesus's proclamation that the time had come for him "to be glorified" (12:23; 13:1; 17:1). In this section Jesus is speaking almost exclusively with his immediate disciples, teaching them the truth about himself and his mission. The Gospel then closes with an epilogue (21:1–25), which may well have been added by the same person who wrote the prologue and combined the two books into one.

Yet narratives are not always well served by the imposition of rigid structure systems, so we should avoid placing too much interpretive weight on reconstructions of literary prehistory. If we simply consider John's story at the level of the unfolding narrative, the plotline that emerges is fairly straightforward (see the table "The Structure of John").

What Does John Teach Us about the Work of God in Christ Jesus?

John's opening prologue provides readers with a glorious constellation of images designed to orient us toward his distinctive portrait of Jesus. Recall that Matthew's Gospel begins by focusing on Jesus's *ancestral* beginning: his was "an account of the *genealogy* of Jesus" (Matt. 1:1, emphasis added). Mark starts later in time, at "the beginning of the *good news* [*gospel*] of Jesus" (Mark 1:1, emphasis added), with

The Structure of John

Theological Prologue (1:1–18)		
Part One (1:19–12:50)	1:19–51	Background: John and the Calling of Jesus's First Disciples
	2:1–4:54	Early Ministry: Initial Signs and Dialogues
	5:1–8:11	Increasing Opposition: Signs, Dialogues, and Discourses
	8:12–10:42	Confrontation in Jerusalem
	11:1–54	The Raising of Lazarus and the Decision that Jesus Must Die
	11:55–12:36	Beginning of the End: Entry, Anointing, Arrival of Greeks
	12:37–50	End of Part One: Summary of Jesus's Teaching
Part Two (13:1–20:31)	13:1–30	Footwashing and Prediction of Betrayal
	14:1–17:26	The Farewell Discourse
	14:1–16:33	The Discourse
	17:1–26	The Prayer
	18:1–19:42	Arrest, Trial, and Passion
	20:1–31	Resurrection Scenes
Epilogue (21:1–25)		

John preparing the way, baptizing people "in the wilderness." Luke, in turn, provides a glimpse from the perspective of one in the period *after* Jesus's earthly pilgrimage, investigating "events" as they had been "handed on to us by those who from the beginning were *eyewitnesses* and *servants of the word*" (Luke 1:1–2, emphasis added). Each of the Synoptic Gospel openings, then, orient us toward a particular *historical* moment surrounding the life of Christ, before (Matthew), during (Mark), and after (Luke).

In stark contrast, John places the story of Jesus in a far grander frame. This Gospel starts long before Jesus's earthly ministry was inaugurated, before his human conception, before the ancestors of Israel, even before creation itself: "*In the beginning* was the Word, and the Word was with God, and the Word was God. He was in the beginning with God. All things came into being through him" (John 1:1–3, emphasis added). The Jesus whom John introduces isn't simply the **Messiah** of Israel (as in Matt. 27:42), crucified "to give his life a ransom for many" (Mark 10:45), in order to reveal the way of salvation for the whole world (Luke 2:10–11, 32). This Jesus is the Word of God by whom all things were made, the center of all that exists, the interpretive lens that is able to unlock the meaning and purpose of all things because he is the very means of creation itself.

This majestic opening claim can help us make sense of Luke's ending. On the road to Emmaus, Jesus castigated his downcast companions, saying, "Oh, how foolish you are, and how slow of heart to believe all that the **prophets** have declared! Was it not necessary that the Messiah should suffer these things and then enter into his glory?" "Then," Luke reports, "beginning with Moses and all the prophets, he interpreted to them the things about himself in all the scriptures" (Luke 24:25–27). Soon thereafter Jesus stands among the disciples and insists, "These are my words that I spoke to you while I was still with you—that everything written about me in the **law** of Moses, the prophets, and the **psalms** must be fulfilled" (24:44).

The phraseology employed here makes it plain that Luke doesn't have particular OT prooftexts in mind. Luke is thinking of "*all* that the prophets have declared!" (24:25), "*all* the scriptures" (24:27), "the law of Moses, the prophets, *and* the psalms" (24:44).[5] Without providing particular details, Luke's Gospel concludes with the unequivocal insistence that the whole story of Israel's Scripture comes to its climax in the person and work of Jesus.

John's Gospel can be read as an explication of this Lukan claim. Right in the opening chapter we hear Philip echo Luke's Jesus, saying, "We have found him about whom Moses in the law and also the prophets wrote, Jesus son of Joseph from Nazareth" (John 1:45). For his part, Jesus himself says to the Jewish leadership, "You search the scriptures because you think that in them you have eternal life; and it is they that testify on my behalf. Yet you refuse to come to me to have life. . . . If you believed Moses, you would believe me, for he wrote about me" (5:39–40, 46). The claim is not that the **Torah** of Moses witnesses in explicit and direct ways to the first-century man Jesus of Nazareth. No, the Torah—along with the Prophets and Psalms—witness to God, and thus these texts witness to Jesus who

---

5. Emphasis added in the Scripture quotations.

is the Word of God made flesh. This is why Jesus can say to Philip, "Whoever has seen me has seen the Father. . . . Do you not believe that I am in the Father and the Father is in me? The words that I say to you I do not speak on my own; but the Father who dwells in me does his works" (14:9–10).

In this manner John's Gospel goes beyond the others to articulate the *unity* of God "the Father" and Jesus "the Son." Some readers have thus been led to conclude that the Synoptic Gospels proclaim Jesus's *humanity* and John presents his *divinity*. Yet this is clearly a mistaken view, for the Synoptic Gospels proclaim Jesus's divinity quite overtly in his mastery over water, his miraculous provision of food, his authority to forgive sins, and his capacity to give sight to the blind and life to the dead (not to mention his own resurrection from the dead!). No, John does not play up divinity because of a lack in the Synoptic witness, but instead leads his readers in a lengthy meditation on what it means to believe that Jesus is, in the words of the **Nicene Creed**, "of one being with the Father."

Jesus asserts this repeatedly in the Gospel of John: "The Father and I are one" (10:30); "The Father is in me and I am in the Father" (10:38); "Whoever has seen me has seen the Father" (14:9). And yet the Father and the Son are most certainly *not* presented as being the *same person*. Their unity does not erase their difference, for the Word is both "God" and "with God" (1:1). The Jesus who is one with the Father still prays to the Father (e.g., 11:41; 12:28; 17:1–26) and repeatedly differentiates between them (e.g., 2:16; 5:17–47). No, their oneness is a unity, not a uniformity; they are presented as being perfectly one in love and will and mission, one in the outworking of God's **redemptive** purposes in the world. Thus the Father is the one who "sends" the Son (see esp. 5:17–47), works through the Son (e.g., 3:35–36; 5:17, 36), speaks through the Son (e.g., 14:10; 17:8), and is glorified in the Son (e.g., 8:54; 11:4; 14:13). Their union is so perfect that Jesus can confidently assert, "No one comes to the Father except through me" (14:6). Thus we read in the prologue, "No one has ever seen God. It is God the only Son, who is close to the Father's heart, who has made him known" (1:18).

John wants us to know that because Jesus is God, he is the central means by which we can understand what God is up to in our lives and in our world. Because he is God's Word, we can trust that he is "the way, and the truth, and the life" (John 14:6). And as we've already asserted, reading in sequence from Luke to John allows us to see how John is especially focused on Jesus as the interpretive lens through which we read the OT Scriptures. In Jesus we learn that the Jerusalem temple, the place where God dwells, is to be understood as a symbol of the person of Jesus (2:13–22). The same is true of the manna that Israel received in their wilderness wanderings (6:25–58), as well as the Passover lamb that Israel ate to remember their deliverance (1:29). The stories and teaching of the great OT characters Abraham (8:31–59), Jacob (1:51; 4:5–15), and Moses also point to Jesus.[6] The judgment of God, which so many fear after reading parts of the OT, is revealed to rest in the hands of Jesus (5:22–30), the one who "came not to judge the world, but to save the world" (12:47).

Viewing the Gospels as a collection, then, we discover that where the Synoptics present *a Jesus who fulfills the* OT, John presents *an OT that prefigures Jesus*. The Synoptics encourage us to read from front to back, from OT to NT, from prophecy and promise to fulfillment and reward. John, by contrast, invites us to read from back to front, from NT to OT, to start with Jesus and find in him the meaning and purpose of all that came before.[7]

What Does John Teach Us about the Spiritual Formation of Christian Disciples?

The prologue of John includes a paragraph that tells us in advance about the kind of reception the Word made flesh will receive by those he encounters:

> He came to what was his own, and his own people did not accept him. But to all who received him, who believed in his name, he gave

6. John 1:17, 45; 3:14; 5:45–46; 6:32; 7:19–23; 8:5; 9:28–29.
7. For more on John's distinctive use of Jewish Scripture, see Richard B. Hays, *Reading Backwards: Figural Christology and the Fourfold Gospel Witness* (Waco: Baylor University Press, 2014), 75–92.

power to become children of God, who were born, not of blood or of the will of the flesh or of the will of man, but of God. (1:11–13)

Scholars have long noted that this section appears to parallel the two "parts" of John's Gospel. Jesus comes to his own people (Israel, people born of the same "blood" and "flesh"), and though they will consider the possibility that he is their expected Messiah (John 7:25–31, 40–44), they will ultimately fail to recognize him as such. This is the story of the first twelve chapters of John, the so-called Book of Signs. Indeed, as that section comes to an end we are sadly informed, "Although he had performed so many signs in their presence, they did not believe in him" (12:37).

Nevertheless, the prologue tells us that there will be others who will actually "receive him" and "believe in his name," and to these the Word will give "power" or "the right" (*exousia*) to become children of God—children by God's power and not by right of country or kin (cf. John 1:12–13). This appears to parallel the content of the latter half of John's Gospel, the so-called Book of Glory (chaps. 13–20), where Jesus speaks more directly with those disciples who do believe in him. In a kind of transition speech where these two halves intersect, Jesus delineates the difference between "his own people" Israel and those who will become "his own" by believing in him. Jesus's emphasis now is *not* on the crowds or the people of Israel as a whole, but on individuals:

> Whoever [*the one who*] believes in me believes not in me but in him who sent me. And whoever [*the one who*] sees me sees him who sent me. I have come as light into the world, so that everyone who believes in me should not remain in the darkness. I do not judge anyone who hears my words and does not keep them, for I came not to judge the world, but to save the world. *The one who* rejects me and does not receive my word has a judge; on the last day the word that I have spoken will serve as judge. (12:44–48, emphasis added)

Hearing this reminds us that John's Gospel appears intent to teach the way of the Word not by overt instruction to crowds but by means of interactions with individual people. We will therefore explore John's portrait of discipleship by looking at four case studies, two from the first half of the Gospel and two from the latter half.

Nicodemus

Nicodemus is introduced as "a Pharisee, . . . a leader of the Jews" (John 3:1). To his credit, he seeks out Jesus to engage him respectfully, though of course he does so under cover of darkness, presumably to protect his reputation. Later Jesus will say, "Those who walk at night stumble, for the light is not in them" (11:10), which, we will see, ends up being initially the case for Nicodemus. We notice that Nicodemus is the first to speak in their encounter, and his words emphasize *his own* religious authority: "**Rabbi,** *we know* that you are a teacher who has come from God; for no one can do these signs that you do apart from the presence of God" (3:2, emphasis added). He thinks he knows Jesus's identity already (merely that of a teacher) and attempts a conciliatory posture by letting Jesus know that the authorities he represents have accepted that he works in "the presence of God." The irony, of course, is that it is *Nicodemus* who is in the presence of God, though he doesn't even know it.

Jesus's response draws attention to Nicodemus's ignorance, and indeed, his inability to receive what Jesus brings: one must experience a new birth, be born "again" or "from above" (the Greek word used here can be translated either way). Nicodemus's incredulous response isn't simply due to a misunderstanding of the pun; it doesn't even occur to him that he, a religious authority figure, would have to start anew with God! Jesus attempts to explain what he means, but Nicodemus can only mutter, "How can these things be?" (John 3:9). At this point in the story at least, Nicodemus cannot "receive" what Jesus says and thus cannot believe. As the chapter progresses, Jesus keeps talking, but Nicodemus fades away in his ignorance.

The Samaritan Woman

The story immediately following in the Gospel of John appears designed to provide a contrast. On the journey back home from Judea, Jesus meets a Samaritan woman at Jacob's well. She is in many ways the exact opposite of Nicodemus: her female gender places her in a subservient role; her Samaritan ethnicity leaves her hated by Jews; and her multiple marriages and current extramarital relationship appear to have made her an outcast in her own village. (Why else is she collecting water by herself during the heat of the day, rather than in the early morning with the other women?) This time Jesus is the first to speak, crossing gender, ethnic, and religious boundaries by asking the woman for a drink of water. In contrast to Nicodemus, who thinks he knows precisely who Jesus is, the woman simply acknowledges his impropriety and refers to Jesus as "you, a Jew" (John 4:9). Jesus's response is no less enigmatic than what was offered to Nicodemus, yet the woman's speech reflects increased receptivity: she calls him "Sir" (*kyrios*, "Lord") and asks for more information. As the conversation continues, she wonders if this man is "greater than our ancestor Jacob," who gave them the well in the first place (4:12). As Jesus says more, her estimation increases further: "I see that you are a prophet" (4:19). As the dialogue progresses, she engages tenaciously to understand Jesus's identity. When at last she says that she believes the Messiah will come to accomplish everything Jesus describes, her patient engagement is rewarded: Jesus tells her, "I am he [*egō eimi*], the one who is speaking to you" (4:26).

At this point the woman leaves Jesus to proclaim in her village what she has heard and seen, inviting others to "come and see a man who told me everything I have ever done! He cannot be the Messiah, can he?" (John 4:29). She ends up becoming the first apostle in the Gospel of John, for we are told, "Many Samaritans from the city believed in him because of the woman's testimony" (4:39). They invite Jesus to stay with them, and when they listen to Jesus himself, they tell the woman, "It is no longer because of what you said that we believe, for we have heard for ourselves, and we know that this is truly the Savior of the world" (4:42).

This final "we know" declaration provides us with an interesting echo. Nicodemus's failed encounter with Jesus *began* with the presumption of what he thought he already knew: "*We know* that you are a teacher who has come from God" (John 3:2, emphasis added). Being locked in his own understanding, his meeting with Jesus dwindled inevitably into deeper misunderstanding. This subsequent successful encounter with Jesus, however, is characterized by initial receptivity to Jesus, followed by increasing perception through hearing his word, and culminates in the clearest of understandings: "*We know* that this is truly the Savior of the world" (4:42, emphasis added).

Discipleship in the Synoptic Gospels is focused on *following*; discipleship in John is centered on *believing* who Jesus is and trusting in what he has come to do for humankind. It would be a grave error, however, to polarize these two by assuming that this "believing" involves a purely rational affirmation of disembodied "truths" about Jesus. Indeed, Jesus will later insist, "The one who believes in me will also do the works that I do" (John 14:12). Believing seems to have more to do with humble openness to receive what Jesus offers, to abide with Jesus until understanding emerges, and then to allow that understanding to transform oneself into a witness to God's work. Because of her encounter with Jesus, the Samaritan woman was transformed from a person experiencing communal isolation into a leader whose testimony led her village to believe in Jesus as the Savior. Just as Jesus is the Word of the Father, so also those who believe in him experience healing restoration so that they may, in turn, provide witness to the word of Jesus.

The Beloved Disciple

The latter half of John's Gospel focuses more intently on Jesus's instruction to those who *do* believe in him. Most prominent among these is the disciple cryptically identified as "the one whom Jesus loved." Our first clear encounter with this individual is in John 13. Having just washed the disciples' feet during supper to provide them with "an example, that you also should do as I have done to you" (13:15), Jesus grows troubled in spirit and declares, for the first time in the Gospel, "One of you will betray me" (13:21). As the disciples in attendance look at one another to figure out whom Jesus has in mind, Peter catches the eye of this disciple "whom Jesus loved" and motions to him to ask Jesus who it is (13:23–24). This disciple is described as quite literally "reclining in the bosom" of Jesus (as the Greek puts it). He is apparently there, at the table, leaning comfortably at rest directly against Jesus's chest. Peter apparently cannot ask Jesus because he is not close enough, but because of this disciple's intimacy with Jesus, he is able to hear Jesus identify his betrayer.

This snapshot of a moment in the relationship between Jesus and a beloved disciple is intended to communicate far more than

may appear at first glance. First, the specificity of his repose in
Jesus's "bosom" recalls what the prologue said about Jesus's relation to God the Father: "It is God the only Son, who is close to
the Father's heart [literally, "bosom"], who has made him known"
(John 1:18). Once again we see that those who believe in Jesus do
what Jesus does: just as Jesus, who resides close to the bosom of
the Father, is the only one able to make the Father known, so also
this disciple, who reclines on *Jesus's* bosom, is the only one able to
make *Jesus* known.

This personal connection brings to mind the many other metaphors in John that describe the close union between the Father and
the Son and in turn between the Son and those who believe in him.
As Jesus says:

Those who eat my flesh and drink my blood abide in me, and I in them.
Just as the living Father sent me, and I live because of the Father, so
whoever eats me will live because of me. (6:56–57)

Very truly, I tell you, I am the gate for the sheep. . . . Whoever enters
by me will be saved, and will come in and go out and find pasture.
. . . I am the good shepherd. The good shepherd lays down his life
for the sheep. . . . The works that I do in my Father's name testify to
me; but you do not believe, because you do not belong to my sheep.
My sheep hear my voice. I know them, and they follow me. (10:7–11,
25–27)

I am the true vine, and my Father is the vinegrower. . . . Abide in
me as I abide in you. Just as the branch cannot bear fruit by itself
unless it abides in the vine, neither can you unless you abide in me.
I am the vine, you are the branches. Those who abide in me and I in
them bear much fruit, because apart from me you can do nothing.
(15:1–5)

As you, Father, are in me and I am in you, may they also be in us, so
that the world may believe that you have sent me. The glory that you
have given me I have given them, so that they may be one, as we are
one, I in them and you in me, that they may become completely one,
so that the world may know that you have sent me and have loved
them even as you have loved me. (17:21–23)

Disciples whom Jesus loves reside close to his heart and make him known. Just as Jesus is one with the Father in love and will and mission, so also faithful disciples are those who dwell in similarly close unity with Jesus. They stay so close to Jesus that he is able to feed them the way food nourishes a body, the way a vine carries nutrients to the fruit, the way a shepherd cares for his sheep. In this way they will be able to stand firm when trouble comes. When they are persecuted, they will take comfort in knowing that Jesus was persecuted first (John 15:18–25). They will not run away from the cross, but will testify to it in word and deed (19:26–37). Thus, when Jesus is suddenly revealed among them, they will be able to recognize him and respond in faith (21:7).

Peter

We end our case-study survey with a look at the apostle Peter in John. As in the Synoptics, John presents Peter as the leader of the twelve disciples, referring to him by name more often than any other of Jesus's followers. When many disciples turn away because of the difficulty of Jesus's teaching, Peter steps forth as the spokesperson of the twelve, saying, "Lord, to whom can we go? You have the words of eternal life. We have come to believe and know that you are the Holy One of God" (John 6:68–69). When Jesus washes the disciples' feet (13:1–11), it is Peter who struggles, refusing at first to allow Jesus this act of service, only to turn right around and ask to be washed head to foot! When Jesus describes his betrayal and death, Peter boldly proclaims, "Lord, . . . I will lay down my life for you" (13:37), only to cower in shameful denial of Jesus a few hours later.

All four Gospels portray Peter as a bold leader who is far from perfect, but John adds insult to injury by regularly contrasting him with the unnamed "disciple whom Jesus loved." The beloved disciple sits close to Jesus at the Last Supper, not Peter. The beloved disciple stays with Jesus at the cross, not Peter. When they hear of the empty tomb, both of these disciples run to the gravesite, but the beloved disciple outruns Peter to look in first (John 20:1–10). Bold Peter pushes past him and enters the tomb to look around, and only then does the beloved disciple enter; but it is the beloved disciple who is named as the first believer in the resurrection (20:8) even though there's nothing to see (his capacity to believe stands in sharp contrast to that of Thomas, who insists in the next scene, "Unless I see the mark of the nails in his hands, and put my finger in the mark of the nails and my hand in his side, I will not believe," 20:25). In a final passage, the resurrected Jesus appears to the disciples while they are fishing, and though none of them recognize him at first, it is the beloved disciple who finally announces "It is the Lord!" (21:7). In response to this, eager Peter dives into the water to be the first to arrive at Jesus's side.

Peter struggles, makes many mistakes, and often shows how little he knows, but there is no doubt that he loves Jesus. In the final scene of the Gospel of John (21:15–19), Jesus looks at Peter and says, "Simon son of John, do you love me more than these?" It's a curious inquiry since Peter is clearly *not* the one whom John has highlighted as the disciple whom *Jesus* loved, presumably more than the others. The question draws our minds back to the earlier exchange between Jesus and Peter over the footwashing: Peter didn't understand and at first resisted this act of loving service that Jesus performed as an example to all disciples everywhere. That earlier scene culminated with Jesus proclaiming, "I give you a new commandment, that you love one another. Just as I have loved you, you also should love one another. By this everyone will know that you are my disciples, if you have love for one another" (13:34–35).

"Love one another" is repeated three times for emphasis. So now Jesus asks this of Peter, three times: "Do you love me?" As Peter repeats, "Yes, Lord, I love you," Jesus replies, "Feed my lambs. . . . Tend my sheep. . . . Feed my sheep" (John 21:15–17). Those who believe in Jesus and claim to love him will give their lives in service, loving people to the end, just as Jesus did. Disciples are described as those who believe in Jesus and abide with him, but this call to love is the only *direct* instruction in discipleship offered in John's Gospel.

It is a reminder to us all. "If you love me," Jesus says, "you will keep my commandments" (John 14:15). Indeed, "Those who love me will keep my word, and my Father will love them, and we will come to them and make our home with them" (14:23). But what could it mean to say that the Father and the Son will make their home with those who keep Jesus's word? And how will any of us be able to keep Jesus's word when even Peter himself was unable to do so?

Herein we pick up the narrative thread first dangled before us at the end of Luke, one that is threaded through this Gospel in order to become a major thematic rope of the Acts of the Apostles. Luke ended with Jesus telling the disciples, "I am sending upon you what my Father promised; so stay here in the city until you have been clothed with power from on high" (Luke 24:49). John alludes to this coming dispensation of power when he speaks of "the Spirit, which believers in [Jesus] were to receive," adding "for as yet there was no Spirit, because Jesus was not yet glorified" (John 7:39). Readers of the OT will of course know that though the Spirit has been around since before the beginning of time (when it hovered at the creation over the waters of chaos), God's people expected a powerful outpouring of that Spirit in the last days (e.g., Joel 2:28–29).

Thus, when John's Jesus tells the disciples of his immanent departure, he responds to their panic and fear by saying, "I will ask the Father, and he will give you another **Advocate**, to be with you forever" (John 14:16). Just as the Father sent the Son, so also he will send one much like the Son, "another Advocate" or "Helper" who, unlike Jesus, will stay "forever" (14:16). "This is the Spirit of truth," Jesus says, who will enable a new birth among God's people (3:5–8), the one "whom the world cannot receive, because it neither sees him nor knows him. You know him, because he abides with you, and will be in you" (14:17). This Helper, Jesus says, will "teach you everything, and remind you of all that I have said to you" (14:26); he will "testify on" Jesus's "behalf" (15:26) and "prove the world wrong about sin and **righteousness** and judgment" (16:8); he "will guide you into all the truth; for he will not speak on his own, but will speak whatever he hears, and he will declare to you the things that are to come. He will glorify me, because he will take what is mine and declare it to you. All that the Father has is mine. For this reason I said that he will take what is mine and declare it to you" (16:13–15).

We are not given much more detail about the Spirit than that, but it is enough to enable our transition to the Acts of the Apostles, a book many have suggested would be more appropriately titled "The Acts of the Holy Spirit." That book has much to teach us about the *work* of the Holy Spirit, but John's witness comes first to ensure that we are completely clear as to what sort of *person* this Spirit is: it is the Third Person of the Triune God, the one sent by the Father to continue the work of the Son in the lives of all who believe in God, abide in God, and love as God loves.

─────────────── Questions for Discussion ───────────────

1. Now that you've read this chapter on John, what questions do you have? What do you want to know more about? Make a list to share with your class or reading group.

2. What is the canonical function of John's disruption of the Luke-Acts narrative? Why include this "spiritual" Gospel?

3. What surprised you in the case study of Nicodemus and the Samaritan woman? Had you made those connections before? What was new? What was the same?

4. Reflect on the contrast of the beloved disciple and Peter. How do their respective relationships with Jesus inform a life of discipleship? What is challenging and what is comforting about their presence in John's Gospel?

5. If John's Gospel had been left out of the NT, what would be missing?

6. Now that you know more about the function of the four Gospel accounts in Scripture, what are your conclusions? What questions do you still have? How has your view of the four Gospels developed?

7. Where does John's Gospel locate you on the way of the Word? How has it helped you along? Where has it warned you to slow down? What in your discipleship requires acceleration? Has the route to your destination been at all clarified?

6

The Acts of the Apostles

The Community of Discipleship

"In the last days it will be ... that I will pour out my Spirit upon all flesh."

(ACTS 2:17)

With the close of John's **Gospel**, we come to the end of the New Testament's multiform story of Jesus's birth, his life and ministry, his rejection and crucifixion, and his victory over death. We have learned many things thus far: that Jesus is the Son of God, who came to fulfill God's **covenant** with Israel; that he is God's suffering servant, who gave his life as a ransom for many; that he is the Savior of the world, who teaches a way of salvation that welcomes everyone; that he is indeed the key that unlocks the meaning and purpose of all things in heaven and on earth. Clearly, the fourfold Gospel of Jesus **Christ** functions as the dramatic climax to the larger biblical narrative begun all the way back in the book of Genesis.

Despite this, the story is far from over. Indeed, we are not yet even halfway through the New Testament! With the Acts of the Apostles, the next narrative horizon is revealed for those who are reading along the way of the Word. As **John Chrysostom** once preached, "If this Book had not existed, . . . the very crowning point of our salvation would be hidden, alike for practice of life and for doctrine."[1] As it turns out, God's work was not completed with the sending of the Son into the world. Human sin is certainly forgiven in Christ, but immorality still ravages our lives, and injustice plagues our communities. The good news of God's **reconciliation** has been revealed to us, but the story must somehow be learned and practiced. In short, we may know about the salvation of Jesus, but now we must figure out how to get up and start walking the way of the Word.

Of course, none of this comes as a surprise to those who have attended carefully to the fourfold Gospel. While Luke's part 1 is an important literary guide to understanding part 2, Acts, we must not overlook how the Gospels as a whole have prepared us to receive this book. Matthew's Gospel launched the NT by insisting that **disciples** are to think of themselves as "the light of the world" (Matt. 5:14), and that one of Jesus's primary tasks was to form a new community called "**church**" (Matt. 16:18; 18:15–20) that would go out into the world teaching people to obey all that Jesus taught (Matt. 28:19–20). Mark's Gospel ended with the resurrected Jesus describing the sort of distinctive signs that will accompany those who believe after his departure (Mark 16:17–18). Finally, John's Gospel brought the story of Jesus's life to a close with the promise that Jesus would ask the Father to give us "another Advocate, to be with you forever; . . . the Holy Spirit, whom the Father will send in my name, will teach you everything, and remind you of all that I have said to you" (John 14:16, 26). Throughout the fourfold Gospel, anticipation has been building for the next stage in the outworking of God's saving plan.

In short: there is more to God's story of salvation than the already amazing fact that God became flesh in Christ to live and die as one of us in order to reconcile us to God. God also became a human in the person of the Son to teach us what true humanity looks like, how to live and love and participate in God's victory over the power of

1. John Chrysostom, *Homily on Acts* 1, in *A Select Library of Nicene and Post-Nicene Fathers of the Christian Church*, 1st series, trans. J. Walker, J. Sheppard, and H. Browne, ed. Philip Schaff, 14 vols. (1886–1889; repr., Peabody, MA: Hendrickson, 1994), 11:2.

death. And now in the Acts of the Apostles, God comes in the person of the Holy Spirit to enable the divine will to become flesh in those of us who seek to walk in his way.

Canonical Transition: From John to the Acts of the Apostles

Viewed from the macrolevel of the NT metanarrative, the transition from the Gospels to the Acts of the Apostles is easy to describe: the Gospels portray Jesus as calling people to follow him, and Acts shows what takes place with the first people who follow! But a closer look at the actual mechanics of the transition is worthwhile. We noticed earlier that the **canonical** process intentionally separated Acts from its original literary partner, the Gospel of Luke, so that the fourfold Gospel collection would culminate with the Gospel of John. The larger transition from the Gospels to Acts may be smooth, but what of the specific move from John to Acts?

Three points are worthy of comment. First, to reiterate the comment made at the end of the last chapter, while John provided us with an expanded elaboration on the *person* of the Holy Spirit (another Advocate, like Jesus, sent from the Father and delivered by the Son), Acts relates detailed reports of the *activity* of the Holy Spirit, who fills people (e.g., 2:4; 4:31) to empower their testimony to Jesus (1:8) and direct their mission and ministry (e.g., 8:29; 10:19). The combined witness of John and Acts provides us with a richly trinitarian depiction of a God who has reached out to heal creation, first by sending the Son to be *God with us in human form*, and then by sending the Spirit to be *God among us so that human life might be transformed*.

Second, John's Gospel ends with an immeasurably important exchange between Jesus and Peter. Each of the **Synoptic Gospels** ends by leaving Peter's leadership in what can only be called a highly compromised position. Indeed, in all three, his final recorded words are "I do not know the man!" (Matt. 26:74; Mark 14:71; Luke 22:60). This is hardly an effective way of establishing him as leader of the **apostles** for the next chapter in the story of salvation! But John's ending resolves any possible problem by providing readers with an intimate portrayal of Jesus's reinstatement of Peter's primacy as the chief shepherd who will go on in Acts to feed and tend God's sheep (John 21:15–19). Interestingly, this final scene has Peter and Jesus go on to discuss the fate of the so-called beloved disciple (21:20–25). Though the Gospel leaves the identity of this figure open, church tradition has typically identified this disciple as John, the son of Zebedee, the very person who is repeatedly described as being joined at the hip with Peter throughout the first eight chapters of Acts.[2] Some readers might be left with a sense of competition between these two from John's Gospel, but such concerns dissolve once we see them striving side by side in Acts with one mind for the sake of spreading the gospel.

Finally, in the closing extended speech of John's Gospel, Jesus says, "Very truly, I tell you, the one who believes in me will also do the works that I do and, in fact, will do greater works than these, because I am going to the Father. *I will do whatever you ask in my name*, so that the Father may be glorified in the Son" (John 14:12–13, emphasis added). Readers of Acts will find that followers of the way of the Word are indeed enabled to do the very works that Jesus performed during his sojourn on earth. In fact, just as Jesus made plain in John, the Acts narrative gives primacy to the effective power of Jesus's *name*. As the prologue of John insists, "To all who received him, who believed in his name, he gave power to become children of God" (John 1:12). Acts tells the story of what happens when that first powerful family of God's children is set loose in the world.

The Shape of the Acts of the Apostles

We observed earlier that the Gospel of Luke is an important literary guide to understanding Acts. This is especially the case in understanding the logic of Acts' narrative structure.

In our earlier chapter on Luke's Gospel, we described the important role of Jerusalem in the drama of God's salvation. Luke views Jerusalem as a kind of center point; it seems as though everything that Jesus does leaves him with his face turned toward that great city in

---

2. Peter and John are the first two of the eleven disciples named in Acts 1:13; further, "Peter and John" are named together as a unified team nine times in the first eight chapters (3:1, 3, 11; 4:1, 13, 19; 8:14, 17, 25).

anticipation of the final confrontation that would take place there. Luke's Gospel then ends with Jesus commanding his disciples, "See, I am sending upon you what my Father promised; so stay here in the city until you are clothed with power from on high" (Luke 24:49). The structural movement of Luke's Gospel, then, is focused on *getting to Jerusalem.*

The Acts of the Apostles, in turn, takes this theme up in reverse by carefully describing how the gospel emerged out of Jerusalem and extended outward into the world. "But you will receive power," Jesus tells the disciples, "when the Holy Spirit has come upon you; and you shall be my witnesses in Jerusalem, and in all Judea and Samaria, and to the ends of the earth" (Acts 1:8). Where Luke focused on getting to Jerusalem, Acts focuses on the gospel's spreading out from there "to the ends of the earth." In fact, Jesus's description of the mission functions as a sort of table of contents for Acts:

The Structure of the Acts of the Apostles

Preface and **Ascension** (1:1–11)	Programmatic Statement, 1:8—"You will receive power when the Holy Spirit has come upon you; and you will be my witnesses in Jerusalem, in all Judea and Samaria, and to the ends of the earth."
Witness in Jerusalem (1:12–8:1)	**Baptism** in the Spirit, followed by the story of the earliest Christian mission in Jerusalem, focused on Peter and John's leadership (2:42–8:1).
Witness in Judea and Samaria (8:2–12:23)	The church is "scattered" through persecution; the ministry of Philip, the rise of Saul/Paul, and Peter's first **gentile** converts.
Witness to the ends of the earth (13:1–28:31)	The launch of the gentile mission, Paul's missionary journeys, and his final trip as a prisoner to Rome.

This movement outward from a center ("They were all together in one place," Acts 2:1) to a divinely enforced dispersal abroad ("scattered throughout the countryside of Judea and Samaria," 8:1) appears designed (at least in part) to draw our minds back to a scene from early in the **Bible**, the story of the Tower of Babel (Gen. 11:1–9). Tracing the parallels between the two stories will provide us with a rich **theological** commentary on the literary shape of Acts and, indeed, the proper social shape of all faithful Christian mission throughout the ages.

In Genesis 11 we are told that "the whole earth had one language and the same words" (11:1), and that all the people settled together in one place, saying, "Let us build ourselves a city, and a tower with its top in the heavens, and let us make a name for ourselves; otherwise we shall be scattered abroad upon the face of the whole earth" (11:4). This is despite the fact that God's original creational mandate told humans to "be fruitful and multiply, and fill the earth" (1:28). God made people for a fruitful fullness predicated on *spreading out in multiplicity*, but the human desire is to *gather together in a safe, forced uniformity*. God will have none of this, so God comes "down" to "confuse their language" so that they cannot "hear" (in Hebrew) "one another's speech," and thus "the LORD scattered them abroad from there over the face of all the earth" (11:7–8).

Luke's story of the outpouring of the Holy Spirit can be read in parallel with this earlier event. In both, God expresses the intention that humans would "fill the earth" (Gen. 1:28) or go "to the ends of the earth" (Acts 1:8). Humans then gather together, either in disobedience (Genesis) or in obedience (Luke 24:49; Acts 2:1) to the Lord's direction, which precipitates God's coming down in power to reshape uniform human speech into a multiplicity of languages (Gen. 11:7; Acts 2:2–4). This results in confusion (Gen. 11:7–9; Acts 2:6, 12–13): in the first, the humans can no longer "hear" and understand one another's language; but in the second, the humans are all speaking the different languages of the world, and yet they can all "hear" and understand one another (Acts 2:8). Each event then culminates in a divinely empowered "scattering" abroad over the earth.

In both stories, God rejects the human tendency toward self-securing uniformity and orchestrates the formation of a new human community predicated on diversification around a different sort of unifying center. The earlier story lays the foundation for this new kind of unity by following it with a parallel story of its own, the call of Abram. The Babel story has people gathering together in safe sameness, saying, "*Let us make* bricks. . . . *Let us build* ourselves a city. . . . Let us make a name for ourselves; otherwise we shall be scattered*" (Gen. 11:3–4, emphasis added). But in the call of Abram, God says,

"*Go* from your country and your kindred and your father's house to the land that I will show you. *I will make* of you a great nation, and *I will bless you, and make your name great*, so that you will be a blessing. . . . In you all the families of the earth shall be blessed" (12:1–3, emphasis added).

Here at the birth of God's people Israel, a vision is set forth that rejects any form of unity based on clan or land, blood or soil, family or culture—instead favoring a unity predicated entirely on God's direction and provision. So also in John's Gospel, Jesus said, "I, when I am lifted up from the earth, will draw all people to myself" (John 12:32). No longer would people travel to the Jerusalem temple to worship God, for Jesus himself is God's temple (2:19–22) and true worship only takes place in the Spirit (4:23–24). So also in the Acts of the Apostles: the unity of the Christian church is founded not on one supposedly sacred land or culture or language or leadership, but solely on the powerful name of Jesus and the transforming empowerment provided by the Holy Spirit. Thus, in his very first public speech, Peter offers a quotation from the **prophet** Joel to help his hearers make sense of what God has done in the outpouring of the Spirit:

> In the last days it will be, God declares, that I will pour out my Spirit upon all flesh, and your sons and your daughters shall prophesy, and your young men shall see visions, and your old men shall dream dreams. Even upon my slaves, both men and women, in those days I will pour out my Spirit; and they shall prophesy. . . . Then everyone who calls on the name of the Lord shall be saved. (Acts 2:17–21, quoting Joel 2:28–32)

"All flesh" are invited to participate in this salvation, whether male or female, slave or free, Jew or gentile: "For the promise is for you, for your children, and for all who are far away, everyone whom the Lord our God calls to him" (2:39; cf. Isa. 44:3; 57:19). In what follows we look first at what God does when people call on the name of the Lord Jesus, and then turn to an analysis of what this new human community looks like when it is baptized with the Holy Spirit.

What Does Acts Teach Us about the Work of God in Christ Jesus?

Though Jesus himself directly appears more than once in the Acts narrative,[3] most of what we learn about him derives from the many speeches conveyed in the story (which, all told, account for almost one-third of the entire book).[4] If we were to attempt a summary of what we learn from the speeches about what God has accomplished in Jesus, we might say that Acts portrays Jesus as *God's Messiah*, sent according to *the saving plan of God*, who *suffered according to the Scriptures* and was *revealed to be Lord* of all through his *resurrection from the dead* and *ascension to rule at God's right hand*, so that *anyone who calls on his name might find salvation*. Let us consider each of these claims more closely.

First, Jesus is *Israel's Messiah, sent according to the saving plan of God*. Early Christian preaching in Acts emphasizes that Jesus was not a flash-in-the-pan teacher and miracle worker, and not another Jewish prophet in the long line of prophets. What happened in, to, and through him must not be thought of as a mere accident of history. Luke is consistently concerned to locate Jesus, and the early Christian movement as a whole, specifically *within* the history of God's long relationship with Israel—not as an *alternative* to Israel's history, or something *separated* from Israel's history, but as the next *stage* of Israel's history. Jesus is therefore repeatedly identified as Israel's "Messiah,"[5] the foretold "servant" of God,[6] whose life and work enacted a fulfillment of what was "necessary"[7] for the completion of God's saving will. In his early sermons Peter insists that Jesus was "handed over to you according to the definite plan and foreknowledge of God" (Acts 2:23); he is "the Messiah

3. Though Jesus is present physically with the disciples in Acts 1:3–9, the majority of his appearances come by means of a disembodied voice providing direction and encouragement (9:3–6, 10–16; 10:13–15; 18:9–10; 22:17–21; 23:11).

4. The speeches in Acts take a variety of forms, from missionary speeches (e.g., 2:14–26; 13:16–41; 17:22–31) to defenses before religious and governing authorities (e.g., 7:2–53; 24:10–21; 26:2–23).

5. Acts 2:31, 36; 3:18, 20; 4:26; 5:42; 8:5; 9:22; 17:3; 18:5, 28; 26:23.

6. Acts 3:13, 26; 4:27, 30.

7. Acts 1:22; 9:16; 13:46; 14:22; 17:3; 19:21; 23:11; 25:10; 27:24.

appointed for you, . . . who must remain in heaven until the time of universal restoration that God announced long ago through his holy prophets" (3:20–21); he is the one "anointed" by God "to do whatever [God's] hand and [God's] plan had predestined to take place" (4:27–28). Key point: Christianity is not conceived of in Acts as a religion separate from Judaism; what came to be called "Christianity" emerged as a divinely initiated movement *within* ancient Judaism.

Second, Jesus *suffered according to the Scriptures and was subsequently revealed to be Lord of all through his resurrection from the dead and ascension to God's right hand*. Early Christian proclamation of Jesus as Lord of all was not simply a defensive, overstated apology for the embarrassment of his shameful death on a cross. No, contrary to what most Jews expected, the suffering of Israel's Messiah took place precisely according to the prophetic word of Scripture.[8] Indeed, all the events that had taken place surrounding Christ's death and resurrection are part of scriptural fulfillment.[9] In this way God's mysterious plan, which was hidden from the foundation of the world, would be powerfully revealed to all: as it turns out, God really does intend to bless all the families of the earth as was promised to Abraham (Acts 3:25–26). Much to everyone's surprise, Israel's Messiah ends up being far more than a mere national liberator for an inwardly focused, Babel-like culture; in his victory over the power of sin and death, Jesus is revealed to be the "Author of life" (3:15) and therefore the one and only Savior of the whole world. As Peter announced in his **Pentecost** sermon,

> David spoke of the resurrection of the Messiah, saying, "He was not abandoned to Hades, nor did his flesh experience corruption." This Jesus God raised up, and of that all of us are witnesses. Being therefore exalted at the right hand of God, and having received from the Father the promise of the Holy Spirit, he has poured out this that you both see and hear. . . . Therefore let the entire house of Israel know with certainty that God has made him both Lord and Messiah, this Jesus whom you crucified. (2:31–33, 36)

8. See, e.g., Acts 3:18; 7:52; 17:2–3; 26:23.
9. E.g., Acts 2:16–21, 31–36; 15:15–17; 28:25–28.

The powerful irony must not be missed: the one who was rejected as a false prophet and crucified as a common criminal by the rulers of the day has now been unveiled as the only legitimate King and Lord of all. This crucified King now governs creation from heaven, forgiving sins and transforming people by the power of the Holy Spirit, so that all the earth's inhabitants might one day be renewed, ready to live as God intended all along—as creatures who dwell in faithful, life-giving relationship with their Creator.

Hence, all this took place *so that everyone who calls on the name of Jesus might find salvation*. Indeed, because Jesus is the only legitimate Lord, the only one who bears the life-giving power of renewal, "There is salvation in no one else, for there is no other name under heaven given among mortals by which we must be saved" (Acts 4:12; cf. 13:38–39; 16:30–31).

But what does "salvation in Jesus's name" really entail in this book? Acts teaches us by providing us with narratives of how Jesus's "name" functioned in the life of the earliest followers: they teach the way of the Word in Jesus's name (e.g., 4:17–18; 5:28), they perform miracles of healing and deliverance in his name (e.g., 3:6, 16; 4:30), they set people free from oppressive spirits in his name (5:16; 16:18), the Holy Spirit is received in his name (2:38; 11:15), and the forgiveness of sins is offered to everyone in his name (e.g., 4:12; 10:43). Indeed, in this way all people, both Jews and gentiles alike, are welcomed into the one new family that takes this name as its own.

As we work our way through Acts, we get the clear sense that salvation in Jesus's name simply means being empowered to do the sort of things Jesus did and commanded us to do. This sense is confirmed when we see the apostles replicating Jesus's famous deeds. Just as the Spirit descended on Jesus while he was praying after being baptized (Luke 3:21), so also the believers are baptized by the Spirit while they are praying (Acts 1:14; 2:1–4). Just as Jesus heals a lame man early in his ministry (Matt. 9:2–8 and parallels), so also Peter does the same early in Acts (Acts 3:1–10). Just as it is enough to touch Jesus's cloak to be healed (Matt. 9:20–21 and parallels), so also those who touch articles of clothing touched by Paul receive healing (Acts 19:11–12). Just as religious and political leaders persecute Jesus, so also those same people persecute Jesus's followers (e.g., Acts 4:1–22; 5:17–42).

Just as Jesus, dying on the cross, says, "Father, forgive them, for they do not know what they are doing," and at his death, says, "Father, into your hands I commend my spirit" (Luke 23:34, 46), so also Stephen, dying under a barrage of stones, says, "Lord Jesus, receive my spirit. . . . Lord, do not hold this sin against them" (Acts 7:59–60).

The name "Christian," which occurs for the first time in the Bible at Acts 11:26, means "belonging to Christ." Salvation in Christ's name means becoming Christ's own possession; it means giving Jesus our whole allegiance, which is given in the hope for deliverance from all those things that hinder our flourishing and keep us from living godly lives. All this takes place by the power of the Holy Spirit—called "the Lord, the Giver of life" in the **Nicene Creed**—who (as we've seen) proceeds from the Creator God and the eternal Son, our Savior Jesus the Messiah.

What Does Acts Teach Us about the Spiritual Formation of Christian Disciples?

The salvation described in Acts entails a whole lot more than just going to heaven when we die. In fact, a straightforward reading of Acts leads us to conclude that salvation in Christ involves a complete life transformation orchestrated by the power of the Holy Spirit.

A commonly repeated adage states that the Acts of the Apostles really ought to have been named "The Acts of the Holy Spirit," for it is in this book that the Third Person of the Trinity makes a full appearance on the narrative stage. The presentation here reinforces the Spirit's identification in John as *another* Advocate," distinct alongside the Father and the Son, for in these stories the Spirit bears all the characteristics of a divine Person: the Spirit speaks to believers (Acts 8:29; 10:19; 20:23), sends them places (13:4), and gets involved in their decision making (15:28; 16:6–7). While the Spirit can also be tested (5:9) or opposed (7:51), most often the Spirit is depicted as filling people[10] in order to empower the mission of the church in the world (1:8).

10. E.g., Acts 2:4; 4:31; 8:14–17; 10:44–48; 19:1–7.

Peter's first sermon includes a statement that neatly outlines the mechanics of participation in the Spirit's transforming power: "Repent, and be baptized every one of you in the name of Jesus Christ so that your sins may be forgiven; and you will receive the gift of the Holy Spirit" (Acts 2:38). In response to the gospel message, a decision to change emerges: "Repent." This is followed by a holy ritual that washes away sins, incorporates the believer into the Christian community ("baptized . . . in the name of Jesus Christ"), and enables participation in divine empowerment to serve God in and through that community ("and you will receive the gift of the Holy Spirit").

We watch this communal process take place again and again in the Acts narrative, and what takes shape there appears designed to set a template of sorts for subsequent Christian practice. Much of what is depicted is familiar to any Christian today. The members of this new community "devoted themselves to the apostles' teaching and fellowship, to the breaking of bread and the prayers" (2:42); worship today looks much the same, with singing, Scripture reading, hearing a sermon, receiving Holy Communion, and joining in prayer. "Wonders and signs were being done by the apostles" (2:43); so also today people experience healing and deliverance as lives are transformed to serve God with pure hearts. And both then and now, members of the earliest church "spent much time together in the temple" and "broke bread at home and ate their food with glad and generous hearts, praising God" (2:46–47).

But along the way other things are described that might sound rather jarring to modern Western ears: "All who believed were together and had all things in common; they would sell their possessions and goods and distribute the proceeds to all, as any had need" (Acts 2:44–45). In a later, parallel description, we read, "There was not a needy person among them, for as many as owned lands or houses sold them and brought the proceeds of what was sold. They laid it at the apostles' feet, and it was distributed to each as any had need" (4:34–35). This community does not simply worship together; they also practice radical, daring, openhearted generosity with one another. Christian community is communal. In fact, Acts (right along with the rest of the NT) describes the Christian church as a truly alternative community in the world, a countersociety of sorts, one that draws attention to itself because its life-giving practices are so very different than those of the Babel cultures in which it is embedded.

In a later NT text, the apostle Paul will write something that might draw our attention back to this description of the church in Acts: "As many of you as were baptized into Christ have clothed yourselves with Christ. There is no longer Jew or Greek, there is no longer slave or free, there is no longer male and female; for all of you are one in Christ Jesus" (Gal. 3:27–28). Race and ethnicity, economic class, gender, all sorts of things tend to divide us today: Christian community is supposedly the place where such divisions are somehow overcome. This gathering is called to practice communal unity *in the midst of* true diversity; it is a joining together of real differences without any of the divisiveness that usually accompanies such dissimilarity. What makes this community different, then, is its rejection of the Babel tendency that drives humans to secure themselves in self-enclosed societies of sameness. Such communities find their strength in the walls and towers that keep like-minded people safely inside and "different" people out. By contrast, Christian community is not protected by thick walls, but unified around a common center. What walls there are must be porous, and the doors must stay open, because Jesus is at the center and drawing all the different people of the world to himself.

Paul's threefold assertion of unity provides a helpful framing device for describing the fellowship of the Holy Spirit depicted in Acts. *"No longer male and female"* should not surprise us after reading the Gospels (and especially Luke), but Acts firms up Jesus's witness in a more programmatic manner for the church. "I will pour out my Spirit on all flesh," Joel is quoted as prophesying, "and your sons and your daughters shall prophesy" (Acts 2:17). We know the Spirit anointed both men and women that day, for Acts has already told us that women (including Jesus's mother Mary) were a part of that first fellowship (1:14). The active participation of both genders is underscored throughout the chapters that follow:

> More than ever believers were added to the Lord, great numbers of *both men and women*. (5:14)

Saul was ravaging the church by entering house after house; dragging off *both men and women*, he committed them to prison. (8:3)

When they believed Philip, . . . they were baptized, *both men and women*. (8:12)

Saul . . . went to the high **priest** and asked him for letters to the **synagogues** at Damascus, so that if he found any who belonged to the Way, *men or women*, he might bring them bound to Jerusalem. (9:1–2)[11]

As the story continues, we are introduced to a series of Spirit-empowered women who help lead the earliest church. Paul has a dream of a Macedonian man begging him to come and help them, and when he arrives in Philippi, the Spirit leads him to a business-woman named Lydia, who responds in faith to the gospel and ends up leading the church in her house (Acts 16:11–15, 40). Soon thereafter we meet the married couple Aquila and Priscilla, who partner with Paul and go on to become major leaders in the early movement.[12] We also discover that Philip "had four unmarried daughters who had the gift of prophecy" (21:9). Thus it seems that this is a community that affirms the Spirit's freedom to empower people irrespective of their gender. In the past, a woman's participation in God's covenant was enabled through her relationship with a **circumcised** male relative, but now it comes directly to her through the power of the Holy Spirit.

The story of Acts also makes it plain that in Christian community *"there is no longer slave or free,"* that is, people are not divided by distinctions of class and economic standing. As the Joel prophecy declared, the Spirit will be poured out *even upon slaves* (Acts 2:18). This generous outpouring of spiritual grace transforms followers into generous people who pour out what wealth they have to lift up those in need (2:44–45; 4:34–35). It transforms disabled beggars into

11. Emphasis added in these verses.
12. Paul sends greetings to Prisca and Aquila at the end of Romans (16:3), 1 Corinthians (16:19), and 2 Timothy (4:19). Strikingly, in four out of the six times that the couple is named in the NT, Priscilla (or "Prisca," as Paul calls her in the letters) is named first. The naming of the wife before the husband is unusual in that culture and seems to point to Priscilla's authority and renown.

dancers (3:1–10). It uses "uneducated and ordinary" people to educate the learned in positions of authority (4:13). It brings salvation to an Ethiopian slave (8:26–40), a centurion of the Italian cohort (chap. 10), and a jailer from Philippi (16:27–34). All of these very different people are joined together in "one heart and soul" (4:32) by the Spirit who heals social divisions by drawing all people to Jesus.

Finally, though probably most important for the plot point of Acts in the larger NT story, "*in Christ . . . there is no longer Jew or Greek*" (Gal. 3:28, emphasis added). Our survey of the Gospels made it quite plain that Jesus emerged out of the people of Israel to extend the salvation of God to all the nations of the earth. While we saw that extension already emerging in the Gospel stories, it is in Acts that we witness the formal beginning of a fully fledged Christian mission to the non-Jewish world. It is a conspicuous fact that most of the latter half of Acts focuses exclusively on the ministry of Paul (Acts 16–28), the highly trained Jewish **Pharisee** who was called by Jesus (9:1–19) to preach the way of the Word to the gentile world. Such an extended introduction is needed for someone whose writings make up nearly one-third of the NT! We'll save that introduction for chapter 7 on Paul. For now we'll focus on how Acts narrates the emergence of this mission "to the ends of the earth" (1:8).

First, Acts demonstrates that though Paul might be known as the apostle to the gentiles, the mission to the gentile world did not begin with his work. Before we ever meet Paul, we are told that the Spirit will be poured out on *all flesh* (2:17). This universal outpouring does not happen all at once, yet it emerges in a particular place and on particular flesh: *Jewish* flesh. Acts thus begins with detailed descriptions of the origin of a robust Jewish-Christian mission to non-Christian Jews. Most of the key leaders here are familiar from the Gospel narratives: the opening scenes list the eleven remaining disciples, along with the betrayer Judas and his replacement Matthias (Acts 1)—though most of these have no time on stage, with the speaking parts given to Peter and John in the early chapters.

That first circle also included "certain women, including Mary the mother of Jesus, as well as his brothers" (Acts 1:14). We've already commented on the role of women in earliest Christianity, but what of Jesus's brothers? Unearthing their role requires a bit of canonical

digging. We may recall from the Gospels that Jesus had four brothers: James, Joses/Joseph, Judas, and Simon (Matt. 13:55; Mark 6:3).
We have no clear way of knowing where Jesus falls in the birth order
here,[13] but such issues are outside the scope of our study. Two of
Paul's letters speak of Jesus's brothers. In 1 Corinthians he describes
Jesus's brothers as fellow Christian missionaries (9:5) and mentions
that someone named "James" was the recipient of an appearance
from the resurrected Jesus (15:7). In Galatians, he speaks repeatedly
of "James, the Lord's brother" (1:19), who is listed first alongside
Peter and John as "pillars" of the Jerusalem church (2:9). In that letter Paul also describes a conflict he had with Peter, who was caught
between Paul and certain believers associated with "the circumcision
faction" who "came from James" (2:11–13).

This information helps to clear up a mystery in Acts. The Gospels
made us familiar with an inner group of three disciple-confidants,
Peter plus James and John, the sons of Zebedee, who were present
at Jesus's transfiguration (Matt. 17:1–8; Mark 9:2–8; Luke 9:28–36).
Acts 12 tells us that King Herod began persecuting the church, and
"had James, the brother of John, killed by the sword" (12:2). Peter
was arrested in this oppression, and after his miraculous escape,
he tells the followers he meets to report his experience "to James
and to the brothers" (12:17). We meet this James later in Acts, and
on both occasions he is depicted as being in charge of the Jerusalem church (15:12–21; 21:17–26). Putting all this together, we can
conclude that James, the Lord's brother, was the leader in charge
of the early Jewish-Christian mission to non-Christian Jews centered in Jerusalem. The NT includes a letter from this James and
another from Jesus's other brother Jude, who identifies himself as
"the brother of James" (Jude 1). These two letters frame the seven
NT letters traditionally known as the **Catholic Epistles**, which will
be the subject of chapter 8.

13. Some representatives of the ancient church taught that these were actually
close relatives of Jesus (the official position of the **Roman Catholic** Church). Still
others believed they were Joseph's children from a previous marriage (the view held
by most in the Eastern Orthodox Church). For more on Jesus's extended family, see
Richard Bauckham's fascinating study, *Jude and the Relatives of Jesus in the Early
Church* (New York: T&T Clark, 1990).

Peter, by contrast, appears to have taken up the role of emissary, traveling back and forth between Jerusalem and Jewish-Christian outposts abroad in Samaria (Acts 8:14), Lydda, Sharon, and Joppa (9:32–43), and Caesarea (chap. 10). Before long, the Word spreads to those who are not ethnically Jewish. Philip, who had already been preaching in Samaria (8:4–8), participates in the conversion of an Ethiopian God-fearer (8:26–40). We then read of Paul's conversion to Christ (9:1–19) along with Jesus's statement that Paul is "chosen to bring my name before gentiles and kings and before the people of Israel" (9:15). But while Paul is just beginning his ministry, preaching at this point only to Jews (9:19–30), it is *Peter* who mediates the conversion of the gentile centurion Cornelius and his relatives and friends (chap. 10). In all this it is plain that the mission to the gentiles emerged organically *out of* the mission to Jews that started in Jerusalem. As Paul himself will state, the power of salvation is "to the Jew first and also to the Greek" (Rom. 1:16).

The two groups, Jew and Greek, meet in the story of Cornelius's conversion. Peter himself acknowledges the awkwardness of the situation, saying to Cornelius's community, "You yourselves know that it is unlawful for a Jew to associate with or to visit a Gentile; but God has shown me that I should not call anyone profane or unclean" (Acts 10:28). Because of their interaction, Peter can go on to say, "I truly understand that God shows no partiality, but in every nation anyone who fears him and does what is right is acceptable to him" (10:34–35). And as Peter goes on to preach the Way of the Word in their midst,

> The Holy Spirit fell upon all who heard the word. The circumcised believers who had come with Peter were astounded that the gift of the Holy Spirit had been poured out even on the Gentiles, for they heard them speaking in tongues and extolling God. Then Peter said, "Can anyone withhold the water for baptizing these people who have received the Holy Spirit just as we have?" (10:44–47)

In the midst of social, cultural, and religious differences, the Spirit of God creates a unified fellowship. These people who have no worldly reason to be in the same room together are now joined intimately to one another as companions on the way of the Word.

One final point of clarification is required: it is vital to understand that this spiritual unity is nowhere described as erasing distinctions between people. Spiritual unity is forged *in the midst of differences*, not *at the expense of differences*, as it was in Babel. In Acts, Jews remain Jews and gentiles remain gentiles, but nonetheless both groups are miraculously drawn into one body.

Not all early Christians thought this should be so. We have already mentioned believers in Galatia who were identified as part of "the circumcision faction" (Gal. 2:12). Similar people are described in Acts 15 as Christian Pharisees who travel to the church in Antioch and say to the gentile Christians there, "Unless you are circumcised according to the custom of Moses, you cannot be saved" (15:1). The call to be circumcised created such a stir that a meeting of all the Christian leaders, "the apostles and the elders" (15:6), was called in Jerusalem. Jesus's brother James governed the council and listened to the testimonies given. The believing Pharisees stood up and repeated their insistence that it was "necessary for them to be circumcised and ordered to keep the **law** of Moses" (15:5). Really, how could it be otherwise? Since Abraham, God's people practiced circumcision as the physical sign of the covenant (Gen. 17:9–14), and observance of God's **Torah** had been a basic expectation since it was first delivered to the people through Moses. There was no NT at this point, no Letters of Paul carefully delineating the role of the law and circumcision in God's plan; there was only the **Jewish Scriptures**, what we now call the **Old Testament**. If discerning God's will was a simple matter of finding Scripture passages in support of a position, then the pro-circumcision group appeared to have the case locked up.

Against this, others testified to the work that God was doing in the present among uncircumcised gentiles. Their spokesperson, Peter, stood up and said, "God, who knows the human heart, testified to them by giving them the Holy Spirit, just as he did to us; and in cleansing their hearts by faith he has made no distinction between them and us. . . . We believe that we will be saved through the grace of the Lord Jesus, just as they will" (Acts 15:8–9, 11).

This conflict should be familiar to anyone who has spent time in Christian community. There are occasions where our experience of

God in the present appears to conflict with what seems like the plain testimony of Scripture. How ought Christian leaders to proceed in such situations? Stand rigidly on a particular assessment of Scripture's message, or err on the side of contemporary experience of the Spirit's movement in the world?

James's resolution of the matter points a way forward. He observes what God is doing in the present, and that present experience leads him back to Scripture to help him discern what God is up to. He begins by declaring that God has long been saying through the prophets that salvation will be extended to gentiles (Acts 15:13–17, quoting a version of Amos 9:11–12). If the Spirit has indeed come down on gentiles apart from their being circumcised, then God must intend to bring in these people apart from their becoming full practitioners of Judaism. So James concludes:

> We should not trouble those Gentiles who are turning to God, but we should write to them to abstain only from things polluted by idols and from fornication and from whatever has been strangled and from blood. For in every city, for generations past, Moses has had those who proclaim him, for he has been read aloud every sabbath in the synagogues. (Acts 15:19–21)

The contemporary experience of the Spirit's folding of gentiles into the community of God's people leads James to go back and reexamine Scripture for any precedent that might point a way forward. His reading leads him to conclude that gentile followers need not observe the whole Torah, but should avoid four things: food sacrificed to idols, sexual immorality, improperly prepared meat, and ingestion of blood. Of all the prohibitions in Scripture, why these four? Leviticus 17–18 identifies these four as rules for "strangers" who reside among God's people. In this way fellowship could be maintained between the two different groups living together in unity. Compromise, it turns out, is required on both sides: gentiles must be willing to shift away from certain pagan practices in order to accommodate their observant Jewish brothers and sisters, and Jews must be willing to change their expectations of what is required to be a member of God's covenant people. But it is the Jewish Scripture that determines these things;

gentile followers are guests at the banquet, as Jesus himself reminded us when he insisted, "Salvation is from the Jews" (John 4:22).

James's resolution reflects a brilliant mind that is sensitive to the movement of the Spirit. He rejects a simple either/or distinction between the authority of Scripture and the powerful impact of present experience. Instead, he uses Scripture to interpret his experience of God and, conversely, allows his contemporary experience of God to affect his reading of Scripture. As we move on from Acts to consider the Letters of Paul, the NT canon will provide us with an extended example of a Christian thinker like James, whose task it is to maintain this careful balance in order to teach the way of the Word to the gentile churches he plants.

───────────────── **Questions for Discussion** ─────────────────

1. Now that you've read this chapter on the Acts of the Apostles, what questions do you have? What do you want to know more about? Make a list to share with your class or reading group.

2. More than any other, the book of Acts introduces readers to the Holy Spirit. What impressed you the most about Acts' depiction of this divine Person?

3. Nearly one-third of Acts consists of speeches. What might this tell us about the nature of earliest Christianity? Does this same phenomenon take place among Christians today? If so, how?

4. The Holy Spirit transforms Christian community to function as a very different sort of society in the world. What practices and expectations of American Christianity hold us back from attaining the status of an authentically alternative community?

5. This chapter ended by looking at how James mediated the apparent conflict between Scripture and experience at the apostolic council in Jerusalem. What such conflicts exist in your experience? How are they mediated in your community?

6. If the Acts of the Apostles had been left out of the NT, what would be missing?

7. Where does this book locate you on the way of the Word? How has it helped you along? Where has it warned you to slow down? What in your discipleship requires acceleration? Has the route to your destination been at all clarified?

7

The Letters of Paul

The Pattern of Discipleship

> "I have been crucified with Christ;
> and it is no longer I who live,
> but it is Christ who lives in me."
>
> (GALATIANS 2:19–20)

It is hard to overstate the influence the Letters of the apostle Paul have had on the Christian faith. Despite the fact that Paul had never even met Jesus during his sojourn on earth, by the late second century the church father **Irenaeus of Lyon** was able to rank him right alongside Peter as one of "the two most glorious apostles."[1] Half a century before that, Bishop **Polycarp of Smyrna** could write,

> Neither I nor anyone like me can keep pace with the **wisdom** of the blessed and glorious Paul. When he was with you in the presence of the people of that time, he accurately and reliably taught the word concerning the truth. And when he was absent he wrote you letters; if you study them carefully, you will be able to build yourselves up

1. Irenaeus, *Against Heresies* 3.3.2.

in the faith that has been given to you, which is the mother of us all, while hope follows and love for God and **Christ** and for our neighbor leads the way. For anyone who is occupied with these has fulfilled the commandment of **righteousness**, for whoever has love is far from all sin.[2]

Jesus is the founder of the Christian faith, and James, Peter, and John were its first leaders, but Paul was the first theologian. His writings reflect a sharp mind and a keen pastoral sensibility. Trained as he was in the **Jewish Scriptures**, Paul was able to articulate how God's work in Christ Jesus completes the unfolding pattern of God's saving plan in history. More than that, he offered a detailed description of how God's Holy Spirit enfolds *us* within that pattern of salvation. In the centuries since Paul wrote, God has used Paul's dynamic letters to increase the faith, hope, and love of countless Christians.

Nevertheless, there was a serious problem with Paul's writings in the ancient church. "There are some things in them hard to understand," writes the author of 2 Peter, "which the ignorant and unstable twist to their own destruction" (3:16). Many people were championing Paul in the days of Polycarp and Irenaeus, and not all of them agreed on how to teach the way of the Word. Some used Pauline teaching to support an opposition to Judaism that threatened to detach the Christian movement from its historic and scriptural roots. Others used Paul to support **antinomianism**, the notion that God's grace made obedience unnecessary. Others were gnostics who affirmed a spirit-flesh dualism, believing that the material world, created by a lesser god who trapped our true spiritual selves in bodies, was irrelevant at best or dangerous at worst.

What emerged out of this struggle was the conviction that Paul's powerful teachings required a "frame" that would provide a permanent corrective to these potential misunderstandings. Thus, with the **Gospels** and Acts on one side, and the **Catholic Epistles** and Revelation on the other, we receive Paul in an embrace designed to help us interpret his words aright.

---

2. Polycarp, *To the Philippians* 3:2–3, trans. Michael W. Holmes and J. B. Lightfoot, in *The Apostolic Fathers in English*, ed. Michael W. Holmes, 3rd ed. (Grand Rapids: Baker Academic, 2006), 136.

A complete introduction to Paul's Letters easily merits a book of its own. Our purpose here is not to attempt to cover every element of his life and thought, but to help readers of the NT understand the function of his letters within the **canon** as a whole.

Canonical Transition: From Acts to Paul

The previous chapter introduced Acts by focusing on how it continues the story begun in the Gospels. Now consider for a moment what it would be like if we did not have the Acts of the Apostles to transition readers from the Gospels to the Letters. We would be baffled by the inclusion of letters from someone named Paul. We might assume that the Letter of James was written by the brother of John. And while we would likely celebrate the fact that the way of the Word had made its way to predominantly **gentile** cities like Ephesus, Corinth, Philippi, and Rome, we would certainly be wondering how it got there! It is no wonder, then, that the ancient church separated Luke's Gospel from his book of Acts.

In fact, evidence from canon history suggests that Acts circulated separately from Luke in order to function as an introduction to the NT Letters. The arrangement makes perfect sense. The closing chapter of the Acts of the Apostles leaves Paul under house arrest in Rome. His attempts to evangelize Jews has left him frustrated, as his final words to Jewish hearers make plain: "Let it be known to you then that this salvation of God has been sent to the Gentiles; they will listen" (Acts 28:29). The narrative of Acts closes with these words:

> He lived there two whole years at his own expense and welcomed all who came to him, proclaiming the **kingdom of God** and teaching about the Lord Jesus Christ with all boldness and without hindrance. (28:30–31)

Acts concludes with Paul proclaiming the gospel in Rome; turn the page, and we seem to find a transcript of Paul's proclamation in letter form! Indeed, just as the last line of Acts tells us that he preached the gospel "with all boldness and without hindrance" (28:31), Paul begins his message in Romans insisting, "I am not ashamed of the gospel" (Rom. 1:16). Once again we find a smooth narrative transition governing the arrangement of the NT books.

If we are reading in sequence, then that means the portrait of Paul in Acts is the canonical introduction designed to prepare us to read his letters.[3] What does Acts inform us about Paul? The following items are worth keeping in mind.

First, *the Paul documented in Acts is actually a Jewish Pharisee named Saul.* We first meet him at the stoning of Stephen (Acts 7), when we are told that "the witnesses laid their coats at the feet of a young man named Saul" (7:58), who somehow gave his approval for the killing (8:1). Soon thereafter we are told that he had authority to arrest those "who belonged to the Way" (8:3; 9:2) and that it was on a journey to detain followers in Damascus that Saul first encountered Jesus (9:1–19). Later, when we discover that he studied the Scriptures "at the feet of Gamaliel" (22:3), whom Jewish tradition identifies as the president of the Jerusalem Sanhedrin in his day, we begin to understand that this Saul cut a very impressive figure.

It is common for people to speak of Paul's "conversion" to Christianity and to associate this new orientation with the changing of his name from Saul to Paul. It is clear that he was converted in a sense, for his mind and orientation were radically changed, yet "converted" might not be the best description of what happens in this part of the story. To begin with, there was as yet no religion called "Christianity" for Paul to convert to! The way of the Word was at this point simply a movement within Judaism. Appropriate to such a context, the story of Paul's encounter with Jesus reads very much like a *prophetic calling.*[4] Paul has not changed religions; he has received a call from the God of Israel to preach the way of the Word to non-Jews. And as it turns out, a closer look reveals that his name *did not change* as a result of this transforming event in his life, for he continues to go by the name "Saul" for the next several chapters. Indeed, he remains a Pharisee even after he begins serving Jesus (23:6).

---

3. No one has done more to explore the canonical function of Acts than Robert W. Wall. Most recently, see the book he published with Anthony B. Robinson, *Called to Be Church: The Book of Acts for a New Day* (Grand Rapids: Eerdmans, 2006).

4. The encounter closely parallels OT scenes of the call of Israel's prophets: cf. Isa. 6:1–13 and Jer. 1:4–10.

Several chapters after his call we are suddenly told that he is "Saul, also known as Paul" (Acts 13:9). Saul had a second name, apparently a *cognomen*, which was a common practice among Romans. This insight prepares us for the second thing Acts communicates about Paul: *The Jewish Pharisee named Saul is also a Roman citizen named Paul.* Indeed, Paul "was born a [Roman] citizen" (22:27–28). We are not told how his parents gained their citizenship, but we do know that he was born and raised in Tarsus (21:39; 22:3), capital city of the Roman province of Cilicia (in modern-day Turkey). Tarsus was an important center of **Hellenistic** education, a fact reflected in Paul's Letters, which reveal a learned writer with a keen awareness of Hellenistic rhetorical strategies and the major philosophical systems of the day.

The Paul of Acts is proud of his Roman citizenship (16:37–39; 22:25–29) and appears relatively comfortable in the cosmopolitan settings of Hellenistic cities.[5] His cross-cultural identity formation is a key feature of the third thing Acts clearly portrays about Paul: *he was the most prominent missionary to non-Jews in the early Christian movement.* Acts records three of Paul's major missionary journeys,[6] during which he visited many of the major cities of the northeastern Roman Empire. We recognize these cities from the letters he left behind, like Philippi (chap. 16), Thessalonica (chap. 17), Ephesus (chap. 18), Corinth (chaps. 18–19), and of course Rome (chap. 28). Paul's message is primarily evangelistic; his letters present the gospel in particular contexts, to particular people, facing particular struggles. It is unsurprising, then, that the ancient collectors eventually titled all of his letters according to their recipients: while the Gospels are titled "According to . . ." (*kata* in Greek), Paul's multiple articulations of the gospel he preached are all titled "To the" intended readers (*pros*

5. See, e.g., Acts 17:16–34, which tells the story of Paul in Athens. Despite the fact that he is surrounded by "idols" (17:16), a setting which an observant Jew would typically find abhorrent, Paul is able to honor his hearers, saying, "Athenians, I see how extremely religious you are in every way" (17:22). He even quotes Greek plays and poetry approvingly in support of his argument (17:28).

6. Acts 13:1–14:28, Cyprus and cities in what is now Turkey; 15:36–18:22, Syria, Turkey, Greece (Macedonia and Achaia), and Jerusalem; 18:23–21:16, more cities in Turkey and Greece before returning to Jerusalem.

in Greek). These canonical markers inform our reading of their respective texts: in Paul's case, they remind us that his gospel message is always oriented to his specific readership; he presents a "word on target,"[7] tailored to the needs of his immediate readers.

Fourth, Acts reminds us that *Paul was a partner in ministry*. Despite the extensive focus on his words and deeds, Acts shows us that Paul was not the only Christian missionary to gentiles. Just as Acts depicts Paul as traveling with partners—people like Barnabas (e.g., 11:25; 13:2), Silas (chaps. 15–17), and Timothy (e.g., 16:1–5)—his letters reflect this same reality: seven of the thirteen letters that bear his name also list coauthors, and most of them close with greetings from the many coworkers residing with Paul when he wrote. Paul is on the same side as Peter in the Jerusalem council debate (chap. 15), and he submits without quarrel to James's requests (15:22; 21:18–26). Readers of the canon are therefore unsurprised when we read Paul's report in the Letter to the Galatians, "When James and Cephas and John, who were acknowledged pillars, recognized the grace that had been given to me, they gave to Barnabas and me the right hand of fellowship, agreeing that we should go to the Gentiles and they to the **circumcised**" (Gal. 2:9). Paul is one member of a larger Christian leadership, and his teaching must be received alongside the instruction offered by these others.

A discussion of the canonical transition from Acts to the Pauline Letters would not be complete if we did not also consider some of the discrepancies between the two. While a historian might problematize these differences as contradictory, a canonical approach welcomes them as complementary: *Acts emphasizes certain things about Paul in order to make sure we don't take some of the more extreme statements of his letters in the wrong way.* For example, after Jesus was revealed to him, Paul insists that he didn't confer with anyone and didn't go up to Jerusalem until three years later (Gal. 1:16–18). Acts tells the story differently, with Paul preaching immediately in Damascus before quickly heading to Jerusalem to join the other **disciples** (Acts 9:19–30). Paul reports that the Jerusalem pillars "asked only one thing, that we remember the poor" (Gal. 2:10), and makes no

---

7. The phrase comes from J. Christiaan Beker, *Paul the Apostle: The Triumph of God in Life and Thought* (Philadelphia: Fortress, 1980), 12.

mention of the legal requirements they asked gentiles to observe (Acts 15:22–29). Paul also makes it clear that he no longer thinks of himself as strictly **law** observant, taking up the lifestyle of those with whom he ministers: "To those under the law I became as one under the law (though I myself am not under the law) so that I might win those under the law. To those outside the law I became as one outside the law (though I am not free from God's law but am under Christ's law) so that I might win those outside the law" (1 Cor. 9:20–21). This is despite the fact that Acts presents Paul as a careful observer of the law who had "in no way committed an offense against the law of the Jews, or against the temple" (25:8).

Given the nature of these particular discrepancies, it seems plausible that Acts is concerned to guard readers of Paul's Letters against receiving his words in a manner that detaches them from the heritage of Israel. When we read Acts as an introduction to Paul, we come to his letters knowing in advance that he did not reject Judaism or Israel's Scriptures, much less the essential affirmation that those who believe in Jesus must actually be obedient to the way of the Word. Reading Paul in canonical context frames Paul's message properly within the whole apostolic proclamation and prevents us from twisting it in a manner that suits ourselves at the cost of detaching it from the larger message of the gospel.

The Shape of the Pauline Witness

Modern scholarship has long divided Paul's Letters into two major categories. The first is a group of seven letters considered "undisputed" because most scholars believe they were produced by Paul himself. Romans, 1–2 Corinthians, Galatians, Philippians, 1 Thessalonians, and Philemon all share the same voice and literary style, and they address issues deemed pertinent to the historical time period of Paul's ministry. The remaining letters—Ephesians, Colossians, 2 Thessalonians, 1–2 Timothy, and Titus—are typically labeled "disputed" because of disagreements as to their origin. While some scholars continue to believe that all the letters attributed to Paul are "authentic" documents dictated or written by him, many claim that this latter set derive from a later, post-Pauline period where students of Paul wrote letters in his name to adapt Paul's teaching to new situations.

While there is a good deal of merit to this scholarly discussion, it is important for canonical readers to recognize that the biblical text does not present us with any such distinction. Regardless of who was actually holding the pen at the point of composition, the canon preserves all of these together as letters from Paul that are "useful for teaching, for reproof, for correction, and for training in righteousness" (2 Tim. 3:16). If we are to benefit from all that the canonical Paul has to offer, we must attend to every letter and not just the ones that scholars consider "authentic."

But does the canonical shape of Paul's Letters offer up any other strategies for approaching this body of literature? The following features are worthy of note. First, we see that there are fourteen letters that begin with the aforementioned *pros* title ("to the . . ."), indicating a Pauline text. The first nine are addressed to Christians in seven different cities or regions: Rome, Corinth, Galatia, Ephesus, Philippi, Colossae, and Thessalonica. The next four are addressed to individuals: Timothy (twice), Titus, and Philemon. The last is the letter "to the Hebrews," which bears the Pauline style of title but does not include an opening address indicating that it is from Paul. This fourteenth letter is in a class by itself, so we'll discuss it in our chapter's epilogue. For now, we'll focus on the thirteen letters that are designated Pauline *and* addressed by Paul.

The basic rule of organization for Paul's Letters is length. While readers today typically measure books by page length, ancient people measured length by lines of text, called **stichoi. Scribes** were paid for the number of lines they copied, and writers would cite other authors by referring to the line of the text where the quote was found. When ancient people published collections of material, therefore, it was common to order those texts from longest to shortest.

Paul's letter collection mostly follows the length rule,[8] but there are two interesting deviations. The most obvious, and most under-

---

8. Reconstructions of stichoi lengths are widely available. These numbers derive from the pioneering study of J. Rendall Harris, *Stichometry* (London: C. J. Clay & Sons, 1893).

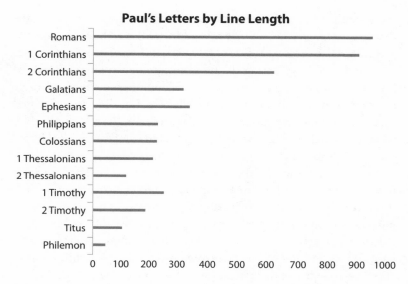

Paul's Letters by Line Length

standable, is that the line count starts over when we reach 1 Timothy, supporting the basic division between letters to churches and letters to individuals. The more unexpected deviation is the slight difference between Galatians and Ephesians. Ancient line lengths are hard to reconstruct, so some have argued that the two letters must have once been determined to be of equal length. Others, however, have proposed an intentional division at this point. In the earlier days of modern German scholarship, the Letters of Romans through Galatians were labeled *Hauptbriefe*, "chief letters," because they were presumed to have been grouped together in light of their (supposedly) greater theological weight. More recently it has been suggested that Ephesians may have served as a cover letter for these first four, which represent the earliest Pauline letter collection (perhaps put into circulation by Paul himself). Others have proposed that the line count starts over here to designate a discrete collection of three "prison letters": Ephesians, Philippians, and Colossians. All of these suggestions are rather speculative, of course, so in the end we probably do best by holding to a basic division between letters to churches and letters to individuals.

The placement of Romans at the beginning of the collection, however, serves a more important function than simply designating it as the longest letter of the set, for Romans also happens to be Paul's theological masterpiece. Since it is addressed to a church he *did not* start himself (see Rom. 1:8–15; 15:14–33), it takes the form of a letter of introduction presenting the most comprehensive articulation of his message that we possess. It includes a number of the memorable topics and themes found in his other letters, but they are presented here in a more universalized (and therefore more widely applicable) format. As such, readers of the canon find in Romans an ideal introduction to Paul's Letters.

But how ought we to summarize Paul's immense body of teaching in what remains of this short chapter? Scholars have often set forth this or that theme as an organizing center of Paul's message. For the purposes of our brief survey, we pick up the phrase Paul himself uses as a rhetorical frame for his Letter to the Romans. In the opening verses, Paul announces that he has "received grace and apostleship to bring about the obedience of faith among all the Gentiles" (Rom. 1:5). A final verse repeats this notion, saying that the proclamation of Jesus Christ "is made known to all the Gentiles, according to the command of the eternal God, to bring about the obedience of faith" (16:26). In Paul's reckoning, *Christ's obedience reveals God's faithfulness to us, and because of this work, the Spirit is able to generate obedient faithfulness in those who believe.* What follows below is a narration of Paul's complex understanding of how this pattern of faithful obedience is taken up by those who follow the way of the Word.

What Does Paul Teach Us about God's Work in Christ Jesus?

As we have repeated several times now, Paul did not know the Jesus who taught his disciples the way of the Word. What he *did* know— extremely well, in fact—were the Scriptures of Israel. Indeed, Paul serves as an important reminder for us that knowledge of Scripture alone isn't sufficient to establish true understanding of God. In Paul's own words,

> I was violently persecuting the church of God and was trying to destroy it. I advanced in Judaism beyond many among my people of the same

age, for I was far more zealous for the traditions of my ancestors. But . . . God, who had set me apart before I was born and called me through his grace, was pleased to reveal his Son to me, so that I might proclaim him among the Gentiles. (Gal. 1:13–16)

Paul's knowledge of God's work in Christ Jesus emerged out of an *experience of personal revelation* that provided him with a new set of lenses to reread the pattern of salvation related in the Scripture he already knew and loved.

But what exactly did this experience reveal to Paul? If we take the story from Acts as our guide, Jesus revealed that the one whom Paul had taken to be a false **Messiah** worthy of death was much more than he appeared to be (Acts 9:4–5). The one who "emptied himself . . . and became obedient to the point of death—even death on a cross" had subsequently been exalted by God and given "the name that is above every name." Paul learned that Jesus was indeed Israel's Messiah, but more than that, he learned that Jesus was the presence and power of God in the world; he learned that "Jesus Christ is Lord" (Phil. 2:5–11).

If Paul was like most other Jews of the day, he probably expected God's Messiah to be a charismatic human leader who would establish the salvation of Israel by freeing them from the Romans. But Paul's experience of the risen Lord revealed something completely unexpected hidden in the message of Scripture: in Jesus, God was "laying in Zion a stone that will make people stumble, a rock that will make them fall" (Rom. 9:33, citing a version of Isa. 8:14–15 and 28:16). Paul is no doubt thinking of his own experience when he writes that the message of the crucified Messiah is "God's wisdom, secret and hidden, which God decreed before the ages for our glory. None of the rulers of this age understood this; for if they had, they would not have crucified the Lord of glory" (1 Cor. 2:7–8). As it turned out, God had a plan for salvation that was much, much larger than Israel's hopes. God's plan in Christ didn't make things right for Israel alone; according to Paul, the good news of Jesus is the complete revelation of God's *own* righteousness for the sake of the *whole* world.

Thus far we have defined righteousness as trusting and faithful **covenant** relationship. Part of the shock of God's revelation in Christ was Paul's realization that no one—neither Jewish Scripture scholars nor Greek philosophers of wisdom—could have ever predicted what God intended to do. This is the case because sin renders all humans "covenantally dysfunctional"[9]—all of us maintain a concept of God that is too small, too insular and self-serving, such that we are not able to live in faithful relationship with the one true God. "There is no one who is righteous, not even one; there is no one who has understanding" (Rom. 3:10–11, citing a version of Ps. 14:3), for "all have sinned and fall short of the glory of God" (Rom. 3:23).

But while everyone was locked in the deadly pattern of thinking only of themselves and their own well-being, God sent Jesus to live out the pattern of obedient faith. Ironically, the single, true model of right covenant relationship with God was rejected and killed by those who believed *themselves* to be the model of right covenant relationship. But amazingly, this rejection would become the very means by which God would establish a new covenant. How? In short, the only way to convince humanity of its complete dependence on the Creator was to overwhelm us with the unimaginable wideness of God's mercy (Rom. 11:33–36). So God came in Christ and proclaimed love, forgiveness, and universal acceptance into God's kingdom. After this offer was rejected, and he was murdered and buried, Jesus broke the power of death by rising from the dead—not to exact vengeance on those who killed him, but in order to establish peace by sharing the power of life with a humanity locked in the pattern of death (Eph. 2:14–17). "God proves his love for us," Paul insists, "in that while we still were sinners Christ died for us" (Rom. 5:8). "Christ died *for* us," died so that death itself would be broken and its power disabled, so that we too might be able to participate in Christ's pattern of obedient faith and "walk in newness of life" (Rom. 6:4).

As Paul puts it, though "the sting of death is sin" (1 Cor. 15:56), God put forth Christ Jesus and "made him to be sin who knew no sin, so that in him we might become the righteousness of God" (2 Cor. 5:21). Thus, in Christ's sacrifice, God "passed over the sins previously

---

9. This helpfully illuminating phrase is borrowed from Michael Gorman. See his superb introduction to Paul, *Apostle of the Crucified Lord: A Theological Introduction to Paul and His Letters* (Grand Rapids: Eerdmans, 2004), 113–34.

committed . . . to prove at the present time that he himself is righteous" (Rom. 3:25–26), that he alone lives out the pattern of obedient faith. Where humanity was seeking salvation in wisdom and power and honor,

> God chose what is foolish in the world to shame the wise; God chose what is weak in the world to shame the strong; God chose what is low and despised in the world, things that are not, to reduce to nothing things that are, so that no one might boast in the presence of God. (1 Cor. 1:27–29)

This great leveling of all humanity before the faithful God leaves us with only one proper response: give up our self-justifying ways, our "boasting" about the things that make us feel secure about ourselves,[10] and acknowledge that God alone is righteous and thus is the only one worthy of our trust and allegiance.

This "trust and allegiance" expressed in Jesus's complete obedience to God is what Paul has in mind when he uses the word "faith," and the establishment of that faith in us is what Paul means when he uses the word **justification**. There is much to discuss here, and it has often been misunderstood in the history of Christianity, so careful attention is required. As a scholar of the Jewish Scriptures, Paul knew that faith had always been the means by which this trust in and allegiance to God was expressed. Way back in Genesis, when God called Abram to trust that what seemed impossible could indeed come true, Abram "believed the LORD; and the LORD reckoned it to him as righteousness" (Gen. 15:6; Rom. 4:3; Gal. 3:6). Righteousness looks like trusting and following God even when doing so seems unreasonable. Later, when Israel was enslaved in Egypt, God saved them by grace, delivering them from bondage and leading them out to a new place. In response, God asked for their trust and allegiance: "Hear, O Israel: The LORD is our God, the LORD alone. You shall love the LORD your God with all your heart, and with all your soul, and with all your might" (Deut. 6:4–5). And later still, one of Israel's prophets said, "Look at the proud! Their spirit is not right in them,

---

10. See, e.g., Rom. 3:27; 4:1–2; 11:17–20; 1 Cor. 1:28–30; 5:6; 13:3; 2 Cor. 10:17; 11:30; Gal. 6:13–14; Eph. 2:8–9.

but the righteous live by their faith" (Hab. 2:4).[11] When we give our trust and allegiance to God, we are **justified** (made right) with God.

For Paul and the Jews of his day, this faithful trust and allegiance was understood to take place solely in the context of God's covenant with the people of Israel. How could it be otherwise? To whom else had this God been revealed, and who else knew what this God expected of people (Rom. 9:4–5)? In this way Israel was set apart as God's "treasured possession out of all the peoples. Indeed, the whole earth is mine," God said, "but you shall be for me a priestly kingdom and a holy nation" (Exod. 19:5–6). Their job was to continue God's project, begun with Abram, to bless the world (Gen. 12:3) by acting as God's **priests**, God's mediators, a "light to the nations" (Isa. 42:6). They would be set apart, that is, they would be *holy*, by observing the commandments of God's law.

But their performance of the law was never intended to *replace* the need for trust and allegiance. While law observance was to be an *expression* of Israel's faith, it was not the *basis* of that faith (Gal. 3:11–12). This is precisely what too many people in Israel forgot. As God's elect, some boasted in their ethnicity (Rom. 2:17) and carefully maintained the social, ethical, and ritual boundary markers of their identity (Phil. 3:4–6). Called to be like father Abraham, they became like the people of Babel. And as they suffered in subjugation under foreign powers, "the dividing wall" of hostility between Jew and Greek grew higher and thicker (Eph. 2:14). As Israel withdrew into itself to protect its holy identity, its capacity to bless the world and be a light to the nations became compromised (Rom. 2:17–24). They circled the wagons, waiting for the day when God would send the Messiah to vindicate them and judge the sinful gentile world.

11. I've quoted Habakkuk here as it is rendered by the NRSV, but it should be noted that Paul's quotations of this verse in Rom. 1:17 and Gal. 3:11 are unique in that they do not agree with either the Hebrew or Greek (**LXX**) OT texts for Hab. 2:4. The Hebrew text has "The righteous will live by *their* faith," and the Greek has "The righteous will live by *my* faithfulness." Paul drops the referent in order to make the case that "faith" is the means of covenant relationship, both God's faith and our own: as he writes in Rom. 1:17, the righteousness of God is revealed "through faith for faith" or (more literally) "out of faith into faith," meaning that God's faithfulness *to* us generates faith *in* us.

It was into this historical context that the Word of God became a human in Jesus of Nazareth. But as our study of the way of the Word has made plain thus far, Jesus was not the Messiah of Israel's hopes. Much to their dismay, Jesus judged the arrogance of Israel's leaders, had a tendency to proclaim gentiles and **Samaritans** more faithful than Jews, and even broke the law by doing work on the Sabbath and flagrantly touching unclean persons. For this he was put to death, in accordance with **Torah**, as a lawbreaker and false Messiah. This was the Jesus of whom Paul knew at first, which is why he worked so vigorously to stamp out the movement to follow Jesus on the way of the Word.

But when the crucified Jesus revealed himself personally to Paul as the resurrected Lord, it turned everything in Paul's world upside down. If Jesus was indeed the Messiah, that meant Jews *were not* the only recipients of God's mercy; it meant that observance of the Jewish law *was not* the only way to be justified with God; it meant that the hope for a Jewish Messiah who would conquer the Romans and **redeem** Israel *as a nation* was mistaken. In short, Paul realized that right covenant relationship with God could now be established on the pattern of Jesus's faithful obedience instead of the pattern of life established by Israel's obedience to the Torah.

This, Paul realized, was the breakthrough, showing precisely how God would "bless all the families of the earth," as promised to Abram (Gen. 12:3). In Christ, God was revealed to be a faithful covenant partner to Jew and gentile alike, for God did indeed enact salvation through the Jews as promised (in sending Jesus as Messiah) and at the same time extended that salvation to anyone who would participate in the pattern of obedient faithfulness (Rom. 4:1–25; Gal. 3:6–9). This was the great gift, or "grace," of what God had done in Christ: *In Christ, God expressed God's own faithfulness in the midst of human unfaithfulness, and in so doing, made faithfulness a possibility for us.* As Paul puts it, in the gospel "the righteousness of God is revealed through faith for faith" or (literally) "out of faith, into faith" (Rom. 1:17). That is, God has demonstrated the pattern of faithful obedience in Christ for the purpose of generating faithful obedience in those of us who follow the way of the Word. This is why Paul says he wants "to be found in him, not having a righteousness of my own that comes from the law, but one that comes through faith in Christ, the righteousness from God based on faith" (Phil. 3:9).

Here we must assert an important correction to one of the ways Paul has been misread over the years. Paul employed a particular verbal formula when he taught the good news of what God had accomplished in Christ:

> We hold that a person is *justified* by *faith* apart from *works prescribed by the law*. (Rom. 3:28)

> We know that a person is *justified* not by the *works of the law* but through *faith* in Jesus Christ. And we have come to *believe* in Christ Jesus, so that we might be *justified* by *faith* in Christ, and not by doing the *works of the law*. (Gal. 2:16)

> [I do not have] a *righteousness* of my own that comes *from the law*, but one that comes through *faith* in Christ, the *righteousness* from God based on *faith*. (Phil. 3:9)[12]

Paul's understanding of salvation in Christ is worked out against the backdrop question of how gentiles would be included in the covenant people of God. Therefore Paul is contrasting faith and works *of the law*: he is *not* contrasting faith and "works" in the general sense of acts of obedience; after all, his calling is to serve God in bringing about the obedience of faith among the gentiles! No, he is contrasting one model of trust and allegiance with another: one model is particular to a single ethnic group and creates a separation between people (the observance of Jewish law, what we might call "Torah works"), and another model is open to everyone and enables communion between people (following the pattern of Christ's faithfulness, what we might call "trust works").

Whenever the Jew-gentile backdrop to Paul's argument did not remain in the forefront, readers have misunderstood Paul by thinking he was contrasting faith and action, or belief and obedience. This misunderstanding was already alive in Paul's own day.

12. Emphasis added in these verses.

And why not say (as some people slander us by saying that we say), "Let us do evil so that good may come"? Their condemnation is deserved! (Rom. 3:8)

What then are we to say? Should we continue in sin in order that grace may abound? By no means! How can we who died to sin go on living in it? (Rom. 6:1–2)

What then? Should we sin because we are not under law but under grace? By no means! Do you not know that if you present yourselves to anyone as obedient slaves, you are slaves of the one whom you obey, either of sin, which leads to death, or of obedience, which leads to righteousness? (Rom. 6:15–16)

Indeed, a close reading of Paul's Letters makes it plain that he cannot imagine any form of "faith" that does *not* involve obedience! Again, the issue for Paul is not whether or not we must obey God; the question is, What will *enable* me to obey God? Paul's answer is "justification by grace through faith." But how is *Christ's* obedience of faith appropriated by unfaithful and broken people like you and me?

What Does Paul Teach Us about the Spiritual Formation of Christian Disciples?

We began the last section by recognizing that Paul came to know Jesus through an experience of personal revelation. On Paul's terms, this knowledge is no mere intellectual awareness: when he describes his personal knowledge of Christ, he uses the language of *participation*. For example, when he relates the story of his calling in the Letter to the Galatians, he says that God revealed the Son "in me," not "to me" (Gal. 1:16).[13] Hence he can go on to say,

I have been crucified with Christ; and it is no longer I who live, but it is Christ who lives *in me*. And the life I now live in the flesh I live by

13. Both NRSV and ESV translate this "to me" but add a footnote saying the Greek is actually "in me." The NIV, NASB, and KJV all translate this correctly.

faith in the Son of God, who loved me and gave himself for me. (Gal.
2:19–20, emphasis added)

*Faith in the Son of God is not simply a truth one claims: it is a
life one lives.* Similarly, in the Letter to the Philippians, Paul says,
"I want to know Christ and the power of his resurrection and the
sharing of his sufferings by becoming like him in his death" (Phil.
3:10). I come to know Christ by becoming "like him," by becoming
one with him and participating in his life, so that he lives in me and
I live my life in him. When we become a Christian, then, we do not
simply *know the truth about Christ*; as Paul says in 2 Corinthians,
"the truth of Christ is in me" (11:10). In Christ, the way of the Word
becomes *our* way.

Herein we discover a wonderful mystery. We said earlier that Christ
rose victorious from the grave to share the power of life with a people
locked in a pattern of death. As it turns out, the life that Christ shares
in his resurrection from the dead is the continual giving of *his own
life*, that is, the very life power of God. At a single point in history
this self-giving took place in the work of the Son on the cross, but
henceforth this life-giving empowerment takes place in the work of
the Holy Spirit, whom Paul calls "the Spirit of life" (Rom. 8:2). In
Paul's reckoning, when Christ, the Son of God, gave himself *for us*,
he was actually giving himself *to us*—and in so doing he was envel-
oping us in his own sonship, so that in Christ we also become God's
"children" (Gal. 4:6).

The classic statement of this trinitarian life sharing is found in
chapter 8 of the Letter to the Romans. Paul says,

Anyone who does not have the Spirit of Christ does not belong to
him. But if Christ is in you, though the body is dead because of sin,
the Spirit is life because of righteousness. If the Spirit of him who
raised Jesus from the dead dwells in you, he who raised Christ from
the dead will give life to your mortal bodies also through his Spirit
that dwells in you. (Rom. 8:9–11)

Paul repeatedly contrasts this new life in the Spirit with a life that
is lived "according to the flesh." Going on, he says,

> So then, brothers and sisters, we are debtors, not to the flesh, to live according to the flesh—for if you live according to the flesh, you will die; but if by the Spirit you put to death the deeds of the body, you will live. For all who are led by the Spirit of God are children of God. For you did not receive a spirit of slavery to fall back into fear, but you have received a spirit of adoption. When we cry, "Abba! Father!" it is that very Spirit bearing witness with our spirit that we are children of God, and if children, then heirs, heirs of God and joint heirs with Christ—if, in fact, we suffer with him so that we may also be glorified with him. (Rom. 8:12–16)

Paul uses the Greek word translated "flesh" in a variety of ways. While it can mean "body" (as in Gal. 2:20), it is more often used as an image for the life of sin, the pattern of death in which humans are perpetually caught.

This "fleshly" pattern of death is opposed to the desires of the Spirit (Gal. 5:16–17). So when Paul describes "the work of the flesh" in Galatians, he lists vices of *selfishness*: "fornication, impurity, licentiousness, idolatry, sorcery, enmities, strife, jealousy, anger, quarrels, dissensions, factions, envy, drunkenness, carousing, and things like these" (Gal. 5:19–21). By contrast, his description of "the fruit of the Spirit" lists virtues of *selflessness*: "love, joy, peace, patience, kindness, generosity, faithfulness, gentleness, and self-control" (Gal. 5:22–23). One life is characterized by taking, but the other by giving; one destroys community, the other builds community; one is embodied in the Babel-logic of self-preservation, the other in the life of Abraham, whose faith enabled him to live the risky life of trust in, and allegiance to, God.

Here, then, is the key to Paul's understanding of life in the Spirit: *personal knowledge of Christ through the Spirit is our participation in God's life-giving power, which is the power to give our lives away to others just as Christ gave his life away to us*. When Paul says he is "crucified with Christ" (Gal. 2:19) by "becoming like him in his death" (Phil. 3:10), he is describing a life characterized by the radical self-giving found in the pattern of Christ's sacrificial life and death.

When the Spirit is working in disciples, then, it is not made manifest primarily in emotional acts of worship, persuasive speech, or powerful signs and wonders. It is made manifest in our capacity to replicate the self-giving pattern of Christ, "who loved me and gave himself for me" (Gal. 2:20), who "did not regard equality with God as something to be exploited, but emptied himself, taking the form of a slave" (Phil. 2:6–7), who "for [our] sakes became poor, so that by his poverty [we] might become rich" (2 Cor. 8:9). It means making our lives "a living sacrifice, holy and acceptable to God" (Rom. 12:1). It means making love the practice that defines our whole identity (1 Cor. 13). It means taking up Christ's obedience of faith—following Christ's radical obedience to God's will by the power of the Spirit.

Earlier we said that the gift of faith in Christ results in justification, which is life in right covenant relationship with God. While the gift of right covenant relationship is offered by God's grace alone, growth in the life of the Spirit requires our active participation. Paul calls this process of spiritual growth *sanctification.* "Just as you once presented your members as slaves to impurity and to greater and greater iniquity," Paul urges, "so now present your members as slaves to righteousness for sanctification" (Rom. 6:19). For "if you live according to the flesh, you will die; but if by the Spirit you put to death the deeds of the body, you will live" (8:13); and "if you sow to your own flesh, you will reap corruption from the flesh; but if you sow to the Spirit, you will reap eternal life from the Spirit" (Gal. 6:8; cf. Col. 3:1–17). The gift of justification is the free offer of God's grace, but that grace sets us on the path of sanctification, which requires us to get on our feet and start walking the way of the Word.

If the pattern of Christ is a life of Spirit-empowered generosity, it should go without saying that the Christian life must be practiced in Christian community. How could anyone grow in the self-giving pattern of Christ in isolation? To whom would they give themselves? Paul calls this community of generosity "the communion of the Holy Spirit" (2 Cor. 13:13), and it is the place where sanctification happens. As in Acts, where the Spirit is made manifest in a community characterized by radical generosity, so it is also in Paul's Letters: though we enter this community as self-enclosed individuals, the Spirit works to break down the walls that keep us divided from one another, filling us with community-building gifts (1 Cor. 12) that transform us from strangers and aliens to fellow citizens and members in the household of God (Eph. 2:13–22).

Given that we live in a culture characterized by unbridled consumption and self-centeredness, we must put this final point as sharply as possible: on Pauline terms, if there is no participation in the life of the church, there is no knowledge of Jesus—for knowledge of Christ is by nature a participation in the pattern of his self-giving. In the Gospels, Jesus says, "Take up your cross daily and follow me" (cf. Luke 9:23). In Paul's Letters, following Jesus along the way of the Word leads us necessarily into the communion of the Holy Spirit, the place where the pattern of discipleship is practiced and proclaimed.

Epilogue: The Letter to the Hebrews

We close this chapter on Paul by returning briefly to a topic we raised when considering the shape of the Pauline letter collection. The Letter "to the Hebrews" bears a title designating it as Pauline ("to the"), but it does not include an opening address indicating that it was written by Paul. The history of its reception into the canon provides fascinating insight into the process by which the NT was formed.

The ending of Hebrews reads very much like a Pauline letter, both in its form as well as its reference to Timothy (13:22–25). Hebrews does not begin like a letter, however, and most of it doesn't read like one either. It identifies itself as a "word of exhortation" (13:22), and it is indeed closest in form to a sermon. We do not know precisely where it came from or who wrote it, but we can say confidently that the language, style, and theme are quite different from the other letters designated Pauline. Second-century Eastern, Greek-speaking Christians like **Clement of Alexandria** maintained a tradition that it was a sermon to Jews originally written by Paul in Hebrew and later translated by someone else into Greek for popular distribution.[14] Early Western, Latin-speaking Christians like **Irenaeus** and **Cyprian of Carthage** either didn't know Hebrews or didn't accept it. **Tertullian of Carthage** thought it was written by Paul's companion, Barnabas.[15] **Origen of Alexandria** (d. 254) had this to say about it:

14. Clement's account is preserved in Eusebius's *Ecclesiastical History* 6.14.4.
15. Tertullian, *Modesty* 20.1.

If I gave my opinion, I should say that the thoughts are those of the apostle, but the diction and phraseology are those of someone who remembered the apostolic teachings, and wrote down at his leisure what had been said by his teacher. Therefore if any church holds that this epistle is by Paul, let it be commended for this. For not without reason have the ancients handed it down as Paul's. But who wrote the epistle, in truth, God knows. The statement of some who have gone before us is that Clement, bishop of the Romans, wrote the epistle, and of others that Luke, the author of the Gospel and the Acts, wrote it.[16]

Ancient biblical **manuscripts** reflected this confusion over the author. Our oldest copy of the Pauline Letters ($\mathfrak{P}^{46}$) places Hebrews immediately after Romans. Other manuscripts place it in its appropriate position by length (after the Letters to the Corinthians), and still others position it between 2 Thessalonians and before 1 Timothy, that is, at the end of the church letters and before the letters to individuals. But the vast majority of ancient manuscripts place it where we find it today: after Philemon, at the very end of the Pauline collection, apparently in reflection of its status as "Pauline, but not written by Paul."

One clue as to its canonical function is found in its self-designation as a "word of exhortation" (13:22), for this is precisely how one of Paul's **synagogue** sermons is described, in Acts 13:15. Acts presents Paul as preaching both to gentiles *and* to Jews in synagogues: Is Hebrews to be received as a transcript of his preaching in the synagogue (to Jews), just as Romans witnesses to his preaching in the Roman world (to gentiles)? Is this why the earliest manuscript of the Pauline Letters placed it immediately after Romans?

The title itself seems to have less to do with the original recipients (how would you actually deliver a letter to "the Hebrews"?) than with its content: the subject matter of the letter is the old covenant, the authoritative writings of the Hebrews, and the addressees are all those who live under the new covenant while continuing to receive the writings of the old covenant as Scripture. Its powerful assertion of the continuity of the two covenants comes as a welcome addition to a collection of Pauline writings that might lead some to affirm

16. Origen's account is likewise preserved in Eusebius's *Ecclesiastical History* 6.25.13–14.

their discontinuity. In this manner its final placement at the end of the collection suggests that it plays the role of an appendix. The literary function of an appendix is the inclusion of additional material that helps to explain or expand upon topics not fully explored in the body of the text. From this perspective, Hebrews is to be received as an important concluding note, an additional reflection designed to shape our ultimate reception of Paul. Against those who might argue that Paul rejected the old covenant in favor of the new, Hebrews helps readers of Paul receive the old covenant *in light of* the new.

Hebrews can also be seen to function as a bridge between the Pauline and Catholic Epistles (CE) collections, which our next chapter will describe as the literary deposit of the leaders of the Jerusalem mission to Jews (a.k.a. those designated "Hebrews"). Just as the Letter to the Hebrews is addressed generally to all those who receive the old covenant as Scripture, so also James (the first letter of the CE collection) is similarly addressed to all Israel, in this instance, "to the twelve tribes in the **Dispersion**" (James 1:1). Thus we might say that Hebrews looks back to the Pauline collection in the form of a needed corrective, and forward to the CE collection as a way of signaling a thematic agreement with the letters that follow.

Questions for Discussion

1. Now that you've read this chapter on Paul's Letters, what questions do you have? What do you want to know more about? Make a list to share with your class or reading group.

2. Have you ever heard Paul's teaching used in a manner that marginalized the importance of the OT or downplayed the importance of obedience? What have you learned in this chapter that would counter such positions? How does our introduction to Paul in Acts help us avoid such misunderstandings?

3. Paul's understanding of God's salvation is richer and more complex than many popular articulations of it. How has your understanding of salvation been expanded as a result of reading this chapter?

4. What does it mean to say that Paul's knowledge of Christ is *participatory*?

5. This chapter defined "faith" as "trust and allegiance." Does that definition differ from what you have heard in the past? What does it introduce that is missing from other understandings?

6. What is your reaction to this chapter's assertion, "If there is no participation in the life of the church, there is no knowledge of Jesus"? In what ways is this statement true? What are the limits of its truth?

7. If the Pauline Letters had been left out of the NT, what would be missing?

8. Where do these letters locate you on the way of the Word? How have they helped you along? Where have they warned you to slow down? What in your discipleship requires acceleration? Has the route to your destination been at all clarified?

8

The Catholic Epistles

The Tradition of Discipleship

"Whoever says 'I abide in him'
ought to walk just as he walked."

(1 JOHN 2:6)

In the late fourth century, **Augustine of Hippo** wrote an essay on *Faith and Works* in an attempt to address what he found to be "a perplexing problem in the writings of the Apostle Paul."[1] Some Christians, it turned out, maintained what Augustine called a "treacherously false security" that "faith alone is sufficient for salvation." Those who believe such things, Augustine says, have a tendency to "neglect to live a good life and fail by good works to persevere in the way that leads to God." That is, they think they can have faith without also practicing obedience; they think they can have God's Word without following God's way. Going on, he says,

> Since this problem is by no means new and had already arisen at the time of the Apostles, other apostolic letters of Peter, John, James and Jude are deliberately aimed against the argument I have been refuting and firmly uphold the doctrine that faith does not avail without good works.

1. Augustine, *Faith and Works*, in *Saint Augustine: Treatises on Marriage and Other Subjects*, trans. Marie Ligouri, ed. R. J. Deferrari, Fathers of the Church 27 (Washington, DC: Catholic University of America Press, 1955), 213–82.

As it turns out, this statement by Augustine represents the earliest articulation of the **canonical** function of the Letters of James, Peter, John, and Jude—a collection that ancient Christians named the **Catholic Epistles** (CE). Augustine's essay goes on to offer an **intertextual** reading of the entire apostolic letter collection, balancing passages from Paul with those of the CE, in order to present a fully apostolic understanding of the life of faithful obedience. His primary Pauline text was Galatians 5:6, which insists, "The only thing that counts is faith working through love." It is repeated ten times, woven together with at least twenty-nine references to passages from the seven CE. He describes how Peter "urged his readers to **holiness** in living and character" (1 Pet. 1:13–16), while "James was so severely annoyed with those who held that faith without works avails to salvation that he compared them to evil spirits" (James 2:19). As for the Pauline passages that suggest one can have faith in **Christ** without being faithful *to* Christ, "another interpretation assuredly must be sought for them, and these expressions of the Apostle Paul must be counted among the passages in his writings which Peter says are difficult to understand and which men must not distort to their own destruction" (2 Pet. 3:16).

History has proved Augustine right. Those who cling too tightly to a particular misreading of Paul (especially those who separate Christianity from Judaism, or divorce faith from obedience) will find it difficult to incorporate his witness into the larger NT canon. This canonical difficulty comes to us by design: as we noticed earlier, Paul is framed by the Acts of the Apostles on one side and the CE on the other, to keep us from falling into the sort of errors that Augustine describes. Though the CE have received far less attention from Christians over the years, we will find that their witness plays a crucial role in the NT's portrayal of the way of the Word.

Canonical Transition: From Paul to the Catholic Epistles

Unlike the major canonical transitions we've considered thus far—from the **Gospels** to Acts, and from Acts to Paul—the narrative logic of the move from the Pauline Letters to the CE is not nearly as overt. For one thing, unlike the Gospels and Acts, these two collections are in reality two subcollections within a single body of NT letters. We have fourteen letters of Paul and seven CE, but they're all part of the NT's twenty-one letters. The transition is also obscured somewhat by the Letter to the Hebrews, which we have identified as "Pauline, but not by Paul" due to its anonymity and its placement outside the logic of line length that governs the rest of that collection. Since the seven CE *also* do not follow the sequence by line length, most scholars have thought it best to lump them together with Hebrews to form a new collection typically called the "General Letters."

Accepting this more recent structure-logic, however, flies right in the face of the canonical markers designed to point readers to the major transition between Hebrews and James. Chief among them is the title form: while the Pauline Letters (including Hebrews) are labeled "To the" recipients, and thus typically address issues specific to the congregation addressed, the CE (beginning with James) are titled "The Letter of" the author and seem to be addressed generally, lacking the sort of elements we expect to see in letters written to particular people or groups. This appears to be why ancient Christians distinguished these letters from Paul's by calling them **catholic**: the Greek *kath'holos* means "according to the whole." These letters are addressed "universally," to all Christians everywhere.

Another marker is the seven-letter form itself: Paul writes to seven **churches**; his collection as a whole includes two times seven letters; and the CE include seven letters. Thus we have a NT letter collection characterized by patterns of seven (a pattern that will become even more obvious when we add the seven letters to seven churches found at the beginning of the Revelation to John!). A final major signal of a transition point is discovered in the sequence *James, Peter, John, Jude*—but now we are moving into questions of the collection's form, so we will forgo any further comment on the canonical transition between Paul and the CE in order to offer more detailed comments on how the shape of the CE communicates the meaningfulness of the two subcollections.

The Shape of the Catholic Epistle Collection

While there was some variation in the collection's sequence early on in the canonical process (especially in the West, which preferred to give Peter the greater honor by placing his letters first), the final ordering *James, Peter, John, Jude* signals a particular narrative context for its reception: "James and Cephas [Peter] and John" (listed in that order) are the figures Paul recognizes in Galatians as the "pillars" of the Jerusalem church and its mission to Jews (Gal. 2:9). Jude comes along at the end of the collection, but refers back to the first letter by identifying itself as a letter from "the brother of James" (Jude 1), conveying to readers the sense that this Jerusalem pillars collection comes in the "embrace" of Jesus's brothers James and Jude. In all, it becomes fairly easy to recognize that the two letter collections are designed to reflect the twofold nature of the earliest Christian church as described in Acts and Galatians: Paul's Letters are texts representing the **gentile** mission, and the CE are letters emerging from the Jerusalem mission to Jews.

The final ordering *Gospels-Acts-Paul-CE-Revelation* is due mostly to the dominant use in the Western church of **Jerome of Bethlehem's** Latin translation, the **Vulgate**. The Greek **manuscript** tradition, however, always placed the CE *before* the Pauline collection. That ordering appears to reflect the narrative logic of Acts, which begins with the mission to Jews headed by the Jerusalem pillars *before* turning to the gentile mission headed by Paul. Our final form, by contrast, seems designed to *extend* the narrative logic of Acts, which ends with Paul in Rome, thereby leading us quite naturally into Paul's Letter to the Romans.

Once we have worked our way through the mighty Pauline collection, however, we run headlong into the Letter of James. His letter is quite different from the letters of Paul. It is not written to a single person or church, but addresses all **disciples** everywhere in a rather commanding tone of voice (James 1:1), leading us to recall the portrayal in Acts of an early church leadership where James held a position of authority *above* Paul—and Peter as well, for that matter! We might then remember the section in 1 Corinthians where Paul ranks James and Peter higher than himself, describing himself as one who had arrived "last of all, as . . . one untimely born" (1 Cor. 15:3–9). And then there is Paul's narration of his calling in Galatians, where he reports that he went to Jerusalem to present the content of his gospel teaching to the leaders there "in order to make sure that I was not running, or had not run, in vain" (Gal. 2:2). He goes on in that letter to describe a conflict he had with Peter when "people came from James" to check on the church at Antioch (Gal. 2:11–14). If we keep all this canonical backdrop in mind as we read James (which includes a portrayal of the way of the Word that even seems to challenge some of what we've learned from Paul), we're left with the strong hunch that this letter and those that follow are placed where they are in the canon precisely for the reason Augustine suggested: they are there, at least in part, to have an effect on our reading of Paul.

In reality, Paul was well aware of his status as a latecomer in the earliest Christian mission. He'd met the risen Lord, but he was not personally acquainted with the Jesus who walked the way of the Word and taught others to follow in his steps. Paul's powerful experience of Christ needed to be checked against the apostolic tradition that had been passed down by those who knew him from the beginning. Indeed, all spiritual experience needs to be tested to see if it is "from God" (1 John 4:1). Who else should be consulted but the eyewitnesses, those who were with Jesus, who saw his deeds and heard his teaching?

Herein we find yet another major difference between the Pauline and CE collections: each of the CE grounds its authority in the eyewitness status of the author. James and Jude, the brothers of Jesus, truly knew the Lord from the beginning of his earthly pilgrimage, and James's Letter in particular is peppered with overt echoes of Jesus's teaching. The First Letter of Peter identifies the author as "an elder" and "witness of the sufferings of Christ" (5:1). The Second Letter of Peter likewise speaks of being among those who were "eyewitnesses of his majesty" (1:16), who heard the voice of God identify Jesus as the beloved Son when they "were with him on the holy mountain" (1:18). And the opening verse of the Letters of John says, "We declare to you what was from the beginning, what we have *heard*, what we have *seen* with our eyes, what we have *looked at* and *touched* with our hands, concerning the word of life" (1 John 1:1, emphasis added).

The two letter collections, Pauline and Catholic, combine to communicate the fullness of the apostolic message. We might say that the Pauline message teaches us about what it is for us to *have faith* in the risen Lord, and the CE teach us what the Lord taught us about *living faithfully*. Paul reminds us that Jesus is *not* a dead figure from the past: he is alive and addresses us today by the power of the Holy Spirit. But the CE remind us that the only way to be certain that it really is Jesus we're experiencing is to check our contemporary experience against the historic witness of Jesus's words and deeds as he lived and taught the way of the Word.

What Do the Catholic Epistles Teach Us about God's Work in Christ Jesus?

As the Letter to the Romans did for the Pauline collection, so also James: the lead letter in the collection is designed to set the stage for our reading of what follows. Given this, it may seem surprising at first to realize that James has very little to say specifically *about* Jesus. He is named only twice (James 1:1; 2:1) and is never overtly set forward as a topic of **theological** or moral reflection. There is no mention at all of his incarnation, death, resurrection, or **ascension**; James has nothing to say about **baptism** or the **Eucharist**; there is no description of a Christian ministry beyond his own, no reference to other ministers or churches in other places, no reference to a ministry to the gentile world, and no discussion of the complexities of the inclusion of gentiles in God's **covenant** community. Indeed, it has often been observed that if the name of Jesus were removed from 1:1 and 2:1, the letter content would have been perfectly acceptable to any Jewish non-Christian reader of the day.

This provides us with our first important insight into James's canonical function. Where Paul can say that Christians are "discharged from the **law**" (Rom. 7:6) because it has been "abolished" in Christ (Eph. 2:15), James identifies the law as the word of God, celebrating it as "the perfect law, the law of liberty" (1:22–25). Where Paul draws attention to himself as a model worthy of imitation,[2] James instructs us to turn to OT examples of faith (e.g., 2:21–25; 5:10–11, 17). Paul can polarize an "old" age characterized by Adam and the law with the "new" age of Christ and the Spirit (e.g., Rom. 5), but James knows of no such distinction: this letter is written by a Jewish follower of Christ to fellow Jewish followers (identified in the address as "the twelve tribes in the **Dispersion** [Greek *diaspora*]," 1:1). Christian readers of James thus discover in reading the letter that a simplistic polarization of "Jewish" and "Christian" will not do. Jesus was the **Messiah** of Israel, and the earliest Christian mission, which James here represents, involved a group of Jews ministering to other Jews. Since "salvation is from the Jews" (John 4:22) and the gospel is given "to the Jew first" (Rom. 1:16), James seems to insist that gentile Christians who seek to remain faithful to Jesus must avoid drawing sharp distinctions between Christian and Jewish identity.

In place of such distinctions, James offers us a letter characterized throughout by an ethical concern rooted entirely in the **Scriptures** of Israel and what sounds a lot like the teaching of Jesus in Matthew (though he never explicitly identifies it as such). James is well known for his dictum "Faith without works is . . . dead" (2:26). If Christians are to "really believe in our glorious Lord Jesus Christ" (2:1), they must "bridle their tongues, . . . care for orphans and widows in their distress," and keep themselves "unstained by the world" (1:26–27). They accomplish this by being "doers of the word and not merely hearers who deceive themselves" (1:22). God "the Father" has sent this "word of truth" into the world; it is "coming down" from God as a "perfect gift" (1:17–18). Indeed, this word of **wisdom** is implanted in us and is able to save our souls (1:21). James never explicitly connects this "word" with the good news about Jesus, but it seems as though he wants his readers to do just that. In reality, it is impossible for us to *avoid* doing so if we read James in canonical context, for his teaching echoes that of Jesus in Matthew (especially the Sermon on the Mount),[3]

2. As in 1 Cor. 4:6; 11:1; Phil. 3:17; 1 Thess. 1:6; 2 Thess. 3:7–9.
3. Compare, e.g., James 1:4 // Matt. 5:48; James 1:5 // Matt. 7:7; James 2:5 // Matt. 5:3; James 2:13 // Matt. 5:7; James 2:14 // Matt. 7:21; James 3:12 // Matt. 7:16; James 5:2–3 // Matt. 6:19; James 5:12 // Matt. 5:34–37.

and Paul has already identified Jesus as "the wisdom of God" (1 Cor. 1:30) and refers to the gospel of Jesus as "the word of truth" (2 Tim. 2:15).

This unusual christological portrait has the effect of increasing the volume of Jesus's ethical teaching *over* teaching about his identity. If James were our only Christian letter, we'd assume that the Word came only to teach a way of walking in the world, a path of wisdom that leads to salvation.

This distinctive witness is extended in 1 Peter. Like James, 1 Peter strongly asserts the ongoing Jewish identity of Christian faith. In fact, although the letter appears to have been written to a primarily gentile audience,[4] the author addresses his hearers as though they were Jews and applies many of the markers of historic Israel to them.[5] Once again, any simplistic distinction between Jewish and Christian identity is blurred.

By comparison to James, however, 1 Peter has a robust and explicit reflection on Jesus's distinctiveness. While the letter is like the Pauline material in reflecting on the significance of Jesus's death and resurrection,[6] the most striking element of 1 Peter's witness is his tendency to point to Jesus's *earthly life* as a model for Christians to imitate:

> If you endure when you are beaten for doing wrong, what credit is that? But if you endure when you do right and suffer for it, you have God's approval. For to this you have been called, because Christ also suffered for you, leaving you an example, so that you should follow in his steps. (2:20–21)

> Since therefore Christ suffered in the flesh, arm yourselves also with the same intention (for whoever has suffered in the flesh has finished with sin), so as to live for the rest of your earthly life no longer by human desires but by the will of God. (4:1–2)

---

4. The case for a predominantly gentile audience is made from passages that describe their "former life" in a way that would make no sense if the readers were Jews. See, e.g., 1 Pet. 1:14, 18; 2:10; especially 4:3–4.

5. See, e.g., 1 Pet. 2:9; especially 2:12 and 4:3, where outsiders are identified as "Gentiles" in a manner suggesting that the readers are not themselves gentile.

6. See, e.g., 1 Pet. 1:2, 18–21; 2:22–25; 3:18.

Christ's suffering on the cross took place to pay the price for our sins (1 Pet. 2:24). But Jesus also suffered to teach *us* how to suffer in a way that honors God. Who else could offer this teaching but one, like Peter, who walked alongside Jesus and observed the manner of his life and the content of his teaching?

Second Peter is designed to pick up where 1 Peter left off:

> This is now, beloved, the second letter I am writing to you; in them I am trying to arouse your sincere intention by reminding you that you should remember the words spoken in the past by the holy **prophets**, and the commandment of the Lord and Savior spoken through your apostles. (3:1–2)

One of the many items underscored in 2 Peter stands in complete agreement with James's earlier teaching that faith without works is dead: 2 Peter opens by insisting that Christians "make every effort to support" faith in Christ with virtues like goodness and self-control and godliness (1:5–7), "for if these things are yours and are increasing among you, they keep you from being ineffective and unfruitful in the knowledge of our Lord Jesus Christ" (1:8). It seems that some Christians (perhaps shaped by a misguided use of Paul's Letters, if 2 Pet. 3:15–17 is any clue) have come to believe that one's ethical life has no real impact on one's salvation. Like James and 1 Peter before it, 2 Peter identifies the "error of the lawless" (3:17) as the tendency to call Jesus "Lord" without making him the "Master" of our lives (2:1). One cannot claim Jesus without also following the way of truth and **righteousness** that he taught (2:2, 21).

Unsurprisingly, the same theme dominates the Letters of John. The one who saw and heard "what was from the beginning . . . concerning the word of life" (1 John 1:1) has a very simple test for determining the difference between authentic Christian faith and its counterfeit:

> Whoever says, "I have come to know him," but does not obey his commandments, is a liar, and in such a person the truth does not exist. (2:4)

> Whoever says, "I abide in him," ought to walk just as he walked. (2:6)

If you know that he is righteous, you may be sure that everyone who does right has been born of him. (2:29)

We know love by this, that he laid down his life for us—and we ought to lay down our lives for one another. (3:16)

Once more it is Jesus's faithful life that provides the model for Christian life in the world. All of this comes to a conclusion in the short Letter of Jude, who complains about those "who pervert the grace of our God into licentiousness and deny our only Master and Lord, Jesus Christ" (Jude 4). As before, there are some who apparently think God's grace and forgiveness provide a license for ongoing sin, as though being a "forgiven sinner" is all God intends for those who claim Christ Jesus as Lord. The CE as a whole stand in the NT canon as a testimony against such dangerous thinking.

Of course, Jesus's faithful life didn't end in his death on the cross, for though he suffered in humility, he was resurrected to a place of glory and honor. In like fashion the CE remind us that the way of the Word leads not just *to* death, but *through* death and into a wonderful inheritance.

Blessed is anyone who endures temptation. Such a one has stood the test and will receive the crown of life that the Lord has promised to those who love him. (James 1:12)

Rejoice insofar as you are sharing Christ's sufferings, so that you may also be glad and shout for joy when his glory is revealed. (1 Pet. 4:13)

Be all the more eager to confirm your call and election. . . . For in this way, entry into the eternal **kingdom** of our Lord and Savior Jesus Christ will be richly provided for you. (2 Pet. 1:10–11)

Do not love the world or the things in the world. . . . The world and its desire are passing away, but those who do the will of God live forever. (1 John 2:15–17)

Now to him who is able to keep you from falling, and to make you stand without blemish in the presence of his glory with rejoicing, to

the only God our Savior, through Jesus Christ our Lord, be glory. . . .
(Jude 24–25)

Jesus both taught and modeled the way of the Word; he walked the
talk and talked the walk. The CE insist that Christians do the same,
always being extremely careful to keep creed and deed in alignment, lest
we be viewed as hypocrites in the world and judged as false by Christ
when he comes again "to judge the living and the dead" (1 Pet. 4:5).

What Do the Catholic Epistles Teach Us about the Spiritual Formation of Christian Disciples?

As it was with Jesus, so it is also with the Spirit: James has frustrat-
ingly little to say on the subject, at least in any overt sense. And yet,
so much of what James says *sounds like* things we've heard elsewhere
in Scripture about the Spirit. For example, James describes a "wisdom from above" that produces precisely the sort of fruit that Paul
attributes to the Holy Spirit (cf. James 3:17–18 with Gal. 5:22–23).
James also calls God the giver of perfect gifts "from above" (1:17) and
talks about living life according to the "wisdom" that comes down
"from above" (3:13–18), using the same word Jesus uses in John when
he tells Nicodemus that those who wish to see the **kingdom of God**
must be born "from above." When Nicodemus is confused by that
claim, Jesus elaborates:

> No one can enter the kingdom of God without being born of water
> and Spirit. What is born of the flesh is flesh, and what is born of the
> Spirit is spirit. Do not be astonished that I said to you, "You must be
> born from above." The wind blows where it chooses, and you hear
> the sound of it, but you do not know where it comes from or where
> it goes. So it is with everyone who is born of the Spirit. (John 3:5–8)

The Spirit births believers into an entirely new orientation, which
reroutes one's life path in a manner that is confusing to those who
have not experienced it.

Paul doesn't use "birth" language in this way. Because his articulation of faith is deeply dependent on the question of the status of

Jew and gentile in covenant community, he typically reserves "birth" language to speak about *ethnicity* (e.g., Gal. 2:15; Eph. 2:11). When the CE speak of birth, however, they are referring to something *spiritual*. As James puts it, desire gives birth to sin, and sin gives birth to death (1:15), but God gave us a different sort of birth, one that comes "by the word of truth" (1:18).

If we are left confused by James's more obscure language, 1 Peter follows to help clear things up:

> Blessed be the God and Father of our Lord Jesus Christ! By his great mercy he has given us a new birth into a living hope through the resurrection of Jesus Christ from the dead. . . . You have been born anew, not of perishable but of imperishable seed, through the living and enduring word of God. (1:3, 23)

Just as God raised the Word to new life by resurrecting Jesus from the dead, so now the living Word of the gospel raises followers to a new life in Christ. By the time we reach 1 John, the "birth" theme has swelled into a recurring motif:

> If you know that he is righteous, you may be sure that everyone who does right has been born of him. . . . Those who have been born of God do not sin, because God's seed abides in them; they cannot sin, because they have been born of God. . . . Beloved, let us love one another, because love is from God; everyone who loves is born of God and knows God. (2:29; 3:9; 4:7)

According to the CE, then, reception of "the word of truth" (James 1:18) does more than simply change the mind; it reorients the whole self, as though followers are born all over again into an entirely different family. First Peter therefore borrows from the prophet Hosea to say of Christians, "Once you were not a people, but now you are God's people" (1 Pet. 2:10; cf. Hosea 1:10; 2:23). Indeed, they are reborn *into* the people of Israel, to become God's "chosen race, a royal priesthood, a holy nation, God's own people" (2:9).

This new ethnicity carries with it a new citizenship and a new politics. Jesus has already told us that his "kingdom is not from this world" (John 18:36), and Paul has insisted that our real "citizenship is in heaven," regardless of our actual birthplace (Phil. 3:20). The CE impress upon readers the seriousness of this notion. Paul's mission was by nature more accommodating in tone and posture. As an **evangelist**, he needed to "become all things to all people" so that he "might by all means save" them (1 Cor. 9:22). This radical openness to the world even led him to ascribe weak faith to those who were *more* observant of purity practices, and strong faith to those who were more relaxed in their approach (Rom. 14:1–15:6). He was severely criticized for this: many accused him of renouncing holiness and purity, embracing sin as part of God's good plan (Rom. 3:8), and rejecting the historic customs and purity practices of God's people (Acts 21:20–21).

But if our foremost citizenship is truly in heaven rather than in the various nations in which we dwell, then our lives must be characterized by holiness, by selective *separateness* from the practices of our surrounding cultures. If our citizenship is in heaven, we must reorient our earthly lives according to the recognition that we are living away from our true homeland. So the first two CE set the tone for what follows in the collection by addressing their letters to people who know they dwell in the "Diaspora" (Greek, meaning "Dispersion," James 1:1; 1 Pet. 1:1). This geographical designation recalls that moment in the OT story when God "scattered" unfaithful Israel away from the Holy Land into **exile** in foreign lands (2 Kings 17–25). The Israelites would need to live as strangers and aliens among a people who held different customs and maintained different values. They would no longer be able to claim holiness simply because they bore the name of Israel or Judah or could travel to worship at the temple in Jerusalem. Now they would have to decide whether or not to actually live as God's "different" people in the world. If they followed God's way, they would stand out as strangers; if they wanted to avoid that estrangement, they could assimilate to the culture in which they lived—but in doing so, they would give up their witness to God's kingdom and would lose their identity as God's people.

The CE exhort Christians to embrace this same diasporic identity. Diaspora people are not at home in this world. They live as refugees, awaiting entry into their true home, "the eternal kingdom" of God

(2 Pet. 1:11). They take up the way of the Word, which turns out to be a difficult road, for the Diaspora is full of trials and temptations that lead followers away from the "narrow" path that leads to God (Matt. 7:13–14). But as James reminds us, "Whenever you face trials of any kind, consider it nothing but joy, because you know that the testing of your faith produces endurance" (1:2–3).

In fact, each of the CE presents readers with a different trial that followers may face as they walk the diasporic way of the Word. These trials purify faith in order to shape one's character to be fit for the kingdom. In James, the trial is life in the Diaspora itself—a life filled with "desire" that "gives birth to sin" (1:14–15) and conflicting values that leave us "double-minded and unstable" (1:7–8), unsure of which direction we ought to walk. This is especially the case in a greedy world driven by money, where we defer to the rich against the needs of the poor (2:1–7; 5:1–6) and engage in business to gain wealth without considering the implications of our actions (4:13–17). James speaks firmly against this, calling us to "cleanse" our hearts and "purify" ourselves from the life practices that increase our friendship with the world but diminish our loyalty to God (4:4–10). According to James, the key proof of our love for God is found in the way we treat the vulnerable among us.[7]

In 1 Peter, the diasporic trial strikes a different chord. It is as though 1 Peter is written to people who have passed the test put forward in James; they *have* lived differently; they *have* avoided the temptations of the world and lived as the diasporic people whom God has called them to be. So 1 Peter describes the struggle of life in a world where Christians live differently and are mistreated as strangers, like misfits who don't belong and suffer abuse as a result. Despite their good conduct they are maligned as evildoers (2:12); slaves are beaten, despite their obedience (2:18–25); Christian wives are mistreated, despite their "gentle and quiet spirit" (3:1–6); Christian husbands pay a social price for treating their wives as coheirs of God's grace in a culture that viewed wives as property (3:7).

Looking to Jesus as his model, Peter instructs his readers to suffer patiently, without taking up normal, "worldly" methods of resistance.

7. See, e.g., James 1:9–11; 1:26–27; 2:1–7; 5:1–6.

> If you are reviled for the name of Christ, you are blessed, because the spirit of glory, which is the Spirit of God, is resting on you. . . . If any of you suffers as a Christian, do not consider it a disgrace, but glorify God because you bear this name. For the time has come for judgment to begin with the household of God; if it begins with us, what will be the end for those who do not obey the gospel of God? And "If it is hard for the righteous to be saved, what will become of the ungodly and the sinners?" Therefore, let those suffering in accordance with God's will entrust themselves to a faithful Creator, while continuing to do good. (1 Pet. 4:14–19)

First Peter thus reminds us that the way of salvation is hard, that it involves a cost that must be paid, a cross that must be carried. The price Jesus paid for our sins wasn't simply a covering for our sins; it was also a **redemption**, a payment designed to buy us back from an abusive master, so that we might live lives of service orchestrated according to an entirely different hope (1:18–21).

The trial in 2 Peter takes things to yet another level. Once again, a progression of sorts may be detected: in this letter the struggle no longer involves worldly people who abuse followers for being different; now some fellow believers have actually taken up the ways of the world. They are "false teachers" who bring "destructive opinions" that lead less mature Christians to "deny the Master who bought them." They live lives of moral licentiousness, with the result that the "way of truth" is being "maligned" by outsiders (2:1–2). They even arrogantly charge the original apostles with promoting "cleverly devised myths" about Christ's return and ultimate "judgment" (1:16–18; 3:1–13).

Against this dangerous teaching, the author of 2 Peter encourages his readers to "remember the words spoken in the past by the holy prophets, and the commandment of the Lord and Savior spoken through your apostles" (3:2). In particular they must recall Jesus's own prediction that this very thing would take place:

> Many false prophets will arise and lead many astray. And because of the increase of lawlessness, the love of many will grow cold. But the one who endures to the end will be saved. (Matt. 24:11–13)

Despite their abandonment of "the way of righteousness" (2:21), the author recalls Jesus's teaching that "the day of the Lord will come like a thief" (3:10) and judgment will disclose all that has taken place. "Since all these things are to be dissolved in this way," says the author, "what sort of persons ought you to be in leading lives of holiness and godliness?" (3:11). Some fellow Christians may forsake the way of holiness, but faithful Christians will remember what Jesus taught and will act accordingly (1:12–15).

As we turn to the Letters of John, the trial has progressed yet again: now the worldly Christians have split off to form a different community (1 John 2:19; 4:1–6), provoking the crisis of schism for God's people. In the face of competing truth claims about God and Christian life, whom should we heed? How do we know which leader represents authentic Christianity? We must not automatically accept the one who claims to have had a powerful spiritual experience (4:1), but only the one who promotes ancient apostolic tradition, that which has been taught "from the beginning"—a phrase repeated ten times in 1–3 John. At its center stands a single, basic claim: "This is the message you have heard from the beginning, that we should love one another" (1 John 3:11). Using this reminder of the center of Jesus's teaching in John's Gospel, the author asserts it against people whom the author calls "antichrists." Popular culture has turned this figure into a single end-time opponent of God, but 1–3 John knows of no such tradition. According to these letters, many people are "antichrist": they deny something about the relation between "the Father and the Son" (2:22–23); in particular, they deny that "Jesus Christ has come in the flesh" (4:2–3).

If we understand this conflict as a debate over some sort of esoteric trinitarian heresy, we miss John's point. Far from engaging a metaphysical battle over the two natures of Christ, John is condemning those whose Christian practice does not "take flesh" in a life that resembles the one they name as Lord. They claim to abide in the Father, but they do not walk in the way of the Son.

> Whoever says, "I have come to know him," but does not obey his commandments, is a liar, and in such a person the truth does not exist; but whoever obeys his word, truly in this person the love of God has

reached perfection. By this we may be sure that we are in him: whoever says, "I abide in him," ought to walk just as he walked. (1 John 2:4–6)

Once again we find a letter insisting on the essential unity between faith and obedience. No Christian reader should ever be surprised by this basic teaching, for it is what the apostles have taught from the beginning.

> Beloved, I am writing you no new commandment, but an old commandment that you have had from the beginning; the old commandment is the word that you have heard. . . . Whoever says, "I am in the light," while hating a brother or sister, is still in the darkness. Whoever loves a brother or sister lives in the light, and in such a person there is no cause for stumbling. But whoever hates another believer is in the darkness, walks in the darkness, and does not know the way to go, because the darkness has brought on blindness. (2:7–11)

The way of the Word is a difficult path. Those who are committed to staying faithful to the way will be able to do so if they hold fast to the center of Jesus's teaching, that we love one another regardless of the cost.

The CE collection ends with the short letter of Jude. The authorial designation "brother of James" (Jude 1) inevitably draws our minds back to the themes of that opening letter of the CE collection. There, followers were addressed as diasporic people, each needing to "keep oneself unstained by the world" (James 1:27). Throughout the CE we've heard the call to keep the faith of Jesus by maintaining holiness and avoiding worldliness. After all this admonition, readers of the NT might wonder if our salvation ultimately depends on our capacity to hold firm to the way of the Word. Didn't Paul insist that **justification** and **sanctification** are *God's* work in us? What is the role of human effort in the outworking of God's salvation in our lives?

Jude can be seen to end the collection by supplying a sort of answer. The letter opening insists that those who are beloved in God are "kept safe for Jesus Christ" (Jude 1). This is good news: the faithful God keeps us, watching over us and guiding our steps as we walk the way of the Word. But immediately thereafter we hear, once again, of false Christians "who pervert the grace" of this safekeeping God "into licentiousness and deny our only Master and Lord, Jesus Christ" (Jude 4). God keeps us safe, but it is easy to abuse that grace in a self-serving manner. To avoid wandering into that dangerous place, Jude instructs believers: "Build yourselves up on your most holy faith; pray in the Holy Spirit; keep yourselves in the love of God; look forward to the mercy of our Lord Jesus Christ that leads to eternal life" (Jude 20–21).

God's love may keep us safe for Jesus, but we must "keep [ourselves] in the love of God." We do this because God is the one "who is able to keep you from falling, and to make you stand without blemish in the presence of his glory with rejoicing" (Jude 24). God keeps us, we keep God, God keeps us: it turns out that a covenant relationship with God is indeed a real relationship, involving responsible agents whose active participation is required. The way of the Word is a path that leads us down a difficult road. But we must always remember that our relationship with God is not a relationship of equals. We cling to God precisely because we have learned from Jesus and his apostles that God alone is the one who can keep us from falling. As Jesus put it in John's Gospel, "Those who love me will keep my word, and my Father will love them, and we will come to them and make our home with them" (John 14:23). And as Paul puts it in the Letter to the Philippians, "Work out your own salvation with fear and trembling; for it is God who is at work in you, enabling you both to will and to work for his good pleasure" (Phil. 2:12–13). We work, we walk, and we struggle to stand firm under the trials of faith we encounter in the Diaspora, knowing that God is at work in those of us who "wait for new heavens and a new earth, where righteousness is at home" (2 Pet. 3:13).

--------------------------- Questions for Discussion ---------------------------

1. Now that you've read this chapter on the Catholic Epistles, what questions do you have? What do you want to know more about? Make a list to share with your class or reading group.

2. While some of the individual CE are well known, most people aren't aware that these seven letters were handed down to us as a singular collection. After reading this chapter, how would you describe the character and canonical function of the collection as a whole?

3. What does the CE's addition of diasporic imagery add to your understanding of the task of walking the way of the Word? What are some concrete implications of identifying oneself as an "alien and exile" in this world?

4. This chapter describes a variety of trials that Christians face. Which ones are familiar to you as you walk the way of the Word? Which ones are unfamiliar? What other trials of faith could be added to those listed in the CE?

5. If the CE had been left out of the NT, what would be missing?

6. Where do these letters locate you on the way of the Word? How have they helped you along? Where have they warned you to slow down? What in your discipleship requires acceleration? Has the route to your destination been at all clarified?

9

The Revelation to John

The Conquering Disciple

**"These follow the Lamb
wherever he goes."**

(Revelation 14:4)

Now we come to the final apostolic writing of the New Testament, the last stop on our journey along the way of the Word. One might imagine some members of the ancient **canonizing** community desiring to bring the biblical narrative to a close in a relatively easy and straightforward manner: perhaps a few final instructions, followed by an encouraging blessing to send us on our way, much like the one we find at the end of Jude (24–25). Fortunately for us, the Spirit was involved in the process, and the Spirit blows where the Spirit chooses (John 3:8). So instead of coming to a simple, straightforward conclusion, the biblical story ends in a mighty crescendo, propelling us forward into the wildly destabilizing orchestra of worship and wonder known as the Revelation to John.

Admittedly, no other text of **Scripture** has been more contested in **church** history. In ancient days as well as our own time, it has been

the haunt of fanatics captivated by its powerful imagery and the al-
lure of its predictive promise. The ancient Western church received
Revelation early in the process of canonization, but later questioned
its validity when it became a favorite of certain groups who were
deemed heretical. The Eastern church rejected it for a very long time,
and despite its eventual canonization, the Orthodox still do not read
it in worship.

The controversy had not resolved by the time of the Reformation.
Revelation was the one book of the **Bible** on which **John Calvin** did
not write a commentary, thereby tacitly expressing his apprehension.
By contrast, **Martin Luther** was quite clear about his concern: his
complete bewilderment about the book led him to conclude that
it was "neither apostolic nor prophetic" and should therefore be
removed from the NT. "I can in no way detect that the Holy Spirit
produced it," he said.

> They are supposed to be blessed who keep what is written in this book,
> and yet no one knows what that is, to say nothing of keeping it. . . .
> Christ is neither taught nor known in it. But to teach Christ, this is
> the thing which an apostle is bound above all else to do; as Christ says
> in Acts 1, "You shall be my witnesses." Therefore I stick to the books
> which present Christ to me clearly and purely.[1]

Luther wasn't the first theologian to admit that he found the book
of Revelation incomprehensible. Hundreds of years earlier, the third-
century bishop **Dionysius of Alexandria** subjected Revelation to careful literary analysis and concluded that it could *not* have been written
by the same person who wrote the Gospel and Letters of John. The
witness he left behind remains instructive for those of us who struggle
to receive it today.

> Some before us have set aside and rejected the book altogether, criti-
> cizing it chapter by chapter, and pronouncing it without sense or
> argument, and maintaining that the title is fraudulent. For they say
> that it is not the work of John, nor is it a revelation, because it is

---

1. Preface to Revelation (1522); cited from *Word and Sacrament*, ed. E. Theodore
Bachmann, Luther's Works 35 (Philadelphia: Fortress, 1960), 398–99.

covered thickly and densely by a veil of obscurity. . . . But I could not venture to reject the book, as many brethren hold it in high esteem. But I suppose that it is beyond my comprehension, and that there is a certain concealed and more wonderful meaning in every part. For if I do not understand, I suspect that a deeper sense lies beneath the words. I do not measure and judge them by my own reason, but leaving the more to faith I regard them as too high for me to grasp. And I do not reject what I cannot comprehend, but rather wonder, because I do not understand it.[2]

I do not reject what I cannot comprehend, but rather wonder. Although Dionysius ultimately did not heed his own advice, we will. Like the **disciples** of old, who continued to follow Jesus despite their lack of understanding, we too will "follow the Lamb wherever he goes" (Rev. 14:4), even if for a time we are led into a fantastic and sometimes fearful place of disorientation.

Canonical Transition: From the Catholic Epistles to Revelation

The Revelation to John includes a number of canonical signals designed to shape our reception of the text within the larger NT canon. To begin with, our author is identified by the familiar name "John" (1:1). Coming as it does without other identifying features, it seems that we are supposed to know who this "John" is. The name was extremely common in the ancient Jewish world, and as Dionysius pointed out long ago, the language and style of this writer is considerably different from that of the person who penned the Gospel and Letters titled by that name. Nevertheless, we find in the following table a number of terminological and thematic connections to the writings of the "John" we've come to know thus far.

These important linkages are not of the sort that would allow us to argue that all the NT writings "from John" were in fact written *by the same* "John" (much like Hebrews in the Pauline collection). But

2. Quoted from Eusebius, *Ecclesiastical History* 7.25.1–5, in *A Select Library of Nicene and Post-Nicene Fathers of the Christian Church*, 2nd series, trans. Arthur Cushman McGiffert, ed. Philip Schaff and Henry Wace, 14 vols. (1890–1900; repr., Peabody, MA: Hendrickson, 1994), 1:309.

Similarities across the Johannine Writings

The openings of the three major Johannine writings bear several similarities.	John 1:6–7—"There was a man *sent* from *God*, whose name was *John*. He came as a *witness* to *testify* to the light, so that all might believe through him." 1 John 1:1–2—". . . concerning the *word* of life—this life was *revealed*, and we have *seen* it and *testify* to it, and declare to you the eternal life that was with the Father and was revealed to us."	Rev. 1:1–2—"The *revelation* of Jesus Christ, which *God* gave; . . . he made it known by *sending* his angel to his servant *John*, who *testified* to the *word* of God and to the *testimony* of Jesus Christ, even to all that he *saw*."
Jesus is the *Word* of God.	John 1:1, 14; 1 John 1:1	Rev. 19:13
Jesus is the *Lamb* of God.	John 1:29	Rev. 5:6–14 and throughout
Jesus uses "I am" sayings.	John 6:35, 51; 8:12; 9:5; 10:7–14; 11:25; 14:6; 15:1, 5	Rev. 1:8, 17; 21:6; 22:13, 16
Jesus gives living water.	John 4:10, 14; 7:37–39	Rev. 7:17; 21:6; 22:1

in canonical perspective these terminological and thematic echoes are such that they enable us to receive the Revelation to John as part of the larger Johannine body of writings.

And yet, as with Luke and Acts, so also with the works of John: the Gospel of John resides with the Gospels, not alongside the Letters, and the Letters are separated from Revelation by the short Letter of Jude. These Johannine writings are clearly related to one another, but the canonical shape does not advise us to read them together as a collection akin to the CE or the Letters of Paul. Indeed, they are separated out by **genre** as distinctive works with particular roles to play within the larger canonical matrix. Clearly, it is important that the Revelation to John be read according to its canonical function as the literary conclusion of the *entire* Christian biblical canon and not simply as an aspect of Johannine literature (as many biblical scholars tend to do).

One further canonical connection must be mentioned. Revelation includes features that would designate it as a letter, especially in the familiar letter opening (1:4–6) and closing benediction (22:21). This unusual letter is sent "to the seven churches that are in Asia" (1:4) and actually includes within it seven letters to seven churches (chaps. 2–3).

With this, the pattern of NT sevens is complete: Paul wrote to seven distinct churches, the CE are seven letters written to all the churches, and Revelation includes seven letters to seven churches. The design as a whole is suggestive of a complete and perfect communication of apostolic tradition. In fact, these seven letters are actually from Jesus Christ himself, as is the revelation as a whole (1:1).[3] We thus find in this final NT text that the Lord himself joins the apostolic task of spreading the way of the Word through letters of encouragement, challenge, and consolation.

The Shape of the Revelation to John

Among the many challenges for modern readers of Revelation is the determination of its genre. Knowledge of the genre of a text allows a reader to form certain assumptions: when we recognize that a writer has produced a piece of poetry, we agree (automatically and unconsciously) to read the poem according to the basic "rules" of poetry; hence we are unsurprised by the presence of figurative language and are not troubled by a lack of punctuation or the bending of grammatical rules. Likewise, when we open a dictionary, we agree to read according to the "rules" of reference works. We would know, for example, that one does not need to start reading a dictionary from the very beginning of the book in order to understand an entry that comes much later. That would be an appropriate reading strategy for a novel, but not for a dictionary.

But what is the genre of Revelation? On this issue most readers have stumbled in their interpretation of the text. In modern times it has become popular to read Revelation as a kind of coded master plan of current and future events, to help followers of Jesus prepare for the "end times," when God draws history to a close. But is that the correct way to read the book? Is that what the genre of this text demands of readers?

3. Revelation is peppered throughout with the number seven (mentioned fifty-five times) and patterns of seven (e.g., the seven churches of chaps. 2–3; sevenfold praises in 5:12 and 7:12; seven groups of people mourn the loss of Babylon in 6:15; and there are seven beatitudes in the book [1:3; 14:13; 16:15; 19:9; 20:6; 22:7, 14]).

In reality, Revelation qualifies for a creative mixture of genre designations. We have already recognized that it bears some markers of an apostolic letter. We should therefore expect Revelation to do what other apostolic letters do: encourage and correct followers by helping them to diagnose their ills and shape their understanding of potential stumbling blocks as they walk the way of the Word. That is to say, reading Revelation as a *letter* helps us recognize that it seeks to shape our faith life *now in the present* and not simply in the distant future when God brings history to an end. Indeed, it has been said before that the message of Revelation is less about the end of history and more about the end or "purpose" of God's creation. After all, if it were written only for the generation of people who happen to be alive at the end of history, why would ancient Christians have identified it as Scripture for all of God's people of every generation?

Revelation is also a prophecy: "Blessed is the one who reads aloud the words of the prophecy, and blessed are those who hear and who keep what is written in it; for the time is near" (1:3). This genre indication calls to mind the prophetic writings of the OT and can perform at least two functions in our reading. First, it invites us to remember the *words* of the OT **prophets**. Much of the strange imagery of Revelation is deeply indebted to the OT in general and the prophetic books in particular, especially the books of Isaiah, Daniel, Ezekiel, and Zechariah. When we encounter the fantastic symbolism of this book, the genre designation invites us to turn back to the prophetic literature of the OT for interpretive help. Indeed, most of us would be a good deal less bewildered by Revelation if we were familiar enough with the OT Scripture to read the texts in conversation with one another.

Identifying Revelation as a prophecy also invites us to keep the *function* of OT prophecy in mind. The word "prophesy" means "to speak on behalf of" someone else. Those who have spent time reading the words of OT prophets know well that the writers of those texts spend far more time "*forth*-telling," that is, "speaking for God," than "*fore*telling," or predicting the future. OT prophets indeed describe the distant future now and then, but they spend most of their time addressing the present life of God's people and its consequences for their immediate future. In the same way, reading Revelation as prophecy should lead us to focus less on its supposed *predictive* power and more on its *descriptive* and *prescriptive* power: through the mystery of its strange and potent words, Revelation seeks to describe what is really going on in the world and prescribe how God's people ought to respond. Indeed, Revelation itself defines "the spirit of prophecy" as "the testimony of Jesus" (19:10; cf. 1:1–3). On Revelation's terms, all those who bear witness to Jesus are prophets.

In addition to being a letter and a prophecy, Revelation's very first word designates it as an **apocalypse** (1:1). While the current Western pop-culture associations with this term might lead us to think of a cataclysmic, end-of-the-world destructive event, the Greek word simply means "unveiling" and is typically translated in English as "revelation." Though it is an unfamiliar genre to most readers today, there was a time in Jewish history when an apocalyptic text would have been immediately recognizable to God's people. Anyone who has read Ezekiel 40–48, Daniel 7–12, or the book of Zechariah would surely recognize that Revelation is written according to similar literary conventions. We actually have copies of various apocalyptic texts produced for Jewish and Christian readers alike in the centuries before and after the life of Jesus.[4] These texts include similar features: A famous person of faith is transported to the heavenly realm to receive a revelation from God. This "unveiling" of God-knowledge is expressed through fantastic symbols, which are often interpreted by angels. More often than not, the communicated message encourages suffering followers to hold fast to the faith amid the seductions and sufferings that so often lead God's people to abandon the way of the Word.

Thus the apocalyptic text can "unveil" the spiritual forces at work beneath the surface of our everyday encounters. The Creator God is the only one worthy of our loyalty, but this world is filled with creatures who seek to take God's place and claim the authority and allegiance that belongs to God alone. Revelation depicts the elders of our faith demonstrating proper worship of God by casting their

---

4. Examples of non-Christian Jewish apocalypses are *1 Enoch* and *2 Baruch*. Apart from the Revelation to John, early Christians also produced *Shepherd of Hermas* and *Apocalypse of Peter*.

crowns (the symbols of *their* authority) at the foot of God's throne (the symbol of *God's* authority), singing, "You are worthy, our Lord and God, to receive glory and honor and power, for you created all things, and by your will they existed and were created" (4:10–11). But we live in a world where God often seems absent, where poverty and death and greed and the lust for power appear to rule without challenge. Revelation tells the story of God's victory over all these things in the person of Jesus, the victorious Lamb, whose sacrificial death unveils the means by which disciples might conquer the powers that strive to keep them from fulfilling their role as **priests** in God's service.

We must acknowledge, however, that the "story" Revelation tells is far from straightforward. This is typical of apocalypses; a basic narrative undergirds the message, but it unfolds across the chapters in a nonlinear manner characterized throughout by symbol and metaphor. For this reason, the book is impossible to structure according to narrative plot points or stages of argumentation. The safest approach is probably the most pragmatic, that is, a structure that simply tracks the major "scenes" Revelation describes (using the pattern of seven as a guide).

A Structure for the Revelation to John

1:1–8	Prologue and letter addressed to seven churches
1:9–3:22	Vision of Christ with seven messages for the seven churches
4:1–8:5	Vision in heaven of God and the Lamb opening the seven seals of God's scroll
8:2–11:19	Seven trumpets of God's judgment
12:1–15:4	A series of visions
15:5–19:10	Seven bowls and the collapse of the city of Babylon
19:11–22:5	Seven unnumbered visions and the arrival of the new Jerusalem
22:6–21	Epilogue

Given the history of its interpretation, the point bears repeating: Revelation is a thoroughly symbolic text and is not to be taken literally. The very first verse says that Jesus "made it known" to John, but the Greek verb translated here is *sēmainō*, which refers to communication by signs or symbols. In this opening, we are invited to read Revelation not as a literal blueprint of current and future events, but as a kind of theological poem—one that is heavily dependent on the imagery of Israel's Scripture, which is directly and indirectly alluded to more than 600 times across its 404 verses. The result is an **intertextual** feast so rich that each sentence evokes wonder and reflection.

To cite just one example, when the fifth trumpet is blown (Rev. 9:1–10), it releases an army of locusts: the description combines imagery from the locust plague God sent against Egypt (Exod. 10:1–20) with Joel's description of a raging army as a swarm of locusts (Joel 1), alongside Ezekiel's proclamation that only those who have God's mark on their foreheads will be protected from judgment (Ezek. 9), which itself alludes back to the mark of protection God put on Cain (Gen. 4:15), and might also bring to mind the **Passover** in Egypt when those who had the mark of the lamb's blood over their doors were spared from destruction (Exod. 12). The image of the army of locusts is not designed to carry one single, simple "meaning," and it does not represent a singular historical event; it is a symbol, rich with meaning, designed to **baptize** the reader's imagination into the depths of Israel's story. It calls to mind the whole story of the Creator God, who opposes the powerful and provides for the weak.

This narrative finds its climax in the Lamb of God, who was faithful unto death in order that death itself might finally be conquered. And the story continues being told by and through all those who follow the Lamb wherever he leads them. In what remains of this chapter, we'll take a closer look at what Revelation unveils about Jesus and about those who would follow him as their King today.

What Does Revelation Teach Us about God's Work in Christ Jesus?

The Revelation to John is very much a revelation about Jesus. But after all that we've read along the way of the Word thus far, what is left to reveal? John's opening greeting focuses the reader's attention on a collection of christological images: Jesus is "the faithful witness, the firstborn of the dead, and the ruler of the kings of the earth" who "loves us and freed us from our sins by his blood and made us to be a **kingdom**, priests serving his God and Father" (Rev. 1:5–6). Here we find Jesus's messianic career distilled to its essential elements: in his life, he provided us with a "faithful witness" to God; in his death, he "freed us from our sins" to enable right relationship with God; in his resurrection, he became "the firstborn of the dead" to break death's power over us; and his **ascension** to God's right hand makes him "ruler of the kings of the earth." Unlike the Gospels, then, which focus primarily on Jesus's humble earthly pilgrimage, Revelation will whisk us up to the heavenly throne room to catch a glimpse of Jesus in full royal array as King of kings and Lord of lords.

But there is one more event in Jesus's mission that Revelation reminds us has yet to come: "Look!" John says, "He is coming with the clouds; every eye will see him, even those who pierced him; and on his account all the tribes of the earth will wail. So it is to be. Amen" (1:7). These verses signal the canonical function of Revelation: this book will conclude Scripture by directing readers away from the limits of their present experience, to announce that this Jesus we love and serve will come again to set things to rights and take up his complete rule as King of kings. His powerful return will be apparent to everyone, though we are told in rather stark terms that not everyone will be happy to see him when he comes.

If we are at all like John, our response to Jesus's sudden arrival would likely be to fall "at his feet as though dead" (1:17)! But King Jesus does not accept groveling servitude; instead, he touches John gently and says, "Do not be afraid; I am the first and the last, and the living one. I was dead, and see, I am alive forever and ever; and I have the keys of Death and of Hades" (1:17–18).

Jesus immediately sets John to work as a secretary, writing letters by dictation to the churches. We'll look more closely at these letters in the next section, but as you read them, notice the authority with which Jesus addresses his people. He does not speak to them as bosom friends. He does not indulge them with soothing words of permissive acceptance. Instead, he speaks to them with stern authority, much like a coach challenging athletes or a general directing troops. Each letter begins with a description of Jesus that underscores his divine lordship: he is the one "who holds the seven stars" and "walks among the seven golden lampstands" (2:1); he holds "the sharp two-edged sword" (2:12); he "has the seven spirits of God" (3:1); he is "the holy one, the true one, who has the key of David" (3:7); he is "the Amen, the faithful and true witness, the origin of God's creation" (3:14). In all, Jesus is characterized as God's authorized agent, the primary actor in the outworking of God's plan. As such, he is the only one who is truly able to offer congratulations or critique to those who imagine themselves to be God's people.

But what makes Jesus worthy to take up this position of power? Soon after John is brought into the heavenly realm to witness creation's worship of its Creator (Rev. 4), a problem is revealed: God holds "a scroll written on the inside and on the back, sealed with seven seals" (5:1–2). God has something to communicate; the Creator holds information, a message that is written down, but sealed. The cry goes forth: "Who is worthy to open the scroll and break its seals?" (5:2). Who among us could be worthy enough to know the Creator's mind and intention? Who can make sense of our world of dark despair, which constantly threatens to undo us? Soon John is weeping bitterly (5:4), right alongside all who lament the confusion and pain that is endemic to the human condition—for it appears at first that no one is worthy to take the scroll from God's hand.

But then comes the good news: one of the elders taps John on the shoulder and says, "Do not weep. See, the Lion of the Tribe of Judah, the root of David, has conquered, so that he can open the scroll and its seven seals" (Rev. 5:5). The description of Jesus as the Lion of Judah and the root of David echoes Genesis 49:9–10 and Isaiah 11:1–10, both of which describe a deliverer who will reign over God's people. John looks up with excitement to see this awesome and powerful human leader, but what he sees instead is "a Lamb standing as if it had been slaughtered, having seven horns and seven eyes" (Rev. 5:5–6a). The conquering leader, the promised ruler of Israel, the one who is worthy to unlock the secret of the Creator's word, turns out to be a sacrificial Lamb. This Lamb is slaughtered, much like the many other Passover lambs sacrificed before it, but somehow this Lamb is still living. Its seven eyes "are the seven spirits of God sent out into all the earth" (5:6b). These seven spirits have been mentioned several times already (1:4; 3:1; 4:5) and appear to refer to the universal Spirit of God, who mediates God's authority and truth to the churches. In the OT, horns represent power (Deut.

33:17; 1 Kings 22:11) and salvation (2 Sam. 22:3; Ps. 18:2); the presence of seven horns on the head of the Lamb indicates perfect power and complete deliverance.

When the Lamb marches up to take the scroll from God's hand, the heavenly host sings a song of worship, which helps us understand why Christ alone can reveal God's ways to us:

> You are worthy to take the scroll and to open its seals, for you were slaughtered and by your blood you ransomed for God **saints** from every tribe and language and people and nation; you have made them to be a kingdom and priests serving our God, and they will reign on earth. (Rev. 5:9–10)

Jesus is the one who is able to unlock the meaning and purpose of our lives because his self-sacrificial life and death provides us with the means to serve God rightly and conquer the forces that seek to destroy us.

As the Lamb begins popping open the seals on the scroll, history begins to unfold before John's eyes. Each seal releases a rider on a horse who delivers something to the earth. The first is a white horse: "Its rider had a bow; a crown was given to him, and he came out conquering and to conquer" (Rev. 6:2). The symbols are not that hard to interpret: the rider has a crown, so this person comes with ruling authority; he carries a bow, a weapon of war, and he comes out "conquering and to conquer." We've already learned from the Lamb to associate conquering with death, so this person is best understood to be a powerful ruler who maintains peace and order through violence. History has shown that this is precisely the sort of leader most people find attractive. But a second rider follows close behind: he is on a red horse, the color of blood. "Its rider was permitted to take peace from the earth, so that people would slaughter one another; and he was given a great sword" (6:4). It seems that a world governed by violent leaders is a world of perpetual war, a world where peace is attained for a few at the cost of widespread death and destruction for others.

Immediately thereafter comes a third rider on a black horse. "Its rider held a pair of scales in his hand" (Rev. 6:5). In ancient days balance scales were an important economic tool, used for measuring portions and weighing precious commodities. The Bible frequently witnesses to people by complaining about the injustice of unfair weights, which cheat customers to maximize the profit margin of bankers and businesspeople who seek gain regardless of the cost.[5] As this horse arrives, a voice from heaven cries out, "A quart of wheat for a day's pay, and three quarts of barley for a day's pay, but do not damage the olive oil and the wine!" (6:6). Wheat and barley are dietary staples, and the prices listed here are exorbitant: an entire day's pay for a mere quart of wheat? But notice that great care is given to luxuries like olive oil and wine. The arrival of this rider after the violent wars of the first two suggests that human conflict results in economic inequity: scarcity and suffering for many, wealth and prosperity for a few.

The final rider is on a horse of a sickly green hue. "Its rider's name was death, and Hades [the grave]" is his companion. The two are "given authority over a fourth of the earth, to kill with sword, famine, and pestilence, and by the wild animals of the earth" (Rev. 6:8). With this, the apparently meaningless cycle of human history is drawn to its inevitable conclusion: death by war, famine, disease, and even violent conflict with nonhuman creation.

This is the way of empire, and many of us have resigned ourselves to it. Life appears to be nothing more than a perpetual struggle for power contested on the backs of the powerless. Some, however, have rejected the way of empire to follow the way of the Word; the fifth seal reveals "those who had been slaughtered for the word of God and for the testimony they had given" (Rev. 6:9). These "souls" cry out to God, "Sovereign Lord, holy and true, how long will it be before you judge and avenge our blood on the inhabitants of the earth?" (6:10). While some of us fall into despair, and others strive to survive by joining in with the pattern of oppression, others take the alternative route of turning their voice of lament to the God and Ruler of the universe. As the sixth seal reveals, the patience of these suffering faithful will be rewarded: the day of the Lord will come,

5. See, e.g., Lev. 19:35–36; Deut. 25:13–16; Prov. 11:1; Isa. 46:6; Hosea 12:7; Amos 8:5.

and the great anger of the Lamb will be revealed (6:12–14). Those who profited from the way of empire, "the kings of the earth and the magnates and the generals and the rich and the powerful" (6:15), will hide in fear on that day.

The following chapters of Revelation unveil a series of scenes describing God's judgment, human struggle, and here and there, depictions of God's victory. Eventually we hear a poem describing the destruction of the earthly powers that perpetuate the death-dealing systems of our world. Its symbol is an imperial city, a place of seduction described as a prostitute, "the whore of Babylon" (cf. Rev. 17:1, 5, 18). We're told that "all the nations have drunk of the wine of the wrath of her fornication, and the kings of the earth have committed fornication with her, and the merchants of the earth have grown rich from the power of her luxury" (18:3). The imagery of **Diaspora** and **exile** that is so common in the **Catholic Epistles** reappears. Babylon is the world: it is the foreign land in which Christians live as resident strangers who do not participate in its ways. So Christians are instructed, "Come out of her, my people, so that you do not take part in her sins, and so that you do not share in her plagues; for her sins are heaped high as heaven, and God has remembered her iniquities" (18:5–6).

Thereafter Babylon—the city of empire, power, wealth, seduction, and inequity—is destroyed by God, much to the shock and dismay of those who wasted their lives investing in it (Rev. 18:9–24). The faithful of God in heaven and on earth, however, celebrate its destruction (19:1–10) and rejoice at the arrival of yet another white rider. This rider closely resembles the earlier white rider in that he is also a ruling warrior, but this one is different. This is the "King of kings and Lord of lords" (19:16) and "is called Faithful and True," for unlike the previous rider, he judges and makes war in **righteousness** (19:11). He wears a robe dipped in blood—his *own* blood, not that of his enemies—and he is identified as "the Word of God" (19:13). He leads the armies of heaven with a sharp sword, only this weapon emerges "from his mouth" (19:15; cf. 1:16). He speaks the word of truth, the only weapon needed, the only one God's people are allowed to use. Although all the earthly and spiritual forces of evil and destruction line up against him for war, the war never takes place, and the enemies are simply captured and destroyed (19:19–21), for the Lamb has already conquered by his death on the cross. No further war is necessary.

Despite its disorienting symbols and occasionally disturbing imagery, the basic point unveiled is this: the Creator God and the Lamb that was slain are the only beings worthy of our worship and allegiance. All other powers that command our loyalty—money, security, relationships, entertainment, power—all of them will lead us ultimately to destruction. Revelation's depiction of Jesus as King of kings and Lord of lords is a final biblical reminder that Christian commitment is never reducible to pious convictions, doctrinal opinions, or emotional sentiments. As Jesus said in the Gospels, "Where your treasure is, there your heart will be also" (Matt. 6:21; Luke 12:34). If Jesus is indeed the King of the kingdom we say we are seeking, it will be revealed in our habits, our orientation to our culture, and our politics.

What Does Revelation Teach Us about the Spiritual Formation of Christian Disciples?

The first verse of Revelation tells us that this book was given by God for the benefit of Jesus's servants and made known through an angel to one servant in particular named John. We've already noticed that this John is not firmly identified, but we are told a good deal about his situation. This brother in Christ had "testified to the word of God and to the testimony of Jesus Christ" (Rev. 1:2), with the result that the governing authorities exiled him to the prison island of Patmos. His hospitable letter opening, which takes for granted that we share with him in "the persecution" and "the patient endurance" required to participate in the **kingdom of God** (1:9), establishes an orienting portrait of discipleship. Indeed, throughout the rest of the book we will repeatedly hear the exhortation that Christians must hold fast to the way of the Word even when doing so brings persecution, suffering, and death. Jesus says as much in his letters to the churches (chaps. 2–3) where he praises those who suffer for his name:

I know your works, your toil and your patient endurance. . . . I also know that you are enduring patiently and bearing up for the sake of my name, and that you have not grown weary. (2:2–3)

You are holding fast to my name, and you did not deny your faith in me. (2:13)

I know your works—your love, faith, service, and patient endurance. (2:19)

Hold fast to what you have until I come. (2:25)

Because you have kept my word of patient endurance, I will keep you from the hour of trial that is coming. . . . Hold fast to what you have, so that no one may seize your crown. (3:10–11)

Not all of the churches receive this praise, however. Paradigmatic in this regard is the final letter to the church in Laodicea, to whom Jesus says,

I know your works; you are neither cold nor hot. I wish that you were either cold or hot. So, because you are lukewarm, and neither cold nor hot, I am about to spit you out of my mouth. For you say, "I am rich, I have prospered, and I need nothing." You do not realize that you are wretched, pitiable, poor, blind, and naked. (3:15–17)

Revelation unveils the truth about our God, our world, and us. Those who are prosperous may tell themselves that they are blessed by God, but Jesus wants them to consider the possibility that their prosperity may actually be a sign of their failure to live as exiles and of their willingness to partner with the ways of empire in order to live a life of comfort.

The call to hold fast and endure intensifies later in the book. When things turn really beastly in the world, when rulers come who claim the power and authority of God for themselves, believing themselves to be worthy of total allegiance, and begin persecuting followers who refuse them in order to hold fast to the way of the Word—then, a choice must be made.

> Let anyone who has an ear listen:
> If you are to be taken captive,
> into captivity you go;
> if you kill with the sword,
> with the sword you must be killed.
> Here is a call for the endurance and faith of the saints. (13:9–10)

Jesus said something similar to this in the first book of the NT when one of his disciples took up a sword to defend him against his persecutors:

> All who take the sword will perish by the sword. Do you think that I cannot appeal to my Father, and he will at once send me more than twelve legions of angels? But how then would the scriptures be fulfilled, which say it must happen in this way? (Matt. 26:52–54)

It must happen in this way. One is reminded of Paul's word that we who know the peace of life with God are enabled to "boast in our sufferings, knowing that suffering produces endurance, and endurance produces character, and character produces hope, and hope does not disappoint us" (Rom. 5:3–5). James also reminds us that the testing of our faith produces endurance (1:3). Disciples of Jesus are followers of a Lamb who was sacrificed, one who took up a nonviolent way of suffering, and called his people to do the same.

Ironically, Revelation unveils the apparent "failure" of suffering unto death as "conquering." Once again, Jesus's opening letters are instructive, for each one ends with a promise to those who conquer as he did:

> To everyone who conquers, I will give permission to eat from the tree of life that is in the paradise of God. (2:7)

> Whoever conquers will not be harmed by the second death. (2:11)

> To everyone who conquers I will give some of the hidden manna, and I will give a white stone, and on the white stone is written a new name that no one knows except the one who receives it. (2:17)

> To everyone who conquers and continues to do my works to the end, I will give authority over the nations. (2:26)

If you conquer, you will be clothed like them in white robes, and I will not blot your name out of the book of life; I will confess your name before my Father and before his angels. (3:5)

If you conquer, I will make you a pillar in the temple of my God; you will never go out of it. I will write on you the name of my God, and the name of the city of my God, the new Jerusalem that comes down from my God out of heaven, and my own new name. (3:12)

To the one who conquers I will give a place with me on my throne, just as I myself conquered and sat down with my Father on his throne. (3:21)

It seems important to recognize that not all forms of human suffering qualify as "conquering," for the vision is very specific. As if to clarify, the voices of heaven sing a song celebrating the victory of the archangel Michael against the forces of Satan, "the accuser of our comrades" in the faith. They sing of these faithful friends, "They have conquered him by the blood of the Lamb and by the word of their testimony, for they did not cling to life even in the face of death" (12:11). What is described here is not the kind of suffering that is forced upon people (otherwise known as abuse); no, this is a kind of suffering that is taken up intentionally by the sufferer. It is *martyrdom*, a witness to Christ that is upheld even against the threat of death.

Jesus's suffering provides both empowerment and model: empowerment, because it opened the way for us to have a transforming relationship with God; and model, because he was the Word who walked a way for us to follow. Those who do indeed follow the Lamb and testify to his kingship will experience suffering in this world. But as Jesus told us in the very first book of the NT, "Those who want to save their life will lose it, and those who lose their life for my sake will find it" (Matt. 16:25). Revelation offers up a vision of what precisely will be found for those who lose their life for Jesus's sake: "a new heaven and a new earth," a new "city" in which to dwell, a home where the one who is "God . . . with us" (Matt. 1:23) will actually *dwell* with us (Rev. 21:1–3). In that place God "will wipe every tear from their eyes. Death will be no more; mourning and crying and pain will be no more, for the first things have passed away" (21:4).

Jesus says, "See, I am coming soon; my reward is with me, to repay according to everyone's work" (Rev. 22:12). As you hear this, do you receive it as a promise, or as a threat? The answer to that question unveils something about the state of our heavenly citizenship. From the beginning of creation those who were faithful to God have "confessed that they were strangers and foreigners on the earth, for people who speak in this way make it clear that they are seeking a homeland. . . . They desire a better country, that is, a heavenly one. Therefore God is not ashamed to be called their God; indeed, he has prepared a city for them" (Heb. 11:13–16).

May we become the sort of people who welcome Jesus when he arrives on that great day. May we keep the vision before us at all times, so that the counterfeit rewards of this life begin to lose their seductive power. May we grow weary of our Babel towers that provide the false security of enforced sameness, towers of nationalism and patriotism, towers of financial security and simplistic demonization of fellow humans as enemies. May we yearn instead to stand with that "great multitude that no one could count, from every nation, from all tribes and peoples and languages, standing before the throne and before the Lamb, robed in white, with palm branches in their hands," singing, "*Salvation belongs to our God who is seated on the throne, and to the Lamb!*" (Rev. 7:9–10).

> The Spirit and the bride say, "Come."
> And let everyone who hears say, "Come."
> And let everyone who is thirsty come.
> Let anyone who wishes take the water of life as a gift. . . .
>
> The one who testifies to these things says, "Surely I am coming soon."
> Amen. Come, Lord Jesus! (22:17, 20)

Questions for Discussion

1. Now that you've read this chapter on Revelation, what questions do you have? What do you want to know more about? Make a list to share with your class or reading group.

2. This chapter has described Revelation as a poetic, theological reflection that strives to "unveil" the spiritual forces at work beneath the surface of our everyday encounters. How does this understanding differ from the more popular understandings available today?

3. If Revelation is Scripture, it must offer a meaningful message to Christians of every generation and not simply describe the situation faced by Christians of the final generation. How does it inform your interpretation of Revelation if its aim is more about the present than the future?

4. What does Revelation's content and placement contribute to the NT canon? To the Christian Scripture as a whole?

5. If Revelation had been left out of the NT, what would be missing?

6. Where does this book locate you on the way of the Word? How has it helped you along? Where has it warned you to slow down? What in your discipleship requires acceleration? Has the route to your destination been at all clarified?

Glossary

Advocate: A word Jesus used to describe the Holy Spirit. The Greek *paraklētos* (Paraclete) describes someone "called alongside"; other English versions of the **Bible** translate the word as "helper," "comforter," or "counselor."

antinomianism: Literally, "lawlessness." Antinomianism describes the posture of the one who believes that God's grace and forgiveness makes morality and obedience unnecessary.

apocalypse, apocalyptic: From the Greek *apokalypsis*, literally meaning "unveiling" but understood to mean "revelation." *See also* **revelation**.

apophasis, apophatic: Combines the Greek prefix *apo-* (meaning "off" or "away from") with *phanai*, "to speak." Apophatic **theology** underscores the unknowability of God and attempts to describe God according to what God is not. *See also* **kataphasis**.

apostle: From the Greek, meaning "one sent" as an emissary or ambassador. Early Christians reserved the term for those who had received a commission to ministry from the risen **Christ**. *See also* **disciple**.

ascension: Jesus "ascended" (rose up) to heaven in bodily form, forty days after his resurrection from the dead, "to sit at God's right hand" and take up his rule in the **kingdom of heaven**. The tradition is found primarily in Luke's writings (Luke 24:50–53; Acts 1:9–11; 2:29–36) but is also reflected in John's **Gospel** (6:62; 20:17) as well as Ephesians 4:8–10; 1 Peter 3:22; 1 Timothy 3:16, and so forth.

Augustine of Hippo (354–430): One of the greatest theologians of Western, Latin Christianity, Augustine's work has had an influence on every area of Christian **theology**. Augustine's witness to the developing biblical **canon** is significant because his works reflect very little on-going debate about the contents of the NT. He therefore functions as a kind of unofficial end point of **canonization** for canon scholars; by Augustine's day, the discernment process of canonization had effectively come to an end.

baptism: The Christian ritual of initiation, practiced by Jesus's command (Matt. 28:18–20), whereby individuals are either sprinkled with or plunged into water to signify repentance (in the case of John the Baptist) and participation in the death and resurrection of Jesus. Baptism is typically linked with the reception of the Holy Spirit (e.g., Matt. 3:16; Acts 2:38; Rom. 6:8).

Bible: From the Greek *ta biblia*, "the books" or "scrolls." The traditional name for the collection of Christian Scripture.

Bonhoeffer, Dietrich (1906–1945): German pastor, theologian, and **martyr** under twentieth-century Nazism, Bonhoeffer's witness and writings are widely revered. He is best known for his book *The Cost of Discipleship* (1937), a study of the Sermon on the Mount (Matt. 5–7) that articulates in detail what is required of the one who seeks to follow **Christ** in the modern, secular world.

Calvin, John (1509–1564): French-Swiss Reformed theologian and pastor whose teaching helped place the **Protestant** movement on more substantial doctrinal footing. His work developed into the system of thought known since as "Calvinism."

canon, canonical, canonization: From a Greek word meaning "measure" or "rule," *kanōn* referred initially to a "rule" (as in a ruler with which one measures) but came to also refer to an official, approved list. Authorized persons, doctrines, and books can be designated as canonical. Typically canon and canonical refer to the collection of Christian **Scriptures**, and canonization refers to the process by which those books were collected into an authoritative whole.

Catholic/catholic: From the Greek word *katholikos*, meaning "whole" or "universal." When capitalized, it typically refers to the **Roman Catholic Church**. When not capitalized, it refers to the ancient tradition of Christianity characterized by a devotion to unity, an embrace of limited but real diversity, and an aversion to division. "Catholicity" is recognized as one of the four classic "marks" of the Christian **church**, according to the **Nicene Creed**: "We believe in one, holy, catholic, and apostolic church." *See also* **Catholic Epistles; church; Nicene Creed; Roman Catholic.**

Catholic Epistles: The NT letter collection including one letter from Jesus's brother James, two from the **apostle** Peter, three from the apostle John, and one from Jesus's brother Jude—figures associated with the mission to Jews in Jerusalem and designated "pillars" of that **church** by the apostle Paul (Gal. 2:9). The ancient church called these letters **catholic**, in part because most of them bear a "universal" address.

Christ: From the Greek *christos*, meaning "anointed one"; the Hebrew equivalent is *mashiakh*, "messiah." In the **Bible** the term refers to anyone empowered for service to God, including **priests, prophets,** and kings. By Jesus's day, the words "Christ" and "**Messiah**" were reserved almost exclusively for the hoped-for coming King of Israel. *See also* **Messiah.**

church: The community of those called out by God to follow **Christ** Jesus by the power of the **Holy** Spirit. Though numerous church families (denominations) and countless church buildings exist, all of them find their unity in the ancient tradition of Christianity known in the Nicene Creed as "the one, holy, catholic, and apostolic church." *See also* **Catholic; Nicene Creed; Eastern Orthodox.**

church fathers: Leaders of the ancient Christian **church** who lived after the time of the **apostles** and were recognized as great teachers or influential bishops.

circumcision: The physical sign of the **covenant** with God for Jewish males, performed on the eighth day of life, wherein the foreskin of the penis is removed.

Clement of Alexandria (ca. 150–ca. 215): **Church father** and theologian who taught at the catechetical school of Alexandria, Egypt. The few writings of his that we possess today provide an important witness to the development of the **canon** in the second-century **Eastern Orthodox Church.**

Communion: A ritual practiced by Christians, by Jesus's command (e.g., Matt. 26:26–29; 1 Cor. 11:23–26), to memorialize **Christ's** death, celebrate Christian fellowship, and anticipate the great feast that will take place at Christ's return. *See also* **Eucharist; Lord's Supper.**

consummation: The point at which something is considered complete or finalized. In the biblical metanarrative, the consummation refers to the completion of God's **redemptive** work at the end of time.

covenant: A relational promise or treaty between two parties. In the **Bible**, covenants are established between God and God's people that set out the terms of their relationship.

Cyprian of Carthage (ca. 200–258): Bishop of Carthage, **martyr**, and **church father**, Cyprian's extant writings provide important insight into the development of the **canon** in third-century North Africa.

Diaspora, Dispersion: From a Greek word meaning "scatter," Diaspora bears both geographical and **theological** meanings in the Bible. Geographically, the Diaspora referred to the places outside the land of Palestine to which Jews had been "scattered," but it also functioned theologically in reference to believers scattered away from their true spiritual home (whether it be Jerusalem or the **kingdom of God**) and living as aliens and exiles in a foreign land as a result. *See also* **exile**.

Dionysius of Alexandria (ca. 200–264): Student of **Origen** at the catechetical school of Alexandria, Dionysius eventually went on to serve as bishop of that city for seventeen years. Among **canon** scholars he is particularly remembered today for his critical analysis of the Revelation to John.

disciple, discipleship: From the Greek word *mathētēs*, meaning "learner" or "apprentice," the term "disciple" is used to designate a follower of Jesus.

Eastern Orthodox: The body of **churches** representing the Eastern, Greek tradition of ancient Christianity.

Eucharist: A ritual practiced by Christians, by Jesus's command (e.g., Matt. 26:26–29; 1 Cor. 11:23–26), to memorialize his death, celebrate Christian fellowship, and anticipate the great feast that will take place at his return. *See also* **Communion; Lord's Supper.**

Eusebius of Caesarea (ca. 260–ca. 340): Greek historian of Christianity and bishop of Caesarea, Eusebius is remembered principally for his *Ecclesiastical History*, which traces the development of Christianity from the first century to the fourth. His history provides invaluable insight into the state of the developing **canon** in the early 300s.

evangelists: From the Greek verb *euangelizō*, meaning "to evangelize," an evangelist is someone who spreads the good news about Jesus. The writers of our four **Gospels** are often called evangelists.

exile: A stock term usually referring to the Babylonian destruction of Judah in 587 BCE. However, the northern kingdom of Israel also suffered an exile previously, in 722 BCE, at the hand of the Assyrians. *See also* **Diaspora, Dispersion.**

Gamaliel the Elder: An authority in the Jewish **law** and a leader of the **Sanhedrin** in Jesus's day, Gamaliel was "a **Pharisee** in the council . . . , a teacher of the law, respected by all the people" (Acts 5:34–39). He also was Paul's teacher (Acts 22:3).

gematria: An ancient practice where letters of the alphabet are assigned a numerical value. Each word then has a number and can be related mystically to other words with the same value or to the occurrence of the same number in nature or history.

genealogy: A list of descendants that traces the lineage of a person or people group.

genre: A means of categorizing artistic works by appeal to the conventions of its production. In literature, the genre forms an unspoken agreement between author and reader, wherein the author agrees to write according to a set of stylistic criteria appropriate to the genre, and the reader agrees (usually subconsciously) to read the text accordingly.

gentile: A term referring to the people of "the nations" other than Israel. It is used specifically to refer to persons who are not ethnically Jewish.

gospel: From the Greek term *euangelion*, meaning "good news," gospel referred initially to preaching on the life, death, and resurrection of Jesus. Later it came to function also as a **genre** of literature focused on the person and teaching of Jesus. The four Gospels make up the first **canonical** unit of the NT.

Gregory of Nyssa (335–394): One of three famous Cappadocian **church fathers** (including Basil of Caesarea and Gregory of Nazianzus), Gregory was bishop of Nyssa and an important contributing member of the Council of Nicaea. The writings he left behind provide an important witness to the developing NT **canon** of the fourth century.

Hellenism, Hellenistic, hellenization: Terms referring to the larger Greek culture that dominated the Mediterranean and eastward world following the conquests of Alexander the Great (356–323 BCE). Hellenism made Greek the common language of the day and introduced aspects of Greek culture to the peoples and religions affected.

holy, holiness: To be holy is to be "set apart" for God's use. People, things, and places can all be considered holy. While the word is classically defined in terms of separation, the meaning in the NT has more to do with being recognizably different as a result of following God's call in **Christ** and the Spirit.

inspiration, inspired: The word inspire derives from the Latin for "breathe into." The biblical term comes from 2 Timothy 3:16, which accounts for the usefulness of **Scripture** by describing it as *theopneustos*, "God-breathed" or "inspired."

intertextual, intertextuality: Refers to expanding the meaning of a text by relating it to other biblical (and sometimes nonbiblical) texts that use similar words and ideas. Biblical texts are often engaged intertextually with others: later texts reference earlier ones to create an intertextual conversation of sorts.

Irenaeus of Lyon (ca. 130–ca. 202): Church father best known for his work *Against Heresies* (ca. 180), an extended **theological** argument in defense of the **church**'s developing orthodox theology. His method appealed especially to apostolic succession, tracing leaders back through the ancient churches to establish the authenticity of the tradition he maintained. Along the way, he became the first Christian theologian to make explicit appeals to NT texts as authorities in their own right.

Jerome of Bethlehem (ca. 347–420): Church father, monk, writer, and pastor, best known for his contribution to the translation of the Christian **Scripture** into Latin. This translation, known as the **Vulgate**, became the commonly used edition of Scripture in the Western **church**.

Jewish Scripture(s): *See* **Old Testament; Septuagint.**

John Chrysostom (ca. 349–407): Archbishop of Constantinople and one of the most influential **church fathers** of his day. He was known especially for his powerful preaching; hence the moniker Chrysostom, "golden-mouthed."

justification, justify: The verbal form of the term "righteous," to "justify" is to "enrighteous," or "to make right." Justification refers to God's work of establishing right relationship with humanity through **Christ** and the **Holy** Spirit. *See also* **righteous.**

kataphasis, kataphatic: Combines the Greek prefix *kata-* (an intensifier) with the verb *phanai*, meaning "to speak"; kataphatic **theology** underscores what can be known of God by speaking of who and what God is. It involves making declarative statements about God's character and identity. *See also* **apophasis.**

kingdom of God/heaven: The place, or situation, where God's rule is acknowledged and God's will is accomplished.

law: The law of God, delivered to Moses on Mount Sinai (Exod. 19–23) and preserved in the first five books of the OT, called **Torah** in Hebrew (meaning "instruction"). *See also* **Torah.**

lectionary: A list of **Scripture** readings appointed for use on a given day or occasion. The two most commonly used today are the Revised Common Lectionary and the **Roman Catholic** Lectionary.

Lord's Supper: A ritual practiced by Christians, by Jesus's command (e.g., Matt. 26:26–29; 1 Cor. 11:23–26), to memorialize **Christ's** death, celebrate Christian fellowship, and anticipate the great feast that will take place at Christ's return. *See also* **Communion; Eucharist.**

Luther, Martin (1483–1546): Augustinian monk and **Bible** professor at Wittenberg, Germany, whose protest against the papacy of his day launched the movement known since as the **Protestant** Reformation.

LXX: *See* **Septuagint.**

manuscript: A handwritten (Latin *manu* + *script*) document. The **Bible** we read is an English translation established on the basis of available ancient Hebrew and Greek manuscripts.

martyr: From the Greek *martys*, "witness," a martyr is someone who witnesses to **Christ**, especially to the point of death.

Messiah: From the Hebrew *mashiakh*, meaning "anointed one"; the Greek equivalent is *christos*, "**Christ.**" In the **Bible** the term refers to anyone empowered for service to God, including **priests, prophets,** and kings. By Jesus's day, the words "Christ" and "Messiah" almost exclusively referred to the hoped-for coming King of Israel. *See also* **Christ.**

Nicene Creed: The profession of faith adopted originally at the Council of Nicaea (325) and revised at the Council of Constantinople (381). It is the creed most widely used by the world's Christians.

Old Testament (OT): The ancient **Scriptures** of Israel, authorized by Jesus and embraced by the **church** throughout history as Christian Scripture. Originally written in Hebrew and Aramaic, these texts were translated into Greek in the centuries before Jesus's birth. This translation, known as the **Septuagint** (abbreviated as **LXX**), was the Scripture used by earliest Christianity. *See also* **Septuagint.**

Origen of Alexandria (ca. 184–ca. 253): One of the greatest theologians and biblical scholars of his day, Origen's work reflects knowledge of **church** practices throughout the world of his day. He is also the first **church**

father who communicates awareness (though not complete acceptance) of all the texts that would eventually be gathered into the NT.

parable: A story, saying, or riddle that compares something—often from nature—with the **kingdom of God**, in order to illustrate what the kingdom is about or to point to who God is. As such, Jesus's parables typically challenge standard worldviews and shock with the radical logic of God's ways.

Passover: The annual Jewish commemoration of their deliverance by God from slavery in Egypt: the houses that had the blood of the lamb on their doorposts were "passed over" in God's judgment (Exod. 12). In the NT, the Passover is associated with Jesus's sacrificial death on the cross and his passing through death and back to life.

Pentecost: A Jewish agricultural festival known in the **OT** as the Feast of Weeks or Feast of the Harvest, one of three major pilgrim festivals of the Jewish year (see, e.g., Exod. 23:14–17). In the NT book of Acts, the outpouring of the Holy Spirit on believers took place during the celebration of this festival in Jerusalem (Acts 2).

Pharisees: A first-century movement of laymen (nonpriests) who were focused on preserving the purity of Jewish religious practice against the defilements of Greek and Roman culture. Made up of teachers and experts in the **law** (**rabbis** and **scribes**), this is the group most closely associated with Jesus, and thus its members are Jesus's primary antagonists in the **Gospel** narratives.

Polycarp of Smyrna (69–155): Bishop of Smyrna and **martyr**, Polycarp was said to have learned from the **apostle** John. His *Letter to the Philippians* and the report of his death, the *Martyrdom of Polycarp*, are important witnesses to early use of Christian texts.

priest: A human who mediates between God and humanity, especially in the offering of sacrifices. In ancient Israel such persons led Israel in its worship of God and served as advisers and leaders. This title is continued in some NT texts to refer to those who serve God in the ministry of the **gospel** (1 Pet. 2:9; Rev. 1:6).

prophet: A spokesperson for God. In the **OT**, various prophets appear in Joshua, Judges, Samuel, Kings, and Chronicles, as well as in the books of the **canonical** prophets Isaiah, Jeremiah, Ezekiel, Daniel, and the Book of the Twelve, often called the Minor Prophets. Persons designated as prophets also appear in the NT (e.g., Matt. 11:9; Luke 2:36; Acts

15:32), and, as in the OT, there are false prophets among them (e.g., Matt. 7:15; Acts 13:6; 1 John 4:1).

Protestant: A representative of one of a number of different groups emerging out of the sixteenth-century Reformation of the Western Christian **church**. Despite their myriad differences, these groups tend to emphasize the authority of **Scripture** over tradition, the centrality of preaching, and the priority of the individual over communal authority.

psalms: Songs and liturgies that are a central part of the prayer and worship of Jews and Christians. The **OT** book of Psalms is a five-part collection including psalms of thanksgiving, praise, lament, and confession.

rabbi, rabbinic literature: From a Hebrew word meaning "my master," a rabbi is a Jewish teacher or religious leader. Rabbinic literature refers to the writings of authoritative rabbis collected over the centuries. The primary texts of rabbinic literature include the Mishnah and the Tosefta, which are collected sayings dating from the period before 200, and the Jerusalem (ca. 450) and Babylonian (ca. 600) Talmuds.

reconciliation: The restoration of right relations. Often synonymous with "atonement," an Old English word referring to the "at-one-ment" created when a broken relationship is restored. Reconciliation is the **apostle** Paul's preferred term to describe what God has done in **Christ** and, by extension, what God is doing by the power of the Spirit in and through the **church**.

redeem, redemption, redemptive: Literally, to gain or regain possession of something by offering a payment. Biblically the word is used most frequently in relation to God's deliverance of Israel from slavery in Egypt and the deliverance of all humanity from the effects of human sin through Jesus's work of **reconciliation**.

revelation: The act of revealing something. In the **Bible** the term revelation may refer to God's self-revealing in the act of creation, in God's relationship with the people of Israel, and principally in the work of Jesus **Christ**. The final book of the Bible, called the Revelation to John or the **Apocalypse** of John, refers to a vision of God's **consummation** received by a **disciple** named John while in exile on the island of Patmos.

righteous, righteousness: A term referring to the character of the person who lives in right relationship with God. *See also* **justification**.

Roman Catholic: The historic representatives of the Western, Latin tradition of Christianity, centered in Rome.

rule of faith: The essential, shared **theological** agreements of Christianity, formalized in the Apostles' and **Nicene Creeds,** and used as a guide or "rule" for interpreting the diverse witnesses of **Scripture.**

Sadducee: One of the dominant sects of first-century Judaism made up of the priestly class and those particularly associated with the temple in Jerusalem. In contrast to the **Pharisees,** the Sadducees recognized only the **Torah** as authoritative Scripture.

saints: From the Greek *hagioi,* "holy ones," the saints are those who have been sanctified in **Christ.** Paul refers to all Christians as saints, though more accurately, "called to be saints" (Rom. 1:7; 1 Cor. 1:2). *See also* **sanctification.**

Samaritans: Inhabitants of the ancient northern kingdom of Israel who in Jesus's day were rivals of Jews associated with the Jerusalem temple. Pious Jews considered them to be religiously impure and thus had no dealings with them.

sanctification, sanctify: The process of being made **holy.** Paul maintains a now-and-not-yet view of Christian sanctification: since Christians have been made holy through **Christ** (i.e., brought into right relationship with God), they must cooperate with the Spirit to actually live like holy people. *See also* **holy; saints.**

Sanhedrin: An aristocratic council presided over by the Jewish high **priest,** to which Rome entrusted some aspects of local government.

scribe: A writer and copier of **manuscripts.** In the **Gospels** the scribes are associated with the **Pharisees** and may be thought of as lawyers or experts in the **law.**

Scripture: From the Latin *scriptura,* "writings," Scripture is the designated term for the ancient writings set apart by Jews and Christians because of their **holiness.**

Septuagint/LXX: The Greek translation of the **Jewish Scriptures** produced as a product of **hellenization** in the third and fourth centuries BCE. The name derives from a tradition of the "seventy" **scribes** who performed the work. This Greek version of the Hebrew texts functioned as the authoritative **Scriptures** for earliest Christians and continues as the basis for biblical texts of Christian groups associated with **Eastern Orthodoxy.**

stichos, stichoi: A stichos is a line of handwritten Greek text. In the ancient world, texts were measured in terms of stichoi (lines).

synagogue: From a Greek word meaning "gather together" or "assembly," the synagogue developed in the postexilic period as a place where Jews living away from Jerusalem might gather for prayers and the reading of **Scripture**.

Synoptic Gospels: A term developed in the nineteenth century to describe the **Gospels** of Matthew, Mark, and Luke, which share a "common view" of the gospel's content and plotline and therefore can be fruitfully studied side by side.

Tertullian of Carthage (ca. 155–ca. 240): North African **church father** and influential theologian of Latin Christianity, Tertullian's many extant writings provide us with insight into the state of the developing NT **canon** in the early third century.

theology, theological: Combining the Greek words *theos* (God) and *logos* (word), theology refers to the study of the things of God, particularly God's word to us, our words to God, and our words about God to others.

Torah: The Hebrew name (Josh. 1:7–8, "**law**") for the first five books of the OT. Meaning "instruction" in Hebrew, the word is also sometimes used to designate the whole instruction of God derived from the **Scriptures**. The Torah includes both narratives and the law of Moses.

typology, typological: The practice of interpretation by means of "types" or symbols, wherein features or characters appearing earlier in a text are thought to prefigure features or characters occurring later in the text.

Vulgate: The Latin translation of the **Bible** produced by **Jerome of Bethlehem** and his school at the end of the fourth century CE. The Vulgate served as the authoritative version of the Bible for the Western **church** for most of its history and continues to serve as an authoritative version for the **Roman Catholic Church**.

wisdom: A way of life dependent on observing how the world in all its dimensions (e.g., political, social, religious, familial, economic) works and then acting appropriately. Wisdom, which comes from God, combines this feature with the necessity of obeying God as well.

Zealots: A sect of first-century Judaism that strove for military victory over Rome and the reestablishment of the Jewish nation.

Suggestions for Further Reading

If you like the approach to Scripture that you've encountered here and want to go further in your study, you might check out the following titles. This list is intentionally incomplete and selective, and it excludes many excellent commentaries. Still, this list will help introductory students get started.

For a deeper exploration of the canonization of the Bible, you'd do well to start with this:

> McDonald, Lee M. *The Biblical Canon: Its Origin, Transmission, and Authority*. Grand Rapids: Baker Academic, 2006.

If you are looking for a more conventional NT introductory textbook that covers a wider range of historical and literary matters than we have in this book, your best bet is this work:

> Powell, Mark Allan. *Introducing the New Testament: A Historical, Literary, and Theological Survey*. Grand Rapids: Baker Academic, 2009.

For a powerful reading of the NT through African American eyes, consider this volume:

> Blount, Brian, ed. *True to Our Native Land: An African-American New Testament Commentary*. Minneapolis: Fortress, 2007.

If you want to know more about the contemporary movement within biblical studies called the "theological interpretation of Scripture," the following books are highly recommended:

Davis, Ellen, and Richard Hays. *The Art of Reading Scripture*. Grand Rapids: Eerdmans, 2003.

Fowl, Stephen. *The Theological Interpretation of Scripture*. Cascade Companions 9. Eugene, OR: Cascade, 2009.

Green, Joel B. *Practicing Theological Interpretation: Engaging Biblical Texts for Faith and Formation*. Grand Rapids: Baker Academic, 2012.

Treier, Daniel J. *Introducing Theological Interpretation of Scripture: Recovering a Christian Practice*. Grand Rapids: Baker Academic, 2008.

For a deeper study of the fourfold Gospel, consider the following:

Burridge, Richard. *Four Gospels, One Jesus: A Symbolic Reading*. 3rd ed. Grand Rapids: Eerdmans, 2014.

Hays, Richard B. *Reading Backwards: Figural Christology and the Fourfold Gospel Witness*. Waco: Baylor University Press, 2014.

Watson, Francis. *The Fourfold Gospel: A Theological Reading of the New Testament Portraits of Jesus*. Grand Rapids: Baker Academic, 2016.

On the Acts of the Apostles, read one of these works:

Robinson, Anthony B., and Robert W. Wall. *Called to Be Church: The Acts of the Apostles for a New Day*. Grand Rapids: Eerdmans, 2006.

Spencer, F. Scott. *Journeying through Acts: A Literary-Cultural Reading*. Grand Rapids: Baker Academic, 2004.

On the Pauline Letters, the best introductory survey is this one:

Gorman, Michael J. *Apostle of the Crucified Lord: A Theological Introduction to Paul and His Letters*. Grand Rapids: Eerdmans, 2003.

You might also consider his far shorter treatment:

———. *Reading Paul*. Cascade Companions 4. Eugene, OR: Cascade, 2008.

On the Catholic Epistles, only one book reads all seven together as an intentionally designed canonical collection:

Nienhuis, David R., and Robert W. Wall. *Reading the Epistles of James, Peter, John, and Jude as Scripture: The Shaping and Shape of a Canonical Collection*. Grand Rapids: Eerdmans, 2013.

On the Revelation to John, the classic, readable text is the following:

Metzger, Bruce M. *Breaking the Code: Understanding the Book of Revelation*. Nashville: Abingdon, 1999.

Scripture Index

Old Testament

Genesis

1:28 92
2:10–14 11
4:15 161
6 11
8:1 43n5
10 19n2
11:1–9 91, 92
12:1–3 93
12:3 20, 122–23
15:6 121
17:9–14 104
19:24 43n3
49:9–10 162

Exodus

3:2 43n3
4:22 25
9:13–23 43n3
10:1–20 161
12 161, 180
13:21–22 43n3, 43n5
15:10 43n5

16:13–35 47
19–23 179
19:5–6 122
19:18 43n3, 43n4
23:14–17 180
25–27 11
33:17–23 42–43

Leviticus

10:2 43n3
12:8 59n5
17–18 105
19:35–36 165n5

Numbers

16:35 43n3

Deuteronomy

6:4–5 121
22:13–30 29
25:13–16 165n5
33:17 163–64

Joshua

1:7–8 183

Ruth

3:18–21 21

2 Samuel

7:13–14 20, 24n6
22:8 43n4
23:3 164

1 Kings

18:23–40 43n3
19:11–13 43
22:11 164

2 Kings

4:42–44 47
17–25 145

Job

9:3–12 44

Psalms

2:6–7 24n6
14:3 120

18:2 164
18:7 43n4
18:8 43n3
22:1 47
22:4–5 47
23 47
65:5–7 47
68:8 43n4
78:26 43n5
89:9 47
89:26–27 24n6
104:7 47
107:23–29 47

Proverbs

11:1 165n5

Isaiah

6:1–13 112n4
8:14–15 119
9:6 24n6
11:1–10 163
28:16 119
40:3–5 57
42:6 122
44:3 93

46:6 165n5
55:8–9 44
57:19 93

Jeremiah

1:4–10 112n4

Ezekiel

1 11
9 161
40–48 159

Daniel

7–12 159

Hosea

1:10 144
2:23 144
6:6 29
11:1 25
12:7 165n5

Joel

1 161
2:28–29 84, 93

Amos

8:5 165n5
9:11–12 105

Habakkuk

2:4 122, 123n11

New Testament

Matthew

1:1 20, 25, 70
1:1–17 19–20
1:1–3:17 24, 38
1:1–4:25 24
1:19 29
1:20 21

1:22–23 22n4
1:23 26, 60, 170
2:1–12 21, 59
2:5–6 22n4
2:15 22n4
2:17–18 22n4
2:23 22n4
3:3 57
3:3–4 22n4
3:16 174
4:1 35
4:1–11 25
4:1–18:35 24, 38
4:3 25n8
4:6 25n8
4:14–16 22n4
5:1–7:29 24, 27,
    28, 174
5:3 59, 139n3
5:7 29, 139n3
5:14 88
5:14–16 27
5:17 22
5:19–20 27
5:34–37 139n3
5:43–48 28
5:48 139n3
6:19 139n3
6:21 167
6:30 34, 49, 60n7
7:7 139n3
7:12 18, 30
7:13–14 146
7:15 181
7:16 139n3
7:21 28, 139n3
7:27 28
8:1–9:38 24
8:5–13 21
8:17 22n4
8:26 34, 49, 60n7
8:29 25n8
9:2–8 96
9:13 29
9:20–21 96
9:27 25n7
10:1–42 24
10:5 58

10:26 36
10:40 26
11:1–12:50 24
11:9 180
11:10 22n4
11:27 26
11:29 17
11:29–30 29
12:7 29
12:17–21 22n4
12:23 25n7
13:1–53 24
13:13 36
13:14–15 22n4
13:20 34
13:35 22n4
13:51 36
13:51–52 34
13:54–17:27 24
13:55 102
14:22–33 30n9, 42
14:27–28 30–31
14:28 30
14:28–33 34,
    35, 47
14:31 34, 60n7
14:33 25n8, 34, 35
15:7–9 22n4
15:22 25n7
16:8 34, 49, 60n7
16:16 25, 25n8
16:18 88
16:25 170
17:1–8 102
17:20 34, 60, 60n7
18:1–35 24
18:5 26
18:15–20 88
18:20 26, 30
19:1–20:33 24, 38
19:1–23:39 24
20:30–31 25n7
21:1–27:66 24, 38
21:4–5 22n4
21:9 25n7
21:15 25n7
21:21–22 34
21:28–31 28

22:23–28 58n4
22:40 18
23:3 28
23:23–24 29
24:1–25:46 24
24:11–13 147
25:31–46 26
25:42 73
26:1–28:20 24
26:26–29 175,
    176, 179
26:52–54 169
26:54–56 22n4
26:63 25n8
26:74 89
27:9–10 22n4
27:40 25n8
27:42 24n6
28:1–20 24, 38
28:16 49
28:18–20 174
28:19 34, 49
28:19–20 vii, 88
28:20 26, 28

Mark

1:1 34, 40, 41, 72
1:1–15 38
1:1–8:26 41
1:2–8 34
1:3 57
1:7 40
1:9 35
1:11 40, 41
1:12 35
1:14–15 35
1:16–20 35
1:16–10:52 38
1:21–28 35, 41
1:21–8:21 41
1:23–25 41
1:23–28 23n5
1:24 40
1:27 35, 40
1:34 40, 41
1:35–39 23n5
1:40–44 41

2:7 40
3:11–12 40–41
3:22 38, 40
4 36n2
4:10–12 36, 41–42
4:13 36, 45, 60n8
4:16–17 61
4:22 36
4:26–29 23n5
4:38 46
4:40 48, 49, 60
4:41 40, 46
5:7 40
5:43 41
6:2–3 40
6:3 102
6:30–34 47
6:45–52 30n9
6:47–52 42
6:48 42
6:49 38
6:49–50 40
6:51–52 35
6:52 45, 60n8
7:18 45, 60n8
7:32–37 23n5
7:36 41
8:4 47
8:11–26 40
8:12 38
8:17 46, 60n8
8:17–18 39
8:18 60
8:21 60n8
8:22–26 23n5,
    39, 41
8:25 39
8:26 41
8:27 39, 40, 41
8:27–16:20 41
8:29 25, 39
8:31–9:1 39–41
8:31–10:45 41
8:34 33
9:2–8 102
9:7 40, 41
9:19 39, 48
9:30–32 40–41

9:32 46, 60n8
9:33–37 40
9:38–40 23n5
10:32–45 40
10:45 47, 59, 74
10:46–52 40, 41
10:52 40
11:1–13:37 38
11:1–16:20 41
12:18–23 58n4
12:38–44 58n4
12:41–44 23n5
14:1–15:47 38
14:68 60n8
14:71 89
15:34 47
16:1 48
16:1–20 38
16:6–7 45
16:8 48, 49, 52
16:9 48
16:9–20 48,
    48n10, 49
16:17–20 48, 88

Luke

1:1 56, 57n3
1:1–2 73
1:1–4 51–52
1:1–4:13 54
1:3 52
1:3–4 49
1:4 53
1:5 55
1:14 61
1:15 57n3
1:20 57n3
1:23 57n3
1:26–56 58
1:28 60
1:32–33 56
1:34–35 60
1:41 57n3, 60
1:44 61
1:45 56, 57n3
1:46–55 62
1:47 59n6, 61

1:53 57n3, 59
1:54–55 56
1:57 57n3
1:58 61
1:67 57n3, 60
1:67–79 62
1:68–75 56
1:69–75 59
1:71 59n6
1:77 59n6
2:1–2 55
2:1–10 74
2:6 57n3
2:7 65
2:10 59, 61
2:12 65
2:13–14 62
2:16 65
2:20 62
2:21 57n3
2:22 57n3
2:25–27 60
2:29–32 56, 62
2:30 59n6
2:32 58, 74
2:36 180
2:36–38 58
2:37 58n4
2:37–38 62
2:39 57n3
2:40 57n3
2:41–52 54
3:1–2 55
3:5–6 58
3:5–8 143
3:6 59n6, 65
3:21 62, 96
3:22 60
3:23–38 57, 58
4:1–13 54
4:3 57
4:6 57
4:14–9:50 54
4:18 59, 60, 61n9
4:18–19 59
4:22 104, 139
4:24–27 58
4:25–26 58n4

5:16 62
5:31–32 64
6:12 62
6:12–16 58
6:20 59
7:1–17 58, 58n4
7:36–50 63, 64
8:1–3 58
8:2 49
8:42 58
9:18 62
9:20 25
9:23 129
9:28–29 62
9:28–36 102
9:31 54
9:38 58
9:51 54
9:51–53 54n2
9:51–19:28 54
9:56–57 54n2
10 70
10:3 54n2
10:17 62
10:21 62
10:30–37 58
10:38 54n2
10:38–42 58, 64
11:1–13 62
11:37–54 63
12:34 167
13:13 62
13:22 54n2
13:33 54n2
14:1–6 63
14:1–24 64
15:1 58
15:1–2 64
15:4–7 58, 62
15:7 62
15:8–10 59
15:9–10 62
15:32 62
17:11 54n2, 58
17:15 62
17:19 54n2
17:20–21 57
17:21 51

18:3–5 58n4
18:9–14 58
18:31 54n2
18:36 144
18:43 62
19:1–10 58, 65
19:4 54n2
19:9 59n6
19:10 58
19:28 54n2
19:29–23:56 54
19:37 61
20:28 58n4
20:47 58n4
21:2–3 58n4
22:19 65
22:41–45 62
22:60 89
23:34 97
23:46 97
24:1–53 54
24:11 49
24:13–35 49, 65
24:25–27 74
24:35 65
24:41 61
24:44 74
24:47 58
24:49 54, 67, 84, 91, 92
24:50–53 62, 173
24:51 49
24:52 62

John

1:1 75, 156
1:1–3 73
1:1–18 72, 73
1:3 70
1:6–7 156
1:11–13 77
1:12 90
1:14 14, 156
1:17 76n6
1:18 75, 81
1:19–51 73
1:19–12:50 72, 73

1:29 70, 76, 156
1:45 74, 76n6
1:51 76
2 69
2:1–4:54 73
2:13–22 76
2:16 75
2:19–22 93
3 70
3:1–2 78–79
3:5–8 84
3:8 153
3:9 78
3:14 76n6
3:15–16 70
3:35–36 75
4 70
4:5–15 76
4:9 79
4:10 156
4:12 79
4:14 156
4:19 79
4:23–24 93
4:26 79
4:29 79
4:39 79
4:42 79
5 69
5:1–8:11 73
5:14–47 75
5:17 75
5:22–30 76
5:24 70
5:36 75
5:39–40 74
5:45–46 74, 76n6
6:15–21 30, 42
6:25–58 76
6:32 76n6
6:35 156
6:35–51 71
6:51 156
6:54 70
6:56–57 81
6:62 173
6:68–69 82
7:19–23 76n6

7:25–31 77
7:37–39 156
7:39 84
7:40–44 77
8:5 76n6
8:12 27, 71, 156
8:12–10:42 73
8:39–51 76
8:54 75
8:58 71
9 69
9:5 71, 156
9:28–29 76n6
10:7 71
10:7–11 81
10:7–14 156
10:9–14 71
10:25–27 81
10:30 75
10:38 75
11 69, 70
11:1–54 73
11:4 75
11:10 78
11:25 71, 156
11:41 75
11:55–12:36 73
12:23 72
12:28 75
12:32 67, 71, 93
12:37 72, 77
12:37–50 73
12:44–48 77
12:47 76
13 69
13:1 72
13:1–11 82
13:1–30 73
13:1–20:31 72, 73, 77
13:15 80
13:21–24 80
13:34–35 83
13:37 82
14:1–16:33 73
14:1–17:26 73
14:6 71, 75, 76, 156

14:9–10 75
14:12 80
14:12–13 90
14:13 75
14:15–17 83, 84, 88
14:23 83, 150
14:26 84, 88
15:1 71, 156
15:1–5 81
15:5 71, 156
15:18–25 82
15:26 84
16:8 84
16:13–15 84
17:1 72
17:1–26 73, 75
17:8 75
17:21 7
17:21–23 81
18:1–19:42 73
18:11 69
19:26–37 82
20:1–10 82
20:1–31 70, 73
20:8 83
20:14 49
20:17 173
20:18 49
20:22–23 70
20:25 83
20:30 72
20:30–31 13
21:1–25 70, 72, 73
21:7 82, 83
21:15–19 83, 90
21:20–25 90

Acts

1 101, 154
1:1–11 91
1:3–9 94n3
1:8 13, 49, 55, 89, 91, 92, 97, 101
1:9–11 173
1:12–8:1 91
1:13 90n2

1:14 96, 99, 101
1:22 94n7
2 61, 180
2:1 91, 92
2:1–4 55, 96
2:2–4 92
2:4 49, 89, 97n10
2:5–8:1 55
2:6–13 92
2:14–26 94n4
2:16–21 95n9
2:17 87, 99, 101
2:17–21 93
2:18 100
2:23 94
2:29–36 173
2:31 94n5
2:31–33 95
2:31–36 95n9
2:33 49
2:36 94n5, 95
2:38 96, 98, 174
2:39 93
2:42 98
2:43 49, 98
2:44–45 98, 100
2:46–47 98
3:1 90n3
3:1–10 96, 101
3:3 90n3
3:6 96
3:11 90n3
3:13 94n6
3:15–16 95–96
3:18 94n5, 95n8
3:20 94n5
3:20–21 95
3:25–26 95
3:26 94n6
4:1 90n3
4:1–22 96
4:12 59n6, 96
4:13 90n3, 101
4:17–18 96
4:19 90n3
4:26 94n5
4:27 94n6
4:27–28 95

4:30 94n6, 96
4:31 89, 97n10
4:32 101
4:34–35 98, 100
5:9 97
5:12 49
5:14 99
5:16 49, 96
5:17–42 96
5:31 49
5:34–39 177
5:42 94n5
7 112
7:2–53 94n4
7:25 59n6
7:51 97
7:52 95n8
7:55–56 49
7:58 112
7:59–60 97
8:1 55, 91, 112
8:2–12:23 91
8:3 100, 122
8:4–8 103
8:5 94n5
8:7 49
8:12 100
8:14 90n3, 103
8:14–17 97n10
8:17 90n3
8:25 90n3
8:26–40 101, 103
8:29 89, 97
9:1–2 100
9:1–19 101, 103, 112
9:2 112
9:3–6 94n3
9:4–5 119
9:10–16 94n3
9:12 49
9:15 103
9:16 94n7
9:17 49
9:19–30 103, 114
9:22 94n5
9:32–43 103
10 101, 103

10:13–15 94n3
10:19 89, 97
10:28 103
10:34–35 103
10:43 96
10:44–47 103
10:44–48 97n10
11:15 96
11:25 114
11:26 97
12:2 102
12:17 102
13:1–14:28 113n6
13:1–28:31 91
13–28 55
13:2 114
13:4 97
13:6 181
13:9 113
13:15 130
13:16–41 94n4
13:26 59n6
13:38–39 96
13:46 94n7
13:47 59n6
14:22 94n7
15–17 114
15:1–11 104
15:12–21 102
15:13–17 105
15:15–17 95n9
15:19–21 105
15:22 114
15:22–29 115
15:28 97
15:32 180–81
15:36–18:22 113n6
16 113
16–28 101
16:1–5 114
16:6–7 97
16:11–15 100
16:17 59n6
16:18 96
16:27–34 101
16:30–31 96
16:37–39 113

16:40 100
17 113
17:2–3 95n8
17:3 94n5, 94n7
17:16 113n5
17:16–34 113n5
17:22 113n5
17:22–31 94n4
17:28 113n5
18 113
18–19 113
18:5 94n5
18:9–10 94n3
18:23–21:16 113n6
18:28 94n5
19:1–7 97n10
19:11–12 96
19:21 94n7
20:23 97
21:9 100
21:17–26 102
21:18–26 114
21:20–21 145
21:39 113
22:3 112, 113, 177
22:17–21 94n3
22:25–29 113
23:6 112
23:11 94n3, 94n7
24:10–21 94n4
25:8 115
25:10 94n7
26:2–23 94n4
26:23 94n5, 95n8
27:24 94n7
27:34 59n6
28 113
28:3–6 49
28:25–28 95n9
28:28 59n6
28:29–31 111

Romans

1:5 13, 118
1:8–15 118
1:16 103, 112, 139

1:17 122n11, 123,
  182
2:17 122
2:17–24 122
3:8 125, 145
3:10–11 120
3:23 120
3:25–26 121
3:27 121n10
3:28 124
4:1–2 121n10
4:1–25 123
4:3 121
5 139
5:3–5 169
5:8 120
6:1–2 125
6:4 120
6:8 174
6:15–16 125
6:19 128
7:6 138
8:2 126
8:9–13 126–28
9:4–5 122
9:33 119
11:17–20 121n10
11:33–36 120
12:1 128
14:1–15:6 145
15:14–33 118
16:3 100n12
16:26 118

1 Corinthians

1:2 182
1:17–18 47
1:27–29 121
1:28–30 121n10
1:30 140
2:7–8 119
4:6 139n2
5:6 121n10
9:5 102
9:20–21 115
9:22 145

11:1 139n2
11:23–26 175,
  176, 179
12 128
13 128
13:3 121n10
15:3–9 137
15:7 102
15:56 120
16:19 100n12

2 Corinthians

5:7 45
5:21 120
8:9 128
10:17 121n10
11:10 126
11:30 121n10
13:13 128

Galatians

1:13–16 119
1:16 125
1:16–18 114
1:19 102
2:2 137
2:9 102, 114, 136,
  175
2:10 114
2:11–13 102
2:11–14 137
2:12 104
2:15 144
2:16 124
2:19 127
2:19–20 15, 109,
  126
2:20 127, 128
3:6 121
3:6–9 123
3:11 122n11
3:11–12 122
3:27–28 99
3:28 52, 101
4:4–5 21
4:6 126

4:26 110
5:6 134
5:16–21 127
5:22–23 127, 143
6:8 128
6:13–14 121

Ephesians

2:8–9 121n10
2:11 144
2:13–22 128
2:14 122
2:14–17 120
2:15 138
4:8–10 173

Philippians

2:5–11 119
2:6–7 128
2:12–13 150
3:4–6 122
3:9 124
3:10 126, 127
3:17 139n2
3:20 145

Colossians

3:1–17 128

1 Thessalonians

1:6 139n2

2 Thessalonians

3:7–9 139n2

1 Timothy

3:16 173

2 Timothy

2:15 140
3:16 116, 178
3:16–17 5
4:19 100n12

Hebrews

11:13–16 171
13:22–25 129, 130

James

1:1 131, 136, 138,
  139, 145
1:2–3 146
1:3 169
1:4 139n3
1:5 139n3
1:7–8 146
1:9–11 146n7
1:12 142
1:14–15 146
1:15 144
1:17 143
1:17–18 139
1:18 144
1:21–22 138, 139
1:22–25 16
1:26–27 139,
  146n7
1:27 149
2:1 138, 139
2:1–7 146, 146n7
2:5 139n3
2:13 139n3
2:14 139n3
2:19 134
2:21–26 139
3:12 139n3
3:13–18 143
4:4–17 146
5:1–6 146, 146n7
5:2–3 139n3
5:10–11 139
5:12 139n3
5:17 139
5:19–20 16

1 Peter

1:1 145
1:2 140n6
1:3 144
1:13–16 134

1:14 140n4
1:18 140n4
1:18–21 140n6,
    147
1:23 144
2:9 180
2:9–10 140n5, 144
2:12 140n5, 146
2:18–25 146
2:20–21 140
2:21 14
2:22–25 140n6
2:24 141
3:1–7 146
3:18 140n6
3:22 173
4:1–2 140
4:3–4 140n4,
    140n5
4:5 143
4:8 16
4:13 142
4:14–19 147
5:1 137

2 Peter

1:5–8 141
1:10–11 142
1:11 145
1:12–15 148
1:16 110
1:16–18 147
1:18 110
2:1–2 141, 147
2:21 141, 148
3:1–2 141
3:1–13 147
3:10–11 148

3:13 150
3:15–17 141
3:16 110, 134

1 John

1:1 138, 141, 156
1:1–2 156
2:4 141
2:4–6 149
2:6 133, 141
2:7–11 149
2:15–17 142
2:19–23 148
2:29 141, 144
3:9 144
3:11 148
3:16 141
4:1 137, 148, 181
4:1–6 148
4:7 144

Jude

1 102, 136, 149
4 142, 150
20–21 150
24 150
24–25 142–43,
    153

Revelation

1:1 155, 157, 159
1:1–2 156
1:1–3 159
1:1–8 160
1:2 167
1:3 157n3, 158
1:4 156, 163

1:4–6 156
1:5–6 161
1:6 180
1:7 162
1:8 156
1:9 167
1:9–3:22 160
1:16 166
1:17 156
1:17–18 162
2–3 156, 157n3,
    167
2:1 162
2:2–3 168
2:7 169
2:11 169
2:12 162
2:13 168
2:17 169
2:19 168
2:25 168
2:26 169
3:1 162, 163
3:5 170
3:7 163
3:10–11 168
3:12 170
3:14 163
3:15–17 168
3:21 170
4 11, 163
4:1–8:5 160
4:5 163
4:10–11 160
5:1–6 163
5:6–14 156
5:9–10 164
5:12 157n3
6:2 164

6:4–15 164–66
6:15 157n3
7:9–10 171
7:12 157n3
7:17 156
7:21 156
8:2–11:19 160
12:1–15:4 160
12:11 170
13:9–10 169
14:4 153, 155
14:13 157n3
15:5–19:10 160
16:15 157n3
17:1 166
17:5 166
17:18 166
18:3–6 166
19:1–10 166
19:9 157n3
19:10 159
19:11–22:5 160
19:13 156
19:16 166
19:20–21 167
20:6 157n3
21 11
21:1–4 170
21:6 156
22:1 156
22:6–21 160
22:7 157n3
22:12 171
22:13 156
22:14 157n3
22:16 156
22:17 171
22:20 171
22:21 156

Subject Index

Abraham, 20–21, 51, 56–57, 71, 76, 95, 104, 122, 127
Acts, book of
    baptism in, 98, 100, 103
    Holy Spirit in, 84–85, 87–106
    as introduction to Paul, 12, 101, 111–15
    John the disciple in, 90n2, 101–2
Adam, 57, 139
antinomianism, 110, 173
apocalyptic, 159–60, 173. See also Revelation to John
apophasis, 36–37, 46, 173, 178
Augustine of Hippo, 10n5, 33, 33n1, 34, 46, 46n7, 133, 133n1, 134, 137, 174

baptism
    in Acts, 98, 100, 103
    of Christians, 138, 161
    Great Commission, 28
    of Jesus, 25, 35, 41, 60, 62, 68, 91, 96
    John the Baptist, 57, 73
    in Paul, 93, 99
beloved disciple, 70, 80–85, 90
Bonhoeffer, Dietrich, 45, 45n6, 174

Calvin, John, 154, 174
Catholic Epistles, 9n3, 10, 12, 102, 110, 131, 133–51, 155, 166, 175
church fathers, 9–10, 12, 36, 68, 175

circumcision, 100–105, 114, 175
Clement of Alexandria, 68, 129, 129n14, 130, 175
Communion, Holy, 16, 98, 175. See also Eucharist; Last Supper
communion, interpersonal, 124, 128–29
covenant
    and circumcision, 104, 175
    covenantal community, 122n11, 138, 144
    God as covenant partner, 7, 26, 56, 87, 100, 105, 119, 120, 122n11, 123–24, 128, 138, 150, 176
    human inability, 120
    new covenant, 69, 120, 130–31, 176
    old covenant, 122, 130–31, 176
Cyprian of Carthage, 125, 176

David, 20–21, 25, 51, 56–57, 95, 163
demons, 23n5, 35, 38, 40–41, 48–49, 62, 96, 134
Diaspora/Dispersion. See also exile
    at Babel, 91–93
    in Catholic Epistles, 131, 139, 145–46, 150, 151, 166
Dionysius of Alexandria, 154–55, 176

Eastern Orthodox, 3, 102n13, 154, 175
Eucharist, 138, 175, 176. See also Communion, Holy; Last Supper

Eusebius of Caesarea, 68, 68n1, 129n14,
     130n16, 155n2, 176
evangelism, and Paul, 111, 113, 145, 176
evangelists (Gospel writers), 33, 60, 176
exile. *See also* Diaspora/Dispersion
  in the Catholic Epistles, 145–46, 151
  and Christians, 151
  and Israel, 145, 176
  in Revelation to John, 166–68, 181

forgiveness
  in Christ, 36, 42, 88, 96, 98, 120, 142,
     173
  in discipleship, 64
  Jesus's authority to forgive, 75
  Jesus's offer of forgiveness, 97

Gamaliel, 112, 177
gematria, 20, 177
genealogy, 19, 19n2, 20, 21, 57, 72, 177
genre, 156–59, 177
gentile, 21, 58, 93, 96, 111, 118–19, 130,
     138, 139, 140, 140nn4–5, 144, 177
  Christian mission to, 11, 13, 91, 101,
     103–6, 114–15, 122–24, 136
  predicted inclusion of, 56, 105
God
  as Creator, 7, 10–11, 14, 30, 42, 46,
     96–97, 120, 147, 159, 161, 163, 167
  as Father, 20, 25–26, 28–29, 54, 69, 71,
     75, 80–85, 88–91, 95, 97, 127, 139,
     144, 148, 150, 156, 161, 169–70
  and the Trinity, 7, 10, 75, 81, 83–85,
     88–90, 97, 126, 148
grace, 28, 100, 104, 110, 114, 118–19, 121,
     123, 125, 128, 142, 146, 150, 173
Great Commission, 28
Gregory of Nyssa, 46, 46n8, 47, 47n9, 177

Hellenism, 22n3, 51, 113, 177
Holy Spirit
  in Acts, 84–85, 87–106
  as Advocate, 84, 88–89, 97, 173, 180
  in canonization, 8–10
  and holiness, 56, 59, 63–64, 66
  in Johannine writings, 70, 84–85, 88,
     134, 145, 148, 177, 182
  in Luke, 55–66, 61n9

as Paraclete, 173
  in Paul, 110, 126–29
  sanctification, 128, 149, 182

idolatry, 46, 105, 113n5, 127
inspiration, 6, 14, 68, 178
  Scripture as inspired, 5, 12, 68, 178
intertextuality, 134, 161, 178
Irenaeus of Lyon, 109, 109n1, 110, 129,
     178

James, brother of Jesus, 102, 104–6, 110,
     114, 136–37, 175
James, disciple (brother of John), 69, 102
James, Letter of, 9, 12, 111, 131, 133–51,
     169, 187
Jerome of Bethlehem, 136, 178, 183
Jesus Christ
  ascension, 10, 26, 67, 91, 94, 95, 138,
     162, 173
  baptism, 25, 35, 41, 60, 62, 68, 91, 96
  birth, 20–22, 22n3, 59, 68, 87, 102, 179
  death, 11, 24, 27, 40, 62, 73, 82, 87–89,
     95, 97, 119–27, 138, 140, 142, 160–62,
     164, 167, 174–80
  forgiveness, 36, 42, 75, 88, 96, 97, 98,
     120, 142, 173
  incarnation, 33, 138
  Jewish ethnicity, 20, 79, 94, 101
  king of Jews, 21
  law, 21, 22, 29–30, 74, 123
  Messiah of Israel, 11, 13, 19, 20, 24–25,
     24n6, 39, 42, 57, 59, 73–74, 77, 79,
     94–97, 119, 122–23, 139, 162, 175, 179
  rabbi, 78
  resurrection, 24, 27, 38, 64, 71, 73, 75,
     83, 88, 94–95, 102, 123, 126, 138, 140,
     142, 144, 162, 173, 174, 177
Jews/Jewish, 17, 20–22, 22n3, 74, 78,
     93–96, 101–6, 112, 113, 115, 122–24,
     129–31, 138–40, 144, 155, 159, 159n4,
     175–78, 180–83
  Abraham as, 21
  ancient, 11, 20
  in Catholic Epistles, 138–40, 140n4
  festivals, 72, 180
  and gentile inclusion, 52, 93, 96, 99,
     101–6

Jesus as king of, 21
Jesus's ethnicity, 20, 79, 94, 101
Jewish-Christian mission to Jews,
    11–12, 102, 111, 136, 175
Jewish scriptures, 22, 22n3, 25, 68,
    76n7, 110, 120–21, 178, 182
Judaism, 95, 105, 110, 112, 115, 118,
    134, 182, 183
Paul as, 112–13, 113n5, 115, 118–24
John, Gospel of, 9, 11, 27, 67–85, 89–91,
    154–56
John, Letters of, 2, 9, 12, 133–51, 154–56
John Chrysostom, 18, 18n1, 88, 88n1, 178
John the Baptist, 57, 73, 174
John the disciple, 15, 69
    in Acts, 90n2, 101–2
    pillar of Jerusalem, 102, 110, 114, 136
Jude, 12, 102, 102n13, 133–51, 153, 156,
    175, 187
justification, 1, 36, 68, 121–25, 128, 149,
    178, 181

kataphasis, 36–37, 46, 173, 178
kingdom of God/heaven, 20, 27, 28, 51,
    56, 57, 59, 63, 64, 69, 71, 111, 120,
    122, 142–46, 161, 164, 167, 173, 176,
    178, 180, 182

Last Supper, 65, 69, 80, 82, 175, 176, 179.
    See also Communion, Holy; Eucharist
law
    in James, 138–39
    and Jesus, 21, 22, 29–30, 74, 123
    lawlessness, 141, 147, 173
    of Moses, 74, 103–4, 115, 179, 183
    in Paul, 115, 123–25, 138–39
    and the prophets, 18, 30
    as Torah, 29, 74, 104, 105, 123, 124,
        179, 182
lectionary, 3, 179
Luther, Martin, 154, 179

manuscript, 48, 130, 136, 179, 182
martyr, 15, 170, 174, 176, 179, 180
Mary, mother of Jesus, 21, 29, 58, 59n5,
    60, 68, 99, 101
    Song of, 56, 61–62
Mary, sister of Martha, 64, 70

Mary Magdalene, 48–49
mercy, 28–30, 56, 63, 66, 120, 123, 144,
    150
Moses, 23, 42–43, 54, 74, 76, 104–5, 179,
    183

new birth, 78, 143–44
Nicene Creed, 75, 97, 175, 179, 182
Nicodemus, 70, 78–79, 85, 143
numbers, symbolism of, 11–12, 20–21, 23,
    25, 71, 134–35, 157, 157n3, 160, 177

Origen of Alexandria, 52, 52n1, 68, 68n2,
    129, 130n16, 176, 179

parable, 23, 23n5, 24, 28, 36, 41–42, 45,
    58, 62, 69, 180
Passover, 72, 76, 161, 163, 180
Paul, 15, 21, 96, 99–104, 100n12, 136, 143,
    149–50, 169, 175, 177, 181, 182
    baptism, 93, 99
    book of Acts as introduction to, 12,
        101, 111–15
    Catholic Epistles as corrective to, 10,
        110, 133–39
    evangelism, 111, 113, 145, 176
    Letters of, 2, 9, 12–13, 102, 104, 106,
        109–32, 135–37, 141, 155–57, 186
    missionary/evangelist, 55, 91, 113–14,
        144–45
    Pharisee, 110, 112–13, 113n5, 115
    as Saul, 91, 100, 112–13
Pentecost, 95, 180
Peter, 15, 39, 69, 70, 80, 82–85, 89–90,
    90n2
    Cephas, 114, 136
    and gentile mission, 102–5
    leader/spokesperson of the Twelve, 25,
        30, 35, 39–41, 47, 89, 90n2, 91, 93–96,
        98, 101
    Letters of, 9n3, 12, 110, 133–51
    pillar of Jerusalem, 102, 110, 114, 136
Pharisee, 23, 27–28, 30, 38, 64, 70, 78,
    101, 104, 112–13, 177, 180, 182
Polycarp of Smyrna, 109–10, 110n2, 180
prayer, 7, 61–62, 66, 69, 73, 75, 96, 98,
    150, 181